KV-541-255

REACTION AND REFORM
1793–1868

PROBLEMS OF HISTORY SERIES
[General Editor—R. W. Harris]

DISSOLUTION OF THE MONASTERIES	G. W. O. Woodward
EXPANSION OF EUROPE IN THE EIGHTEENTH CENTURY	Glyndwr Williams
FRANCE AND THE DREYFUS AFFAIR	Douglas Johnson
COLONIES INTO COMMONWEALTH	W. D. McIntyre
PAPISTS AND PURITANS UNDER ELIZABETH I	Patrick McGrath
THE REIGN OF HENRY VII	R. L. Storey
THE CHURCH AND MAN'S STRUGGLE FOR UNITY	Herbert Waddams
ROYAL MYSTERIES AND PRETENDERS	Stanley B.-R. Poole

THE HISTORY OF ENGLAND SERIES
[General Editor—R. W. Harris]

REFORMATION AND RESURGENCE · 1485–1603	G. W. O. Woodward
THE STRUGGLE FOR THE CONSTITUTION · 1603–1689	G. E. Aylmer
ENGLAND IN THE EIGHTEENTH CENTURY · 1689–1793	R. W. Harris
REACTION AND REFORM · 1793–1868	John W. Derry
DEMOCRACY AND WORLD CONFLICT · 1868–1969	T. L. Jarman

THE HISTORY OF EUROPE SERIES
[General Editor—R. W. Harris]

ABSOLUTISM AND ENLIGHTENMENT · 1660–1789	R. W. Harris
THE AGE OF TRANSFORMATION · 1789–1871	R. F. Leslie
THE END OF EUROPEAN PRIMACY · 1871–1945	J. R. Western
RUIN AND RESURGENCE: · 1939–1965	R. C. Mowat

HISTORY AND LITERATURE SERIES
[General Editor—R. W. Harris]

THE TRIUMPH OF ENGLISH · 1350–1400	Basil Cottle
REASON AND NATURE IN 18TH-CENTURY THOUGHT	R. W. Harris
ROMANTICISM AND THE SOCIAL ORDER · 1780–1830	R. W. Harris

1793–1868

REACTION AND REFORM

England in the Early Nineteenth Century

JOHN W. DERRY

M.A., Ph.D.(Cantab)

Fellow of Downing College, Cambridge

LONDON

BLANDFORD PRESS

First published in 1963
Reprinted 1965
New edition 1970

© Copyright by Blandford Press Ltd
167 High Holborn London WC1

Printed in Great Britain by Richard Clay (The Chaucer Press), Ltd.,
Bungay, Suffolk

2874

TC 05332

TOLWORTH SECONDARY
GIRLS SCHOOL.

1 2 MAY 1993

c

F

AME | DATE I

MAY 197

CONTENTS

LIST OF ILLUSTRATIONS

ACKNOWLEDGEMENTS

Photograph number 10 has been reproduced by gracious permission of Her Majesty the Queen.

The remaining photographs have been reproduced by permission of the following:

1, 2, 3, 4, 5, 6, 11, 12, 14, 15, 16 and 17   The Trustees of the National Portrait Gallery

7, 9 and 13   The Trustees of the British Museum

8   The Trustees of the Science Museum

18   The Radio Times Hulton Picture Library

LIST OF MAPS

Introduction

THE seventy-five years which separate the outbreak of the war with revolutionary France and the first and greatest of Gladstone's ministries were marked by intense—often dramatic—political, social and economic change. Men were thinking in new ways about the world in which they lived, and the world itself was undergoing a decisive transformation. In political controversy the ideas of the American and French Revolutions mingled with those of more homely reformers. In philosophy and religion the old certainties were being questioned, criticised and occasionally discarded. The reorganisation of industry, and the redistribution of population, constituted a profound and far-reaching revolution in modes of production and habits of life. An advancing technology gave men an increasing control over their environment, and although the new techniques in spinning and weaving had their origins far back in the eighteenth century, it was only in the last twenty years of the old century, and in the first quarter of the new, that a radical alteration took place in the ways in which men earned their daily bread, and in the places where they lived. At the close of the eighteenth century most Englishmen were country-born. If they came to the towns, to be near the factories where more of them worked, they could still recall the village life of a predominantly agricultural community. Fifty years later, the English were a nation of town dwellers—ugly, insanitary and overcrowded as many of the towns were. This urban society posed new and perplexing problems, however much the system's arch-critic, Karl Marx, later boasted of the advance made over the alleged 'idiocy' of rural life. But then Marx's outlook was permanently coloured by his continental upbringing, and it may be doubted whether he ever understood the English and their ways.

Although the rich seemed to be getting richer, the poor were not always getting poorer. The industrial magnates were often self-made men, toughened in the grim struggle for existence and frequently contemptuous of those less able, or less fortunate, than themselves. Every success story demonstrated the apparent truism that honesty and hard work were the sure recipes for personal happiness and national prosperity. And, despite the horrors of the Industrial Revolution, the new society ultimately made possible a fuller and freer life for the common people. As the emergent nations of Africa and Asia realise today, industrialisation is the speediest path to a higher standard of living, the complaints of those devoted to the moral superiority of the spinning wheel notwithstanding. If English society in the early nineteenth century seems brutal and insensitive, it was not merely the inhuman jungle so often portrayed in history books. It had its critics, its writers and artists, even its comedians, as well as its factory owners and profiteers. As it became more sure of itself and more conscious of its power, society became more impatient of its faults. Men were conscience stricken in their desire to put them right. Throughout the period parliamentary reform was eagerly and acrimoniously debated, and two Acts, defining the franchise and amending the system of representation, were placed on the statute book. Their immediate effects have been exaggerated —corruption did not come to a sudden stop in 1832—but they form a significant part of that process which, albeit spasmodically and incoherently, finally changed the structure of politics and government to meet the needs of a new society. The position of the Crown, of the King's ministers, of the Cabinet, and of party, all altered in important ways, during the period which embraces the traditional oligarchy of the eighteenth century, and the restless and tumultuous world of Peel, the Chartists and the Anti-Corn Law League; of Palmerston and the young Victoria.

Too much has been made of the joys of life before the Industrial Revolution. The picture of 'Merry England', symbolised by the maypole and the madrigal, and endowed with the elusive charm of a folk culture, is as misleading as a portrait of the nineteenth century dominated by the workhouse and child labour, by noisome slums and loathsome disease, and the sinister figure of the legendary bloated capitalist. The new society had many faults, but frequently they were those of the old writ large. The employment of children had been an indispensable feature of the domestic system. Long hours of work, low rates of pay, the neglect of safety precautions in mines and factories, and an indifference to planning, were not new. The lack of insight so often displayed by men of culture, education and intellect was the consequence of attitudes so deeply ingrained that they could not readily be jettisoned. The distrust of all government—so distinctive of the *laissez-faire* outlook—was a thoroughly eighteenth-century characteristic, born of men's experience. Tom Paine, the self-appointed apostle of reason and progress, never lost it. Men looked at the sort of government they had had—or thought they had had, which is even more to the point—and decided that, whatever its virtues, the less the government interfered in their affairs the better. In its own day this attitude was progressive and radical, however absurd it may seem today.

Too much has also been made of the abstract trends at work during the years which saw England's emergence as the foremost manufacturing country in the world. The Marxist interpretation of history, with its rigid and monotonous emphasis on the class struggle, and its unyielding attempt to squeeze historical events into a pre-ordained pattern leading to the final victory of the proletariat, does not of itself explain the complexities of Regency England, or the subtleties of the first thirty years of Victoria's reign. Despite the impressive edifice erected in the name of historical inevitability, such language is no more than a convenient shorthand which the historian must use with tact and discretion. Men may not be the masters of their fate, but they still feel that they are the captains of their souls, and their response to their environment is more decisive in influencing the outcome of any crisis than any of the illusory laws of historical development. Because they feel themselves to be both free and morally responsible, men think and feel deeply about the choices which confront them. To see the way in which men respond to a situation which they themselves did not make, and to realise that in so doing they create problems with which their children will grapple, is part of the fascination of historical study.

This book seeks to describe and analyse a society in transition, when honest doubt dispelled many creeds, when the condition-of-the-people question became a matter of national concern, and when, at the close of our period, despite its distance in time and its strangeness of thought, we stand on the brink of a world recognisably like our own. It is ironic that the Victorian Age should be regarded, with more than a trace of envy, as one of confidence, security and comfort. For contemporaries life was hard and testing. The future was uncertain. Men were afraid and anxious, perplexed by new sciences and old faiths, and fearful of social and political revolution, and of the dangers of democracy—not then the respectable word it has now become. The choice often looked like one between Rationalism and Rome, Reaction and Democracy, Barbarism and Philistinism. The complacent tranquillities of the second half of the century could not be foreseen during its stormy opening. No historical period has a completely satisfying unity—history is too untidy for that—but there is more thematic integration and development between 1793 and 1868 than might at first appear. The period sees the working out, in English terms, of the French and Industrial Revolutions. And since the most obvious consequence of the French Revolution was a long and gruelling war, with which some of the most famous names in our history—Pitt and Fox, Nelson and Wellington—are associated, it is just as well to start with an account of the hostilities. It is platitudinous to point out how lacking Jane Austen's novels are in any preoccupation with the war, even though two of her brothers were in the navy, but no one who had fought with Nelson at the Nile or Trafalgar, who had heard Pitt and Fox compete in splendid eloquence for the favour of the House of Commons, who had marched with Wellington across the dusty plains of Spain or seen the Imperial Guard broken at Waterloo, was ever likely to forget it. And, while these dramatic events unfolded, the busy wheels of industry were forging the weapons of war and the tools of peace; the sinews of a new life and a larger hope.

1 : William Pitt and the Revolutionary War

The Character of the War

Wᴴᴇɴ the French Republic declared war on Britain in February 1793 it was impossible to predict the length and scale of the conflict. Nothing in a century's experience of colonial rivalry and continental and oceanic warfare had prepared men for what was to come. For the French Revolution precipitated an ideological srtuggle. The clash of arms reflected a battle for the minds of men. There could be no compromise between the Old Order and the New. The ideals of liberty, equality and fraternity, allegedly the inspiration behind the bayonets of the young Republic, questioned the assumptions underlying the old empires and established monarchies of Europe. The days of the familiar, limited wars of the eighteenth century were over. There was no place for the leisurely tactics of the *ancien régime*. Professional armies were confronted with vast levies of conscripts, fired with a zeal which was reminiscent of the wars of religion. A war for righteousness had begun.

Although they disliked and distrusted the French, the English did not desire war. They were only beginning to sense their recovery from the humiliation of losing the American colonies. The early stages of the French Revolution had aroused mild attention and varied interest. Some were glad that the French were now paying for the help they had given to the American rebels, and rejoiced at the sight of the traditional enemy torn by internal feuds and discord. Others—mostly Dissenters and Whigs —sympathised with the French Revolution, interpreting it as the French version of the 'Glorious Revolution' of 1688. Very few men shared Edmund Burke's passionate conviction that the French Revolution would result in domestic tyranny, international chaos and military dictatorship. And no one was less attracted to a policy of intervention than William Pitt.

Pitt's Character and Career

He had been First Lord of the Treasury and Chancellor of the Exchequer for nine years. The second son of the great Earl of Chatham, he had been active in politics since he was twenty-one. Honest and industrious, austere and upright, he had few close friends and almost no relaxations. He drank heavily, but refrained from the fashionable vice of gambling. In public he appeared aloof and arrogant, but there were warm feelings behind the cold exterior which he presented to the world. To the few who knew him well he was a true friend and a congenial companion, but his shyness prevented him from winning the affection as well as the respect of his contemporaries. He never married, and there was a tragic loneliness about his life. He gave himself wholly to politics, submerging his private life in his public career. He was a brilliant debater, an able administrator and a first-class financier. He approved of the reform of Parliament and of the abolition of the Slave Trade. He had read Adam Smith and was a convinced free trader. But although he had achieved much during his term of office—the restoration of the nation's finances, the reform of the customs, a new trading agreement with France and an alliance with Holland and Prussia—he had also experienced disappointment. His proposals for the reform of Parliament, moderate and practicable though they were, had been rejected. His attempt to introduce free trade between Great Britain and Ireland had been thwarted, and the Slave Trade was abolished only after his death.

His position was made all the more complicated by the political structure within which he worked. In the 1780s the modern two-party system was unthinkable. Men described themselves, in a general way, as Whigs or Tories, but there was little party discipline within the House of Commons and no party organisation in the country. There were groups of active politicians, eagerly contending for power, but they had to win the support of the independent country gentlemen, as well as the approval of the Court party, which upheld any government, providing that it was not especially unpopular or inefficient. In 1788 Pitt's own supporters in the Commons numbered only 52 in a House of 558 members. His consequent dependence on the rank-and-file members, few of whom appreciated the more far-sighted aspects of his policy, meant that he could not achieve his objects quickly. He became skilled at gradually procuring the solution he favoured and adept at the slow drudgery involved in the courting of multifarious interests. He was not a modern party leader, backed up by a disciplined and obedient array of members in the House and an effective organisation in the country. It was impossible for Pitt to impose his will on the Commons: he had rather to coax them into reluctant agreement.

At one time it was thought that Pitt's relationship with George III was like that of a Victorian Prime Minister with his sovereign. But even after Pitt's accession to power in 1783 George III retained his constitutional right to select ministers and to influence policy. Pitt could not afford to ignore the King, or to underestimate George III's obstinacy in clinging to his point of view. On the one occasion when Pitt misjudged the situation—over the proposed emancipation of the Catholics in 1801—the King forced him to resign. On many issues George III thought Pitt dangerously advanced, but because Pitt respected the King's position, and did not compel him to change his mind, and because Pitt was far preferable to Charles James Fox, George III acquiesced. Yet it should be clearly understood that the King still possessed considerable political influence, despite advancing years and bouts of insanity. Pitt had a double loyalty, to the King and to the Commons. In dealing with both he had to show restraint and tact, for he knew how fragile was the ascendancy which he wielded.

Nor was Pitt's relationship with his colleagues in the Cabinet as unchallenged as the pre-eminence accorded to a modern Prime Minister. Within the Cabinet opinion was divided on several of the most controversial issues of the day: Parliamentary Reform, the abolition of the Slave Trade, and, later, Catholic Emancipation. Doctrines of collective responsibility were in their infancy. Although Pitt was the ablest of the King's ministers, he could not insist that his colleagues accept his own opinion on every matter of consequence. Had he done so his ministry would have fallen. He preferred to accept the conventions of the time, and to permit divergences as long as they did not threaten the existence of the ministry. But in dealing with the King, the Cabinet and the Commons, Pitt had to display immense patience and considerable tolerance.

At first Pitt had sympathised with the more moderate of the French Revolutionaries. He was convinced that the disturbances would terminate in the establishment of a constitutional monarchy on the English model. But he watched the decline into terror with mounting anxiety: France had become the object of pity even to a rival. His own hopes for peace, confidently expressed in his budget speech in February 1792, were soon exposed as delusions. Yet he strove to avert war. In order to facilitate negotiations, the French ambassador was allowed to remain in London in an unofficial capacity, after the fall of the French monarchy in August 1792. But in November the so-called Edict of Fraternity promised French aid to any people struggling against tyranny: the revolution was about to spread to all Europe. The French Minister of Marine talked about hurling 50,000 caps of liberty to England, where the people were thought to be awaiting the chance to rebel against George III. Inaccurate though these notions were, the position took a turn for the worse when the French broke their obligations under several treaties and refused to respect the neutrality of the Scheldt. Their invasion of the Low Countries added to British anxieties, always sensitive on any point touching the independence of the Netherlands. Pitt hated war. Peace was necessary if he was to consolidate his financial achievements. War would upset the delicate balance of national solvency. But he could not escape from the responsibilities of power in an age of revolution.

For most of the 1790s the war went badly for Britain. Her allies, Austria and Prussia, were incompetent and unreliable, and they were more interested in partitioning Poland than in restoring the French monarchy. Yet without them England was powerless to wage war on the continent. The Duke of York's little expeditionary force was soon involved in a frustrating campaign in the Nether- lands, and only Howe's naval victory of the 'Glorious First of

June' (1794) cheered English hearts, though it failed to prevent the safe arrival of a grain convoy which was eagerly awaited in a France desperately short of bread. The mid-nineties brought only disappointment: Prussia left the coalition, Spain changed sides and Austria alone could not meet the French challenge.

Radicalism and Repression

At home the government succumbed to the 'Anti-Jacobin' scare, repressing radical societies with an excessive enthusiasm. A largely illusory enemy at home compensated for the all too successful enemy abroad. The London Corresponding Society, which was primarily interested in the reform of Parliament, had foolishly had dealings with the French Convention. The fact that its secretary was a shoemaker called Hardy, and that it sought to organise agitation for Parliamentary Reform on a national scale, frightened the authorities still further. It seemed that the artisans were beginning to take the lead in some types of political action. Disturbances in several of the northern industrial towns, particularly those in Sheffield, added to the sense of alarm. Without a police force, and easily deluded by the exaggerated reports of informers and spies, the government introduced legislation to stamp out disaffection. The Aliens Act of 1792 empowered the authorities to control and supervise foreign immigration. In 1794 Habeas Corpus was suspended in order to facilitate the detention of conspirators against the King and his government. In 1795 the Seditious Meetings Act stipulated that all meetings at which more than fifty people were present, and all lectures outside schools and universities, were to be licensed by the local magistrates. In the same year the Treasonable Practices Act proscribed all who plotted against the King, who planned to aid any invasion, or who attempted to intimidate Parliament. Anyone who denounced the British Constitution could be transported for seven years. The Anti-Combination Laws of 1799 and 1800 declared that all societies taking secret oaths, or with branches throughout the country, were illegal, and anyone who collaborated with another to achieve a reduction of working hours or a rise in pay could be brought before the magistrates and gaoled for three months. These

B

Acts were intended to nip Jacobinical conspiracy in the bud: even the Combination Laws were primarily aimed at the London Corresponding Society. In so far as they were concerned with 'trades unions' they were an attempt to reinforce old statutes, and modern historians, such as Professor T. S. Ashton, have claimed that they have been given an unwarranted prominence in the history of the Labour movement. The laws were, in fact, rarely invoked: perhaps because the penalties imposed were relatively light. And, despite the government's belief that the country was on the verge of insurrection, the submissive reception of this legislation by the majority of Englishmen suggests that the extent of unrest was greatly exaggerated. The trials of the radical leaders, Horne Tooke, Thelwall and Hardy, on charges of treason, ended in triumphant acquittal for the accused, and the public was entertained by the sight of William Pitt himself in the witness-box, testifying to his own support of the reform associations in the 1780s.

The Radicals seemed more revolutionary than they really were. Their talk of 'Citizen' and 'Convention', and the wild language they used about tyrants and bloodshed, obscured the fact that their political programme was closer to that of the Chartists than the Jacobins. But by identifying legitimate agitation with bloody revolution, and timely reform with dangerous change, the French Revolution postponed the reform of Parliament for a generation. It is easy to condemn the government for its repressive action, but the memory of the disastrous Gordon Riots, as well as the fear of Jacobinism, was in men's minds, and it is possible to over-emphasise the effects of the scare. Some magistrates applied the law leniently; others took every advantage of the opportunities for repression. There was considerable variation up and down the country, and the dull-witted Duke of Portland, who succeeded Dundas as Home Secretary in 1794, was not the man to direct an energetic campaign of co-ordinated suppression. In any event, it is questionable whether any such idea was in the minds of the Cabinet. They were all men familiar with the predominantly rural world of the eighteenth century, and the obvious means of maintaining order was to strengthen the powers of the traditional officers of the law—the Justices of the Peace. They relied on the man on the spot to enforce the law, and even after Waterloo the Liverpool ministry was obstinately old-fashioned in its conviction that there was very little which could not be dealt with by the local magistrates. Not that disturbances did not take place: in 1795 and 1797 there were riots and popular demonstrations against the government. The London mob shouted 'No War! No famine! No Pitt!', breaking the minister's windows in Downing Street by way of driving their point home. There was even an attempt to assassinate George III, though the authenticity of the 'Pop-gun Plot' was doubted by the Whigs. But these instances of unrest were inspired by poor harvests, food shortages and hunger, not by Tom Paine and the French.

Fox and the Opposition

While Pitt struggled to carry on the war against France and to maintain order at home, Fox and the other Whigs who had broken with Burke and Portland over the French Revolution opposed the government's repressive policy and its conduct of the war. Charles James Fox symbolised resistance to the King, to Pitt and to repression. Ten years older than Pitt he had started his political career as a Tory, but after being unceremoniously dismissed from a minor post in 1774 he became one of the most scathing critics of the policy of coercion in America. This brought him into closer association with Rockingham and the Whigs, and when North's ministry fell in 1782 Fox was Foreign Secretary in the Rockingham administration. But after Rockingham's death Fox quarrelled with his successor, Shelburne, resigning in protest at Shelburne's appointment as head of the ministry. He was only able to get back into office by joining forces with his old enemy, North. This cost him much of his popularity, and his India Bill gave George III the pretext for dismissing the Coalition. For the rest of his life, with the exception of a few months in 1806, Fox was in opposition.

He was always an individualist, his impetuous and volatile nature making him an unpredictable and unreliable colleague. His private life was the antithesis of Pitt's. He was warm and passionate, Pitt was withdrawn and aloof. Fox was a heavy gambler, a keen racing man, and an enthusiastic—but unskilful—amateur cricketer. After a liaison of many years he eventually married Elizabeth Armistead—his 'own dear Liz'. He had great personal charm, an outstanding oratorical gift and immense ability. But there was a flaw: he was too prone to act on a momentary impulse. He was also unlucky: he was never given the opportunity to undo his mistakes or to prove his true worth in office, though during his final spell at the Foreign Office he earned golden tributes. After his death even George III, his lifelong enemy, confessed that he had not thought he would miss Mr Fox so much. He was no doctrinaire in politics. His inspiration was an all-consuming, but ill-defined, devotion to liberty. He could be unscrupulous, ruthless and overbearing, as ambition prompted him.

He had responded with all the ardour of his character to the appeal of the French Revolution. He described the fall of the Bastille as 'How much the greatest event that has happened in the world, and how much the best!' But later developments in France saddened him, and in 1792 his position was very close to Pitt's. When Burke and his friends went over to the ministry, however, Fox became more violent and intransigent in his opposition to the government. He said that he would oppose everything which was brought forward by Pitt. His emotions had dimmed his judgment, not for the first time, betraying him into attitudes which were theatrical in their extravagance. All his sympathies were roused by the prosecution of the Radicals. 'God help the nation that has such judges!' he exclaimed, when Lord Braxfield sentenced Palmer and Muir to transportation during the Scottish Treason Trials in 1794. Fox could take comfort that his Libel Bill, entrusting juries with the responsibility of deciding whether a publication was libellous or not, had been passed in 1792. Throughout the war he advocated peace with France, pointing out contradictions in government policy and arguing the necessity for negotiations with the French. Fox ignored the cataclysmic and aggressive aspects of the Revolution. Heartbroken as he was over the September Massacres and the Reign of Terror, he clung to his belief that the cause of the Revolution was that of liberty and enlightenment. He was less altruistic than has often been supposed, and he was as guilty of inconsistency as the government, but in opposing Pitt he performed a valuable service, almost in spite of himself. He reminded men of the need for free speech and open discussion at a time when many panicked into repressive and intolerant attitudes. Several of his colleagues were even more determined. Grey introduced motions calling for Parliamentary Reform in 1792, 1793 and 1797, only to be told that it was foolish to mend a roof in a thunderstorm. Sheridan, so often depicted as no more than a witty drunkard, was tenacious in his opposition to the war. When Fox seceded from the Commons, in frustrated disgust with politics and in eager contemplation of the joys of private life, Sheridan remained. But he was more selective and more discriminating in his criticism of government policy. He supported the ministry whenever he thought it right to do so—as over attempts to improve naval recruitment—and consequently his criticisms were all the more telling. Unlike Fox, he did not gloat over the defeats suffered by his country.

The Course of the War

But there could be no disguising the dismal course of events. Pitt was no strategist. He hoped that inflation would bring about the collapse of the French economy: instead, he saw the Republican armies triumphant. In deference to the commercial interest, and in unhappy imitation of his father's strategy, he dabbled in West Indian expeditions. British troops died in their thousands, the victims of disease, not of French bullets. The trouble was that Pitt did not want to get too involved in the war in Europe. He had no desire to commit England to a royalist crusade, although he believed that the restoration of a moderate constitutional monarchy in France offered the best hope of a settlement. His main preoccupation was with the protection of British interests, which he thought could be well enough secured by the acquisition of new trading stations. Nor did he appreciate the potentialities of seapower as a means of concentrating, not dispersing, his resources. He fell back on its defensive advantages—yet it is hard to see what else he could do when his continental allies failed him. Even Chatham had required effective allies in Europe. Attempts to help the royalist peasants of La Vendée and Brittany in their resistance to the Jacobins ended in misery and futility, and in the meantime young Napoleon Bonaparte inflicted defeat after defeat upon the Austrians in his brilliant Italian campaign. In 1797 Francis II of Austria sued for peace. When the British government put out cautious peace feelers, in 1796 and again in 1797, Malmesbury, the British envoy, found the French arrogant, unyielding and insolent, and on two occasions he was ordered to leave within forty-eight hours. England remained defiant, but she stood alone. Her ally Holland had been reduced to the status of one of the satellite republics through which French dominion was perpetuated. And it was now the turn of the British economy to wilt under the strain of war. In 1797 the Bank of England suspended cash payments, and though Pitt vainly and misguidedly strove to preserve his Sinking Fund, the National Debt continued to rise. New and unpopular taxes, such as the income tax, were imposed. Others, such as the famous window tax, were increased. A voluntary loan was raised in an effort to meet the cost of the war. Life was grim in England during the last years of the eighteenth century, and hardship at home was all the more difficult to bear when stalemate was the only reward for the nation's exertions. The French Republic seemed invincible.

Not all misfortunes were endured at the hand of foreigners. In 1797 the fleets at Spithead and the Nore mutinied. England lay exposed to the threat of invasion. While the North Sea fleet was paralysed by mutiny Admiral Duncan patrolled the seas with his flagship and a solitary frigate, bluffing the Dutch into believing the British fleet was at sea by sending messages to fictitious squadrons over the horizon. But the sailors were not traitors: they promised to put to sea to meet any enemy threat. They had many grievances. Many of the men had been pressed into service. Leave was inadequate and food and pay were poor. Discipline was harsh and justice was rough. But though the mutineers at Spithead affirmed their loyalty, the outbreak at the Nore took a more serious turn. Richard Parker, a gifted and unscrupulous agitator, seized the opportunity to become the acknowledged leader of the mutineers. But his spell was broken when the sailors learned that he had withheld the offer of a royal pardon. He and the other ringleaders were hanged, and the most serious of the men's complaints were met. Duncan's crews soon showed that they had lost none of their mettle by defeating the Dutch at the battle of Camperdown. Earlier in the year Sir John Jervis had defeated the Spaniards at Cape St Vincent, and the war now ground to a halt. At sea the British had more than held their own, but they were powerless to break the French stranglehold on Europe.

In 1798 the French sought to turn the scales by dispatching Bonaparte to Egypt. Eluding the British fleet, he soon established himself in Egypt by his victory over the Mamelukes at the battle of the Pyramids. Napoleon himself dreamed of an empire in the east and toyed with the idea of becoming a Moslem. The first stage of the strategic threat to India had been accomplished. But Nelson destroyed the French fleet at the battle of the Nile (August 1st, 1798), and when Bonaparte attempted to march into Asia Minor he found his way blocked at Acre. There the great invasion came to an ignominious conclusion. The siege was abandoned and the Ottoman Empire saved. Napoleon deserted his army and sailed back to France. He had learned from a newspaper thrown into his camp during the siege of Acre that the corrupt and inefficient Directory was faring badly in the new war against Austria and Russia.

Pitt had formed the second coalition against France. He was now broken in health, but he braced his shattered frame to face the test. By the distribution of subsidies he roused the nations of Europe against France. He was trying to create a more effective alliance. Prussia's place was taken by Russia, and for a time the allies were in sight of victory. But Bonaparte's return transformed the situation. The *coup d'état* of Brumaire overthrew the Directory and set up the Consulate with Bonaparte at its head. Soon the allies were reeling under massive blows. The defeats of Marengo and Hohenlinden compelled the Austrians to sue for peace. By the treaty of Lunéville the Austrians lost their Italian territories, receiving Venice in compensation. The historic Venetian Republic had vanished, and its demise inspired Wordsworth to commemorate the event in a sonnet. The Russians left the coalition, their mad Tsar Paul conceiving a passionate admiration for Napoleon. With the Prussians, Swedes and Danes, they formed the Armed Neutrality of the North, hoping to throttle English commerce in the Baltic, thereby cutting the British navy off from much-needed marine stores. But Nelson's daring foiled the stratagem. The destruction of the Danish fleet at Copenhagen (April 2nd, 1801) meant the end of the Northern League. Tsar Paul had been murdered in March and Russian policy underwent another dramatic change. But although Britain maintained her naval supremacy, the second coalition had been as futile as the first. The French Republic, now firmly governed by the most ruthless genius of the age, was triumphant. The continent had no choice but to accept the New Order. The war had failed to achieve any of its objectives. Revolution and regicide remained unpunished, and the Netherlands were still bound to France. Men were weary of war. Anxiously and fretfully they looked for some escape from their predicament. Was peace possible? And upon what terms? The question was made all the more difficult by the fact that Pitt was no longer the King's chief minister.

The Irish Problem

For, in addition to the burdens of war, Pitt had been struggling with the problems of Ireland. The long, sorry tale of British indifference and unimaginative blundering reached a climax in the rebellion of 1798. The rising's causes were deeply rooted in the past. There were three distinct peoples in Ireland, each jealous of the others. The Anglo-Irish aristocracy, who were Anglican in religion, controlled the Dublin Parliament and fiercely defended its recently won independence. They were the landowning and ruling class, and they guarded their privileges vigilantly. In Ulster the Presbyterians resented their exclusion from political power. In the south and west the Catholic peasantry, who had remained faithful to their religion through innumerable trials, were treated as a subject race. A minority owned the land; a minority enjoyed the privileges of the established Church; only the majority were without rights and without privileges. The country lacked mineral resources, and was too dependent on the potato and the linen industry. Absentee landlords neglected their estates and rack-rented their tenants. Pitt had tried to invigorate the Irish economy by freeing trade between Great Britain and Ireland, but his resolutions had been defeated. Although the 1780s saw some improvement, the essential problem remained unsolved.

The French Revolution brought a new spirit into Irish politics. Grattan and his friends, who represented the more liberal section of the dominant class, were devoted to the vision of a free and united Ireland. They distrusted any action by the British government which could be interpreted as impinging upon the legislative independence of the Dublin Parliament. They were willing to emancipate the Catholics, believing that the timely concession of full citizenship would reconcile them to the Protestant ascendancy. In 1793 the Catholic freeholders were given the vote, though it was still impossible for a Catholic to sit in Parliament. But Grattan and his companions were eighteenth-century Whigs in outlook. They were constitutionalists and they abhorred democracy. And only a minority of the Anglo-Irish shared Grattan's liberal approach to the Catholic problem.

Far different were the ideas of the United Irishmen. Young men who had seen the spectacular success of the French Jacobins became disillusioned and impatient with the niceties of Parliamentary debate, especially after the fiasco of Earl Fitzwilliam's Lord Lieutenancy in 1795. Fitzwilliam was in sympathy with the Irish Catholics and had been sent to Dublin to prepare the way for some measure of relief. Unfortunately he exceeded his instructions, and by dismissing several government officials he alerted opponents of emancipation. Amidst a storm of controversy Pitt had little choice but to recall him. The difficulties of the Catholic problem had been fully exposed, and young Irishmen thought that the methods of the French revolutionaries held out the best prospect for a speedy cure to the ills of Ireland. It was hoped to create an Irish republic, one and indivisible, where liberty, equality and fraternity would transcend the traditional rivalries between Catholic and Protestant. Aristocrats such as

Lord Edward Fitzgerald threw themselves wholeheartedly into the movement. Embittered and ambitious men, of more humble origins, such as Wolfe Tone, saw in the movement the salvation of their country and the satisfaction of their own desires. In the north radical ideas were sympathetically received. In the south many Catholic priests (especially those who had been trained in France) gave the revolutionary caucus their blessing. The Irish looked to France for aid: French bayonets and Republican ideas would form an irresistible combination.

But the United Irishmen were inexperienced and imprudent, and this was their undoing. They talked wildly and loosely of their plans. They could terrorise the peasants into silence or complicity, but they lacked the stamina for the more testing and responsible tasks of patient preparation and careful planning. The authorities sensed their danger. In Ulster the peasantry was disarmed with a determination which shrank from no brutality. The well-to-do leaders were either arrested—like Lord Edward Fitzgerald, who was mortally wounded while resisting arrest in a Dublin boarding house—or driven into exile. When the rebellion came it was far different from what had been envisaged by the leaders. Ulster was still enfeebled, and was swiftly crushed, but Leinster rose in arms. The Catholic Bishops counselled obedience to George III, but their advice was brushed aside by the more bigoted parish priests. The insurrection took on a religious character. Ancient grievances, such as tithe and rent, meant more to the peasants than French opinions. Protestants were butchered, landlords executed. But a terrible reckoning awaited the rebels. The troops and yeomanry, acutely conscious of the dangers of the rebellion, answered atrocity with atrocity. After several illusory successes the rebels were routed at Vinegar Hill and their principal camp destroyed. The rising was ruthlessly put down. The dream of an Irish Republic was cruelly dispelled. Wolfe Tone was arrested on board ship and after being tried was condemned to death. He committed suicide in prison. When General Humbert landed with 1,100 French troops in Killala Bay, two months after the suppression of the insurrection, he won a few skirmishes but was eventually driven to surrender at Ballinamuck. He had been too late. The

Irish tragedy moved into a new phase, less bloody, but even more decisive.

William Pitt had watched events with keen interest. He had always followed Irish affairs with close attention, and now all his misgivings had been justified by events. He was unhappy with the status and character of the Irish Parliament, and he favoured a liberal solution to the Catholic problem. The rebellion confirmed him in his opinion that far-reaching reform was necessary. With the precedent of the Union with Scotland to guide him his thoughts turned to a similar solution for Ireland, and, as an indispensable part of the same policy, he contemplated political emancipation for the Catholics. Yet his task was formidable. Opinion within the Cabinet was divided. Several of the staunchest supporters of a Parliamentary Union were vehemently opposed to any suggestion of removing the religious test for political office. The King's anti-Catholic prejudices were well known, and Pitt knew that George III required the most tactful handling if he was to agree to the measure. In Dublin the Irish aristocracy saw its precious legislative independence threatened. Pitt recognised that Union would have to precede relief for the Catholics. A united Imperial Parliament would be able (so he thought) to take a more disinterested view of the Irish question, and the Catholic peasantry, perhaps a dangerous majority in their own land, would be safely submerged in a greater whole—the United Kingdom of Great Britain and Ireland. A divided Ireland was a permanent threat to British security. Only good fortune, and a happy coincidence of prevailing winds, had foiled French invasion at a time when it would have constituted a major danger.

But Pitt and his Irish advisers—chiefly Cornwallis, the Lord Lieutenant, and young Viscount Castlereagh, now on the threshold of his political career—knew how difficult it would be to persuade the Irish Parliament to vote away its own existence. It was notoriously venal and corrupt, and the Irish borough-mongers well knew the value of their property. The government therefore competed with the Irish politicians on their own terms. Compensation was paid for the loss of seats in the Irish House of Commons, and in the squalid negotiations Cornwallis and Castlereagh did not flinch, though they could not disguise their disgust. Their devotion to duty has earned them the unworthy jeers of posterity, while the Dublin Parliament has acquired a spuriously romantic charm. Eventually the government bought up a sufficient number of Irish proprietors. The corrupt legislature came to an appropriately corrupt end. The Union was carried in both Dublin and London, and in January 1801 the new Imperial Parliament assembled at Westminster.

But Pitt's troubles were not over. He had hoped to gain the support of a united Cabinet before approaching the King on the Catholic issue, but his efforts to carry his colleagues with him had been frustrated. While Pitt thought that time would bring his colleagues round, Loughborough, the Lord Chancellor, had put the King on his guard. George III was convinced that to agree to the emancipation of the Catholics would be to violate his Coronation Oath to uphold the Protestant religion, as by law established. He was oblivious to rational argument, and the knowledge that the King was adamant in his opposition to the proposed concession stiffened the determination of the more conservative members of the Cabinet. Pitt was in a sad predicament. He faced the opposition of many of his ministerial colleagues and the stubborn refusal of the King to give way. He knew that many (probably the majority) of the ordinary members of Parliament were also against his proposal, and that public opinion, in so far as it could be gauged, was antagonistic. No formal promise had been given to the Catholics, but Pitt's honour was at stake. The implications of Union were known to have influenced Catholic opinion. Pitt had no choice. For the first time in his career he used the threat of resignation. But George III did not budge: he had an alternative minister in Addington. So, in March 1801, Pitt went out of office.

Pitt's Resignation

It has sometimes been suggested that Pitt used the Catholic issue as a pretext for leaving office when his real motive was a recognition of the failure of his war policy, and of the necessity to make peace with Bonaparte. But Pitt had never subscribed to the 'no-negotiation' thesis advocated by Burke and Windham throughout the war, nor was he as rigid in his approach to international affairs as his cousin, Grenville. He was essentially pragmatic in his conduct of policy, and he was prepared to admit the necessity of peace. Later, when Addington negotiated the peace of Amiens, Pitt gave it his approval. Perhaps a greater measure of truth lies in the broken state of Pitt's health—but he had committed himself to the Catholic cause, and it is difficult to see how he could have resolved the situation in any other way. He was convinced that Union and Catholic emancipation were both necessary for the pacification of Ireland. One was useless without the other. This was one instance where he could not content himself with a job half done.

Yet he soon gave a pledge to refrain from raising the Catholic issue again during the King's lifetime. This has been seen as a betrayal, as an unscrupulous stratagem to prepare the way for his return to office. (Although it should be pointed out that Pitt was criticised by his own friends for his reluctance to take an active part in bringing about his own return to office.) But when George III went mad in 1801 it was obvious that his breakdown had been caused, partly at least, by the strain of the emancipation controversy, and when he recovered the King made no attempt to hide his own strong convictions on the matter: Pitt was responsible for his mental collapse. Naturally Pitt was distressed by this accusation, and when it is remembered that it was now evident that there was a danger that the King would collapse in the same way should the matter be reopened, the awkwardness of Pitt's position can be appreciated. The King was still active in politics, as head of the executive. Another bout of madness would disrupt the government of the country and perhaps provoke another Regency crisis. Everyone knew that it was unlikely that George III could ever be persuaded to give way on the Catholic question. His failing mind clung to its prejudices like a drowning man to a lifebelt. Pitt was doing little more than recognising several embarrassing, but ineluctable, factors in the current situation. In any case he probably thought that he was doing little more than postpone the issue. George III was now ageing. Few people thought that he would live for another nineteen years. Nor was Pitt alone in making this concession to the King. Castlereagh, Tierney and Canning all gave a similar undertaking. Even Fox, when taking office in 1806, told his friends that he did not intend to embarrass his sovereign by bringing the Catholic issue forward. No formal pledge was given, but, so far as George III himself was concerned, it seemed to be implied. Later this confusion led to the downfall of the 'Talents' ministry in 1807, when the unyielding and dogmatic Grenville—whose attitude was less flexible than that of the opportunistic Fox—refused to give an undertaking not to raise emancipation for the Catholics in any form whatsoever. The fact that Grenville, too, was driven from office when confronted with the King's intransigence, emphasises the problems which compelled Pitt to resign and to give his promise to the King.

The Union had been accomplished, but without emancipation it exacerbated the bitterness of Irish politics. Yet it is misleading to look at 1801 with too vivid a recollection of the history of the nineteenth century. Had Union been followed, as Pitt desired, by the speedy emancipation of the Catholics, the long sequence of misunderstandings and treachery might have been broken. Without the agitation for relief Irish politics might have assumed a more hopeful character. When Pitt's scheme was wrecked by the iron will of George III the Irish nation moved forward to new tragedies.

Peace of Amiens

The Addington ministry soon embarked on peace negotiations. The nation was so anxious for peace that they agreed to terms which were excessively favourable to the French. Britain returned all her conquests to France, with the exception of Ceylon and Trinidad, and promised to hand over Malta to the Knights of St John. The French undertook to recall their troops from Naples, the Papal States and the central Italian duchies. The independence of Holland, Switzerland and northern Italy seemed to be guaranteed by the treaty of Lunéville. But while the British hoped for peace in their time, Bonaparte never doubted that a new war against England would be necessary. Peace would be no more than a breathing space during which he could consolidate, not diminish, his power on the continent. In the meantime the English celebrated the end of the war. Holiday-makers poured into France. The grim austerities of the 1790s were forgotten, and, as yet, men were happily unaware of the new perils which were soon to be faced in the years ahead.

2 : The War Against Napoleon

THE first phase of the war had been dominated by fear of the ideas of the French Revolution as well as apprehensions over the conquests of the Republic; but when the peace of Amiens came to an end the war was envisaged in more personal terms. It was a struggle against Napoleon. Whatever the rights and wrongs of the question, he was chiefly responsible—in British eyes—for the breakdown of the uneasy peace. A minority of intellectuals perversely regarded him as the personification of liberal hopes, but to the majority of Englishmen he was the embodiment of tyranny and deceit. 'Little Boney' became part of popular legend, and grotesque parodies of his figure appeared in countless cartoons.

Breakdown of Amiens Settlement

Certainly the deficiencies of the Amiens settlement were soon apparent, for the British had sacrificed too much in their desire for a speedy termination of hostilities. They had overlooked the need for that measure of security which Pitt had consistently championed throughout the 1790s, and anxieties were soon aroused by Napoleon's conduct in Europe. He annexed Piedmont and Elba; occupied Switzerland, where he was duly installed as 'Mediator' of the Swiss Republic; and maintained his armies in Holland and northern Italy. Nor had he forgotten his dreams of empire in the east, and when the French government newspaper *Le Moniteur* published Sebastiani's Egyptian Report British suspicions of French designs in the Mediterranean were confirmed. The Addington government felt that the spirit of the Amiens agreement had been broken and refused to withdraw British troops from Malta—a particularly valuable base should hostilities be renewed, and if Egypt should once again become a major objective of French strategy. When Bonaparte demanded that Malta should be handed over to the Knights of St John Addington stood firm.

In Paris the British ambassador was publicly humiliated, and in May 1803 war was declared. Everyone knew that Malta was merely the occasion, not the fundamental cause, of the conflict. The real explanation lay in Napoleon's plans for the continued domination of the continent: a supremacy which could not be tolerated by Britain, especially if it became the springboard for a threat to her communications with India.

But however determined he had been over Malta, Addington had no military ambitions. Without allies on the continent Britain could do little but stand on the defensive, and since this had the advantage of being less expensive than a more spectacular campaign, Addington was content. But dissatisfaction with the government grew until even Pitt and Fox found themselves in the same opposition lobby. Pitt had deliberately refrained from intriguing against Addington, but his more enthusiastic supporters urged him to play a more active role in bringing the government down. Canning was bitterly hostile to the Addington ministry, ridiculing it in his clever political verses. Though there were several attempts at negotiation, these proved abortive: Pitt had no desire to accept a subordinate post under Addington's leadership. While energetically performing his duties in the Volunteers Pitt saw no purpose in returning to politics unless he shouldered the responsibility for the direction of the war. In May 1804 the resignation of Addington made way for Pitt.

Pitt's Second Ministry

He tried to form an all-party government, uniting men of all political opinions in one patriotic endeavour. The controversies of the 1790s were forgiven, if not forgotten, and Pitt offered Fox the post of Foreign Secretary. But George III's obstinacy ruined his plans. The King refused to accept Fox as a member of his Cabinet. In doing so he was within his constitutional rights, but his action made a national government impossible. Although Fox urged his friends to go ahead without him, they rejected Pitt's generous allocation of posts in the new ministry. Grenville, now a staunch ally of Fox, also declined Cabinet office. Pitt accepted the situation with resignation. He knew his health to be such that the strain of

C

ministerial duty would probably cost him his life, and his Cabinet was so weak that it was jeered at as the ministry of Billy and Pitt. Several of the more important members of Addington's government stayed on—though this was less unusual at that period than it would be today.

Pitt had now profited from his errors during the Revolutionary War. He courageously set about creating the third coalition against the French. He encouraged Russia and Austria to take up arms, and tried to concentrate, not disperse, his resources. He wanted to force the French to commit themselves to a protracted campaign in Italy, where British sea-power could be used to facilitate co-operation between the Russians and Austrians. But until Pitt's negotiations had their effect England was threatened by invasion. Napoleon, who proclaimed himself Emperor of the French in March 1804, marshalled the so-called 'Army of England' on the hills above Boulogne, and prepared a huge fleet of transports. He dismissed allegations that he was attempting the impossible, striking medals in advance to celebrate his conquest of England. But without command of the sea the invasion was doomed to failure. Earlier thoughts of a speedy night crossing were succeeded by the sober realisation of the decisive nature of British sea-power. With Spain as an unwilling ally, Napoleon set about devising the overthrow of the British fleets. He intended that the French squadrons at Toulon and Brest should evade the blockade, meet in the Atlantic and seize control of the channel. Then the Grand Army would be ferried across the sea and England overwhelmed.

Despite their apparent invincibility, these schemes miscarried. Villeneuve, the French Admiral at Toulon, slipped through Nelson's blockade and escaped to the West Indies. But on his return he could do no more than fight an indecisive battle with Calder off Cape Finisterre. Then he put into Corunna to refit, and, abandoning all hope of a junction with the Brest squadron, sought refuge in Cadiz (August 1805). Napoleon was furious. The chance of naval supremacy in the channel was lost. Barham, the old but outstandingly able First Lord of the Admiralty, ordered the British fleets to concentrate off the Spanish coast. And now other factors upset Napoleon's timetable. In April the Anglo-Russian convention had been signed, and in July the Austrians joined the coalition, which also included Sweden. Napoleon, recognising the failure of his invasion project, and aware of the need to strike a swift blow at the Austrians before the Russian armies could reach central Europe, took the Army of England off to Germany. He surprised the Austrian General, Mack, and forced him to surrender at Ulm (October 1805). A month later he was in Vienna: the coalition was already reeling. But Nelson's victory over the French and Spanish fleets at Trafalgar on October 21st shattered Napoleon's sea-power. England was already safe from invasion, and for the rest of the war Napoleon's strategy was crippled by the control of the seas which the Royal Navy exercised. Nelson's greatest victory was an offensive triumph, although his death damped the nation's exultation. Even Pitt himself, usually a sound sleeper, was so excited by the news that he rose at three in the morning, trying to master his feelings by beginning the day's work. Victory at sea inspired hopes of a similar triumph on land. Once the Austrian and Russian armies met, Ulm would be avenged. But in December 1805 Napoleon inflicted the crushing defeat of Austerlitz upon the allies. Austria was knocked out of the war: the old familiar tale of disappointment and disillusionment was repeated yet again.

The news of the disaster demoralised Pitt. He knew the magnitude of the blow. The coalition could no longer win that decisive victory for which he longed with all the intensity of a dying man. His health was shattered; his physique was exhausted. Haggard and pain-ridden, he was conscious of his country's misfortunes until the end. He died in the early hours of January 23rd, 1806. After Trafalgar cheering crowds had dragged his carriage through the streets. Now Parliament voted to pay his debts, and buried him by his father's side in Westminster Abbey. England had saved herself by her exertions, but Europe was not yet saved by her example. Pitt's work lay in ruins. This lonely, brave and dedicated man had seen his last desperate effort thwarted, but in the agony of his final months of life he had perceived that the resistance of a people would be fatal to Napoleon's power, and with strange foresight he prophesied that Spain would be the place where this would first be accomplished. And in death he became a symbol of the nation's will to resist.

Fox–Grenville Ministry

With the death of Pitt the King succumbed to the necessity of accepting Fox. Together with Grenville, Fox formed a ministry, but within nine months he too was dead. In collaboration with Wilberforce, who had campaigned against the traffic for many years in the face of misrepresentation and bitter opposition, Fox secured the abolition of the Slave Trade, but he learned from experience the impossibility of a negotiated peace. Fox had never appreciated the difficulties under which Pitt had laboured. Despite his sympathy for the ideals of 1789, he never grasped the nature of the conflict between Britain and France. He thought of the war as open to settlement at any time by the normal processes of negotiation. He clung to the old diplomacy of the eighteenth century until the end of his life. He did not understand the complexities of dealing with a Revolution and a Dictator. He warned Napoleon of an attempt on his life: he soon discovered that chivalry made no impression on Napoleon's outlook. The negotiations in Paris were an appalling mixture of tragedy and farce. They were incompetently conducted by the British representatives, and with victory in sight Napoleon was in no mood to moderate his claims. In September 1806 Fox died, a bitterly disappointed man. Grenville took over as head of the 'Ministry of All the Talents', but the autumn and winter brought more bad news from Europe.

Prussia had put off the decision on whether or not she should join the coalition until it was too late. The French domination of Germany was a reality before the Prussians could do anything about it. The Confederation of the Rhine was a puppet state under French control. It was also an affront to Prussian pride. Then Napoleon turned his attention to North Germany, declaring himself 'Protector' of the Hanseatic towns. In October 1806 war came after a summer of diplomatic wrangling and military manoeuvres. But the legend of Prussian invincibility, already tarnished by Valmy in 1792, was exploded at Jena, where the Prussian army was catastrophically defeated. Napoleon was in Berlin by the end of October, ready to complete his triumph by finishing off the Russians, who still held out in Poland. In 1807 two bloody battles were fought at Eylau (February) and Friedland (June). Napoleon's power was at its zenith. Austria was crushed: the Holy Roman Empire was abolished. Prussia was divided and humiliated. In July Napoleon and the Tsar met at Tilsit and apportioned the world between themselves. Dalmatia and Turkey were assigned to Russia's sphere of influence. The Tsar agreed to close his ports to British ships and to help Napoleon to bring the Danes, Swedes and Portuguese to heel: in order to prevent the Danish fleet from falling into enemy hands the British bombarded Copenhagen in 1807. Napoleon's control over western Europe was also recognised by the Tsar. Never again was Napoleon to know such unchallenged dominion. Imperceptibly and irrevocably his power now slid into gradual decline. His own arrogance was his undoing, for he ignored Talleyrand's warnings that France needed a friend in Europe, not merely a collection of satellite states surrounded by disgruntled and defeated foes. But reconciliation was beyond Napoleon's comprehension, and he was incapable of appreciating the advantages of a moderate peace. He believed in harsh terms, imposed by force. But in 1807 these truths were not apparent. For the British there was little to hope for. It was difficult to see how defiance could be transformed into victory. It was equally difficult for the French to put their continental supremacy to decisive use in defeating Britain.

Ministerial Crises

In England the conduct of the war was bedevilled by ministerial crises. In their anxiety to improve military recruitment Grenville and his colleagues proposed to allow Catholics to hold commissioned ranks in the English army. George III condemned the measure. He saw it as the first step in a sinister conspiracy to procure Catholic emancipation, and demanded pledges from his ministers that the subject would never be raised again. The position was confused. Fox had allowed the matter to drop when taking office, but Grenville was inflexible. He refused to give the required promise, and in March 1807 the Duke of Portland formed a new government. English politics were torn by personal animosity. Addington (who now bore the title of Viscount Sidmouth) hated Canning, Canning envied Castlereagh, and no one could compose these differences. For two years Portland clung on as First Lord of the Treasury, but the ministry went through many anxious moments. The Duke of York was driven to resign as Commander-in-Chief by the revelation that his mistress had sold commissions in the army. Charges of corruption were made against several of the ministers themselves. Military expeditions—inherited from the 'Talents'—failed in South America and Egypt. In 1809 the Walcheren campaign was added to a series of military reverses. By creating a diversion in the Low Countries it had been hoped to help the Austrians, who were once again fighting Napoleon. But the Austrians were defeated at Wagram and compelled to sue for peace, while the British expeditionary force withered away, the ravages of disease taking a severe toll of life. The troops were recalled before the end of the year, but the government was discredited. Portland fell ill and died. Canning and Castlereagh fought a duel and went out of office. Spencer Perceval, the underestimated but competent Chancellor of the Exchequer, took over. His attempts to strengthen his ministry by bringing in Grey and Grenville failed, but he and his colleagues—Liverpool at the War Office, Wellesley (Wellington's brother) at the Foreign Office, Eldon as Lord Chancellor—stuck doggedly to the task of winning the war. They were not men of insight or imagination, but neither were they the fools they are often alleged to have been. Liverpool, for example, stoutly defended the strategic value of the Peninsular War when that campaign was denounced as useless by the defeatist Whig opposition. Despite doubts and rumours, the ministry survived until Perceval's assassination in 1812. In 1810 George III went mad for the last time, and in the following year the Prince of Wales was installed as Regent by Act of Parliament. The Whigs had hoped that the accession of the Prince Regent would bring them into office, but his association with the Foxites now belonged to the past, and after several months of speculation the

Perceval ministry stayed in power. As he grew older the Prince Regent acquired more of his father's prejudices, perhaps by way of atonement for the sins of his youth. He wanted a vigorous prosecution of the war and rejected any concessions to the Catholics. The thought of presiding over a victorious nation appealed to his aesthetic sense. On Perceval's death Liverpool succeeded as First Lord of the Treasury: the most important ministerial appointment was that of Castlereagh as Foreign Secretary.

The Continental System

In the deadlock which followed Tilsit both the British and the French cast about for some means of defeating their adversary. Both resorted to economic warfare. By his Berlin and Milan decrees (1806–7) Napoleon tried to kill British trade with Europe. He confiscated all ships and cargoes which had come from British ports. He envisaged a continent which refused to accept British manufactures, and also ceased to provide England with the necessary marine stores and timber for her fleets. But the techniques of control were insufficiently developed for this policy to be fully effective, and its consequences were almost as bad for the countries of Europe as for Britain. A flourishing smuggling trade sprang up, for the French armies themselves needed British woollens and leather goods. In order to equip his troops for the invasion of Russia Napoleon had to permit the import of British boots and saddles. But if it was only spasmodically applied, the 'Continental System' did adversely affect British trade. In 1808 the British were badly hit. There was some improvement in 1809–10 with new markets in South America and the Near East compensating for the loss of trade in Europe, and with some relaxation in the regulations governing trade with the French Empire. But then Napoleon tried to tighten up the system once more, and in 1811 British exports to northern Europe fell to one-fifth of the 1810 figure. But the strain was too great for Europe to bear: whenever the restrictions began having the desired effect on the English economy Napoleon was driven by the hardships of his own people, and the needs of his own economy, to relax them.

The political consequences of the 'Continental System' were even worse. To enforce his policy Napoleon was compelled to extend his control to new countries and longer coastlines. The device which was to have starved England to surrender by depriving the 'nation of shopkeepers' of their trade became a will of the wisp, luring Napoleon on to destruction. The Peninsular War and the Russian Campaign were both fruits of the attempt to ruin English commerce.

Britain replied to Napoleon's decrees by the issue of Orders in Council. France and her satellites were pronounced to be under blockade. Not only was trade between enemy ports to be prevented but neutrals were allowed to trade with the French Empire only if they were selling British goods or if their vessels first put in at a British port, where their cargoes were liable to a duty. Napoleon had decided that the British were to have no commerce with Europe. They retorted by stipulating that his overseas trade was subject to their direction and control. Both sides finally withdrew from their policy of economic strangulation, for in trying to throttle the enemy, they found they were damaging themselves. In 1812 Liverpool cancelled the Orders in Council, and Napoleon lifted the embargo on British goods. But by this time both had paid the political price. Britain was involved in a War with America, while Napoleon had tasted frustration and defeat in Spain and Russia. That economic warfare should be tried at all was in itself a tribute to the gravity of the conflict, and the ultimate supremacy of sea-power.

Spain and Portugal

And sea-power had made it possible for the British to exploit Napoleon's intervention in Spain. He determined to put his brother Joseph on the throne of Spain, in order to make his Continental System more effective and to protect his lines of communication with Portugal, where he was already meddling with a view to cutting off Portuguese trade with Britain. Squalid disputes between the King of Spain and the heir to the throne gave Napoleon his opportunity. He summoned the Spanish royal family to Bayonne, and deposed them. The insult provoked a national resistance to the French. The Spaniards rose in revolt against the foreign usurper. The moment of decision had arrived. But the Peninsular War began with a mingling of victory and folly. Sir Arthur Wellesley, the younger brother of Lord Wellesley, landed in Portugal and defeated the French at the battle of Vimiero (August 21st, 1808), but his superiors allowed the French to escape by agreeing to the convention of Cintra, which permitted Junot's troops to return to France with their equipment. Dalrymple, Burrard and Wellesley were all brought home to answer the charges levied against them. Meanwhile Sir John Moore, a brilliant soldier who had been primarily responsible for the excellent training given to the British infantry, took over command.

His task was not easy. He had to collaborate with the Spaniards, but their irregular levies were difficult to get on with and impossible to discipline. The quality of his Portuguese allies was questionable, especially if they had to face the French in the field. Moore had hardly set out to bring aid to the Spaniards when he heard that Ney had already destroyed two of the Spanish armies and that the French were poised to crush what remained of Spanish resistance in the south. Moore boldly used his force to draw the French off. He struck at their lines of communication and saved the Spaniards from the full fury of the French assault. Napoleon himself joined in the pursuit of the English, only to abandon it in order to quell the Austrians, who were once again in arms. Meanwhile Moore's heroic campaign in central and northern Spain had ended in victory and death. The retreat to the sea had been arduous and exhausting, but the British drove off their pursuers at Corunna and made good their escape. Their commander was mortally wounded: his soldiers buried him on the field of battle and left him alone with his glory. The army had suffered heavy casualties, but the taste of victory heartened men who now knew for certain that the British infantry were a match for the massed columns of the French. More significantly the Spaniards were still in the fight. This was doubly valuable when the Austrians submitted to Napoleon's humiliating demands after their defeat at Wagram. A Habsburg Princess, Marie Louise, married their conqueror, and for three years the Austrians kept on good terms with Napoleon until the after-effects of the Russian campaign gave them the opportunity of revenge.

In April 1809 Wellesley, cleared of responsibility for the convention of Cintra, returned to Portugal. There he built up a base for his operations. The lines of Torres Vedras formed a refuge to which he could return whenever the French armies threatened to engulf his small force. Every summer he sallied forth, harrying the French, fighting only when he had to and husbanding his army with parsimonious care. He won victories at Talavera in 1809 and Busaco in 1810, and was raised to the peerage with the title of Viscount Wellington. Then, in the winter of 1810–11 Masséna tried to recover Portugal and pressed on towards Lisbon. Wellington retreated before him, wasting the country as he went. Masséna was halted before Wellington's earthworks, but it was the besieger, not the besieged, who was starved out. In the spring of 1811 Masséna retired. The habit of living off the land had brought a grim retribution, and the French learned the stark truth of the saying that in the Iberian peninsula large armies starved while small ones were defeated. But much tough fighting lay ahead. In May 1811 Wellington won a dearly bought victory over Masséna at Fuentes de Oñoro. Farther south, where the British were investing Badajoz, Beresford stood his ground at Albuera, but his army was fearfully mangled. Marmont and Soult longed to recover Portugal, but they shrank from another winter before the lines of Torres Vedras. Then, in January 1812, Wellington surprised the enemy by taking the offensive. Cuidad Rodrigo fell, as did Badajoz after a ferocious struggle. Several months of manoeuvring culminated in the victory of Salamanca in July, but although he entered Madrid in triumph, Wellington was once again compelled to retreat to Portugal. He still lacked the resources to gain final victory. He could not disguise his chagrin at the disappointing outcome of the campaign, but the French were growing weaker every day. The Spanish guerillas were adding to the strains and stresses which were breaking the nerves of the French army. Napoleon spoke contemptuously of 'the Sepoy General'—a reference to Wellington's early exploits in India—

but the 'Spanish ulcer' was draining his Empire's strength. Though Wellington had to wait another year before accomplishing the liberation of Spain, his nicely calculated strategy and tactics were major factors contributing to Napoleon's downfall.

The Russian Campaign

There was also the Russian campaign. Like the Peninsular War, it sprang from Napoleon's Continental System. Since Tilsit relations between the Tsar and Napoleon had deteriorated. Napoleon wanted to tighten his control of Russian trade, especially with Britain, and had also had second thoughts about Russian designs upon Turkey and the possibilities of Russian expansion towards the Mediterranean. The Tsar was increasingly anxious about French policy in central and eastern Europe, and had been insulted by Napoleon's choice of an Austrian instead of a Russian princess as the means of legitimising his régime. The Continental System was already breaking down, torn apart by its internal contradictions, even when it seemed on the verge of success, but as long as the British retained their maritime supremacy, Napoleon was committed to following his ambitious, but impracticable, scheme. The independence claimed and exercised by the Tsar drove Napoleon to the only method left open to him—perhaps the only one he really understood—direct military intervention, fraught with risks as this was. So with an army of 700,000 men recruited from all the nations of the French Empire he crossed the river Niemen, hoping to bring the Russians to decisive battle as soon as possible (June 1812). But he was drawn into the innermost recesses of Russia, his communications becoming ever more tenuous as his huge army floundered amidst a desolated country. Even when the Russians gave battle at Borodino (September 1812) victory was costly and indecisive. The occupation of Moscow did not break Alexander's spirit, and in the burning shell of the city Napoleon experienced the appalling illusion of success. His army was exhausted, and his attempt to retrieve the situation by a strategic retreat failed. The Russian winter inflicted new privations upon his weary troops. Defeated by the sheer size of Russia and the horrors of her climate, he acknowledged his humiliation and made for home. But the agony was not over: half a million men were lost during the long trek: many starved to death, others died of exposure or were killed by the Russian peasantry or marauding Cossacks. The retreat from Moscow became a by-word for suffering, endurance and defeat.

Now Europe saw the chance to throw off French domination. The Prussians, who had been slowly recovering from the catastrophe of 1806, had been compelled to help Napoleon: now they changed sides. After a period of hesitation the Austrians followed their example. In Spain Wellington was triumphant. He outwitted the French, crossed the Ebro and defeated King Joseph and Marshal Jourdan at Vittoria (June 1813). Napoleon faced a continent in arms, but the immensity of the crisis brought out the best in him, much as success usually brought out the worst. At Leipzig he was defeated in a massive contest lasting for three days, the legendary 'Battle of the Nations'. Soon he was exercising his genius to the full in defending France from invasion. Some critics claim that his skill was never more brilliantly displayed than in these campaigns against colossal odds, but his youthful and inexperienced armies were overwhelmed by weight of numbers. In 1814 Napoleon abdicated: the Bourbons were restored. But, though Napoleon was exiled to Elba, France retained her frontiers of 1792. At last the long war was over, and men turned their thoughts to the novel problems of peace.

War with the United States

But England was involved in another war. In 1812 hostilities had broken out between Britain and the United States. The ostensible reason was the right of search exercised by the British in their blockade of France. But before the Americans declared war in June 1812 the British government had decided to cancel its restrictions on trade, and this became operative in July. In fact, dreams of conquering Canada and hopes of expansion entertained by the frontiersmen of the western states were more important in determining American policy. New England—the area hardest hit by the British blockade—was unenthusiastic about the war. It was popular in the western states, where men were impatient to open up new territories. For both sides the conflict was frustrating. The Americans won several fights on the Great Lakes and sacked Toronto, but their invasion of Canada was a failure. The British burned Washington, the Federal capital, but were themselves defeated at New Orleans. The war settled nothing. It stirred old memories of the War of Independence, revived suspicions of British desires to limit American expansion and provided the Americans with picturesque episodes to be celebrated in song, but the maritime controversies were left unresolved and the future development of Canada and the United States was not decisively affected. After all, the Orders in Council had been directed against France and not the United States.

The Hundred Days

Men had scarcely adjusted themselves to a world at peace when the romantic episode of 'the Hundred Days' burst upon them. Napoleon escaped from the tiny island of Elba, which had been given to him, and landed in the south of France. His reception was initially cautious, then rapturous as the old imperial magic brought men flocking to his standard. The disillusionment of the Bourbon restoration had dimmed men's recollection of the retreat from Moscow, the burdens of conscription, the hardships of the Continental System. Ney, who had promised to bring Napoleon back to Paris in a cage, deserted Louis XVIII and went over to his Emperor. Napoleon denied that he had any warlike intentions: the new Empire would live at peace with its neighbours. He claimed that he had always wanted to devote himself to the constructive tasks of peace, and in order to court liberal opinion in France he promised a representative assembly. But the powers of Europe were unconvinced. They doubted Napoleon's sincerity and questioned the practicability of coexistence. So Napoleon's career was played out to its final climax on June 18th, 1815. Wellington, commanding a motley army of Germans, Belgians, Dutch and British, held out at Waterloo until the arrival of Blücher and the Prussians sealed Napoleon's doom. It had been, in Wellington's words, 'a near run thing', but Napoleon was banished to St Helena, where he died in 1821. For a generation

Bonapartism was a myth, then, in the unprepossessing person of
Louis Napoleon, the Emperor's nephew, it became a political
reality. But in 1815 the allies congratulated themselves on dispersing the threat to their security so quickly.

Congress of Vienna

At Vienna the statesmen looked for a principle to guide them
in their efforts to restore order to a ravaged Europe. Talleyrand,
whose shrewdness had enabled him to survive every change of
fortune, suggested legitimacy as the most reliable concept available;
so, wherever it could be managed, the old dynasties were restored
—in France, Spain, Naples, the Papal States and the Italian
duchies. To guard against a renewal of French aggression Belgium
was united with Holland to form the Kingdom of the Netherlands;
Prussia was given territory on the Rhine; and Genoa merged into
Piedmont. The German Confederation, with Austria as President,
replaced Napoleon's Confederation of the Rhine. Prussia acquired
Swedish Pomerania and part of Saxony. The powers recognised
Russian control of Finland and Bessarabia, and when Tsar
Alexander became King of Poland that country too became a
province of the Russian Empire. Norway was taken from Denmark
and given to Sweden. France escaped with the frontiers of 1790,
and an army of occupation until the indemnity of 700 million
francs was paid. Talleyrand had argued that too harsh a peace
would endanger the restored Bourbons, and the settlement can
hardly be regarded as a punitive measure. Britain had little interest
in territory in Europe, and the continental statesmen were prepared to see her gain various colonies and trading stations, most
of which had a commercial or strategic value, and many of which
she had seized during the war: the Cape of Good Hope, Ceylon,
Mauritius, Guiana, Trinidad, Tobago, Malta, Heligoland. Nor
were the statesmen at Vienna as ignorant of liberalism and
nationalism as has often been maintained. Castlereagh could talk
about 'a great moral change coming on in Europe', admitting
that 'the principles of freedom' were 'in full operation'. He
thought it wise, however, to retard rather than accelerate the
development of 'this most hazardous principle'. His caution was

justified. Nationalism had disrupted international relations and had provoked war. Liberalism was still a dubious movement, for it seemed to be the harbinger of revolution, and who, in 1815, could doubt that revolution was a disaster? When the principle of self-determination was applied in redrawing the map of Europe in 1919 the result was neither a stable nor a liberal Europe. The aristocrats of 1815 were practical statesmen, not prophets. By their lights they did their job well. The settlement was not perfect, but it was not vindictive. It was a sensible attempt to solve a complex and monumental problem. It lasted, with a few modifications, for forty years. It sought to maintain the peace by establishing the Concert of Europe—a more realistic answer to the problems of international conflict than the League of Nations. The four victors—Britain, Russia, Prussia and Austria—bound themselves together in the Quadruple Alliance and undertook to confer regularly on the international situation and the best means of dealing with a threat to peace. Thus was born the famous Congress system. The true instrument of repression was the Tsar's ambitious Holy Alliance, which was accepted, in the first place, by the other powers only out of politeness, however much it was later exploited by Metternich, and which Castlereagh dismissed in private as 'a piece of sublime mysticism and nonsense'.

But when Castlereagh returned home from the Congress men were incapable of appreciating his achievement. Britain had won the war because of her control of the seas and her economic power. Now the social implications of that power had to be faced. The immediate situation was depressing. The condition of the people, so long regarded as beneath the dignity of politicians, was forcing itself on their attention. Industrial unrest, unemployment, a recession in agriculture, a colossal national debt and high food prices—these were the blessings of peace. And to understand why this was so it is necessary to discuss the social revolution which had been taking place all through the long war, and the society which Lord Liverpool and his colleagues governed with little comprehension of the profounder issues. It is a curiously paradoxical society: for Regency England was uncomfortably poised between the old way of life and the new.

3 : England in 1815

THE first thirty years of the nineteenth century are usually identified with the complex and controversial process described as 'the Industrial Revolution'. But although the expansion of British industry, the changing structure of the national economy and the emergence of new social problems can be discerned at this period, it is misleading if the extent and degree of these innovations are exaggerated. At the end of the war with France Britain was still very far from being an urban and industrialised society. Out of a population of 13 million, between 9 and 10 million still lived in sleepy villages, remote hamlets or quiet market towns. Most men were employed in rural pursuits, and on the eve of the first Reform Bill the nation was almost exactly balanced between agriculture and industry. The booming cotton industry, which had profited most from the new inventions, accounted for no more than an eightieth of the population. When Victoria came to the throne in 1837 more women were employed in domestic service than in the cotton mills, and the building trade afforded more work than any other single occupation. In 1815 London's tailors and shoemakers outnumbered the miners of Durham and Northumberland. There was much variation from one part of the country to another. Generalisations about farm labourers in the south cannot be applied to those of the north, nor can descriptions of town life in Lancashire or Yorkshire be taken as true of Suffolk or Wiltshire or Kent. Regions retained a distinctive character, and the country was much more diverse in its habits of life than our own more uniform society. Local patriotism and local customs moulded the outlook of ordinary folk. Traditional rituals brought colour to their lives at Christmas, Easter, May Day and Michaelmas. The old order was passing away, but its demise was slow, chequered and protracted.

One confident statement can be made with regard to Regency

England: the population was expanding. Although the figures available are not wholly reliable, they reflect a development of immense significance. In 1688 the population of England had been estimated at 5,500,000 and by 1760 it had grown to 6,500,000. In 1801 the census returns showed that there were 8,331,434 Englishmen, and ten years later this figure had swelled by another million. In 1815 Britain was inhabited by 10,000,000 Englishmen, 2,500,000 Scotsmen and 500,000 Welshmen. The increase continued: 14,000,000 in 1821, 16,500,000 in 1831, 21,000,000 in 1851. This is not to be explained by any gigantic rise in the birth-rate, for it had fallen slightly in the 1780s, and it fell again after 1830. The principal reason was a fall in the infant mortality rate: more children were surviving the dangers of the first six years of life. Other factors contributed to the growth in population: advances in medicine and midwifery; the building of more hospitals (though these were outrageously unhygienic by later standards); improved, but still primitive, sanitation; perhaps a more varied and nutritious diet. The towns of the north-west attracted large numbers of Irish immigrants, and as well as adding to their populations this created problems of a peculiar character. The situation was made all the more difficult by the fact that so many of the new industrial towns were located in the same area. Despite the evils of industrialisation—bad housing, chronic overcrowding and deficient sanitation in towns where public amenities lagged behind chaotic development—men were living longer than their grandfathers had done. With all their faults, the factories meant that the artisan and his family no longer ate and slept in the same room as they worked. But instead of interpreting the multiplication of numbers as evidence of a rising standard of living, men feared it as a potential burden on the rates, and saw in it a symptom of ultimate disaster.

The Growth of the Towns

As the population grew more men came to live in the towns. In 1801 Liverpool housed 82,000 people. Thirty years later the city's population was 202,000. Similarly, the inhabitants of Leeds numbered 123,000 in 1831, compared with 53,000 at the beginning

D

of the nineteenth century. In the same period the populations of Birmingham and Sheffield doubled. In 1815 over a million people lived in London—roughly one in ten of all Englishmen. Within five years over a quarter of a million had been added to this figure. The rise of population, and the mobility of labour which was so important in the Industrial Revolution, made the accommodation problem all the more acute, and during the war the shortage of timber, bricks and glass, together with a high rate of interest which restricted borrowing, crippled the building trade. Even at the best of times it would have been difficult to meet the challenge of over-rapid expansion. With so many clamouring for homes it is not surprising that poor buildings, deficient in workmanship and squalid in design, were hastily erected, all too frequently being huddled meanly together. Much abuse has been heaped on the 'jerry-builders', without regard for the limitations which high taxation and a lack of adequate materials imposed on them. Some of them were the ruthless profiteers of legend, but many were unsophisticated men, unable to see beyond the immediate future, baffled by the problems confronting them and unhappily aware that nothing in their own experience gave them any guidance in dealing with the demands which were being made of them. Between 1811 and 1831 750,000 houses were constructed, but the average number of people per house remained much about the same—somewhere between five and six. Conditions were especially bad in the north-west. In Manchester there were over 20,000 cellar dwellings where the poverty-stricken Irish thronged in prolific confusion. Cobbett indignantly denounced living standards in the north, asserting with his customary vehemence that the factory workers were worse off than villeins or serfs. Yet, during this same period, important improvements were being made in several of the older towns. In London the Prince Regent was pushing on with his grandiose plans to perpetuate his memory as the architect of a nobler capital, and although his schemes were never fully implemented, Regent Street stands as his monument. When the monarchs of Europe visited England after Waterloo the new gas-lamps in the streets of Westminster were the marvel of the age. Although the houses which were being built for the poor conformed to the conventional eighteenth-century indifference to systematic drainage, the new suburbs for the more affluent had drains instead of cess-pools and water-closets instead of the traditional privies. The houses built at Bethnal Green in the early years of the nineteenth century had their foundations rotted by the malodorous overflow of the cess-pools, yet they were thought to be a distinct advance on previous houses, for they were two-storied and were more spacious than many of the older dwellings. In any case, sewage disposal remained unsatisfactory until the manufacture of cheap, glazed earthenware pipes on a large enough scale in the 1840s. Overcrowding more than offset structural improvements, and in the new towns the children of the slums manifested an old problem on a bigger scale. For it was the children who suffered most from the reorganisation of industry. Their parents, who had flocked to the towns in response to the shorter hours and higher wages which were in operation there, had had some experience of the benefits of living in the country. But their children knew only the grim streets in which they were born and the busy factories in which they toiled. The drabness of the towns—so often hastily erected near the handiest source of power —was depressing and unrelieved. There were few parks, playgrounds, gardens or trees. There were almost no facilities for recreation. Beauty was as remote as hygiene. Nor did the accepted attitude towards children make the situation any easier. It was thought right and proper that children should join their parents in the factory as soon as possible, in order to play their part in winning bread for the family. This had been the usual practice in the old domestic industries, where four year olds were given their share of the work. It was believed that lack of employment for the young would lead to habits of idleness and vice. Both morality and economic self-interest were satisfied. But before condemning the employers it is worth recalling that many children knew no sterner taskmasters than their own parents. The gradual realisation of the evils of child-labour was itself a consequence of industrialisation, but it took time to impress itself upon the consciences of men.

For the workers employment in the factories meant both gain

and loss. Gone were the days when the independent weaver could work when he felt like it, taking two or three days off whenever the spirit prompted him to join his drinking companions in the tavern. Now he had to work during the hours fixed by the owners. Although hours in the factories were long—sixteen hours a day were common—they were no more arduous than the weary shifts which men had known in the old days, for the domestic weaver had to make up for lost time by working for protracted spells. Nor were the hours in the mills more exhausting than those of the agricultural labourers. The regularity of working hours was more burdensome than their length. Men did not mind longer hours if these meant higher wages, but they bitterly resented the loss of liberty which was represented by the monotonous and inescapable routine of factory life. Yet even monotony was no new experience. As sober a craftsman as Francis Place bore witness to the soul-destroying nature of the putting-out system:

'I know not how to describe the sickening aversion which at times steals over the working man and utterly disables him, for a longer or shorter period, from following his usual occupation, and compels him to indulge in idleness. I have felt it, resisted it to the utmost of my power, but have been obliged to submit and run away from work. This is the case with every working man I have known . . .'

Nothing is more unrealistic than the portrayal of the artisans of pre-industrial days as skilled and devoted craftsmen. Some were, but in most cases the machines did more speedily and more efficiently what had been done by hand. Even the dangers of unemployment (often blamed by the workers on the new-fangled machines) were no worse than previously, when booms and slumps had threatened the livelihood of village craftsmen. But the workers were in no mood to philosophise over their plight. In 1811 organised machine breaking took place in Nottingham, the movement taking its name from a simple youth called Ned Ludd, who had broken some machinery in a fit of rage. Mythology transformed the boy into 'King Ludd', who was said to have his headquarters in Sherwood Forest. The government replied by making frame-breaking a capital offence, but the troubles spread to Yorkshire and Lancashire. Factories and mills were attacked, some owners defending their property with as much zeal as the deluded Luddites displayed in destroying the machines. Ludd's followers perished bravely in a futile cause. Seventeen Luddites were executed at York early in 1813, but the secret oath-taking went on.

The root of the problem did not lie in the existence of machines, but rather in the assumptions about wages, working conditions and child-labour which were simply carried over from the domestic system. Ultimately the factory destroyed many of the mistaken ideas which had been so integral a part of the old order: the belief that high wages would bring disaster, the acceptance of child-labour as a normal part of manufacture. If the factory hand was substituted for the farm worker who was also something of a weaver or spinner, this was not necessarily a bad thing. The food, clothing and wages enjoyed by the workers in the factories (at least when there was plenty of work to be done) were superior to those of the unfortunate agricultural labourer. What the factory worker missed most were the customary country sports —and occasional profitable poaching expeditions. Particularly badly hit were the handloom weavers, who were in no position to compete with the new methods of production. Though many employers made use of 'parish apprenticeships', by which substantial numbers of pauper children were transported to the new industrial areas, where they were housed by the employer, put to work in his factory and given some elementary education, under the guise of apprenticeship, this method of recruiting labour faded away when it became possible to find 'free' children locally. In 1802 the elder Sir Robert Peel attempted to regulate the conditions under which pauper children were employed, but his Factory Act was ineffective, as was his more ambitious Act of 1819, which sought to prohibit the employment of children under the age of nine in the cotton mills and to limit the working day for young people to twelve hours. Without a satisfactory system of inspection these measures were doomed to failure, but they were portents of things to come.

During the war industry had flourished, despite the difficulties created by Napoleon's Continental System. The iron and steel industries expanded to meet the increased demand for the weapons of war, but their value was not restricted to the production of munitions. Iron machinery improved the efficiency of the coal-mines and made the cost of mining cheaper. The thriving coal trade was largely carried on by sea between the great English ports. Although the first years of the war had deprived the cotton industry of several of its markets, it nevertheless reaped the advantages of invention, particularly when the installation of power looms enabled weaving to exploit to the full the new techniques in spinning. In 1815 50,000 tons of cotton were imported to supply the mills of the north, and ten years later this amount had doubled. The wool trade, which was centred in Yorkshire, took longer to reorganise itself. It suffered more than the cotton industry from the loss of markets caused by the war. Only after the end of hostilities did it take any comparable strides towards mechanisation. The shipbuilding industry, which was chiefly occupied in turning out small vessels of under 100 tons, was concentrated round the Thames estuary. Engineering, though comparatively on a small scale, had benefited from the technical improvements devised by Bramah, Maudslay and Roberts. In transport England led the world. Other countries might boast of better roads or more splendid canals, but none could rival the overall excellence of British communications. Telford and Mac-adam were improving road surfaces, while the canals were enabling manufacturers to ship their heavy goods at economic rates. Yet, in the midst of so much innovation, the strength of old habits and working methods must not be forgotten. Even in Sheffield, where in 1797 a tourist had commented that since the introduction of steam the town no longer abounded in 'cripples and weak, deformed people', some of the cutlery works still refrained from using steam power—the symbol of the new age.

Rural Developments

The horrors of the industrial towns have diverted attention from the equally important changes which were taking place in the agricultural areas. With three-quarters of the people living in small towns or villages the problems of rural distress loomed larger in

1815 than has sometimes been implied. During the war with France English agriculture had enjoyed an intense, transient, golden age. The need to produce as much food as possible, during years when the country was cut off from supplies of continental grain, gave added impetus to the application of new techniques—crop rotation, better tilling, more scientific stock breeding—and also encouraged men to develop land which would otherwise have been left idle or dismissed as a poor investment. The process of enclosing common land was carried through. The old open fields were hedged and neglected waste drained and ditched. As communications improved the farmer found that he could sell his products in more distant towns, and the Board of Agriculture, which had been set up in 1793, was active in disseminating new ideas. In 1815 home-grown farm produce had increased by more than 50 per cent, compared with what had been achieved twenty years earlier. With a heavy demand for his goods, and with high prices being paid, the farmer invested more capital in land. Rents were high, and many men borrowed heavily in order to improve their farms. The more prosperous farmers emulated the gentry, while the middling sort often sold their farms to their wealthy neighbours, carrying on their businesses as tenant farmers. Though it is now believed that the enclosure movement neither destroyed the old yeoman class nor depopulated the countryside, it certainly bore heavily upon the cottagers, whose customary rights were swept away by the onward march of improvement. A great gulf separated the farmers, on the one hand, and the landless labourers, on the other. Some of the deprived made their way to the industrial towns, where they swelled the teeming proletariat. Others remained, their lot made all the worse by the well-meaning decision of the Speenhamland magistrates in 1795, to supplement agricultural wages out of the rates. This was a traditional method of dealing with rural poverty, but it served only to demoralise the depressed still further. Farmers were encouraged to pay low wages, in the knowledge that they would be supplemented from the rates, and at the same time the incentive to demand higher wages was also weakened. It is important, however, to remember that the Speenhamland 'system' was not universally applied. Though it was adopted in the East and North Ridings of Yorkshire, it was principally confined to East Anglia, the Home Counties and the South. In the north-west, where farmers had to compete with the demand for labour in the cotton mills, agricultural wages were higher. Even where the Speenhamland expedient was so unhappily applied the English agricultural labourer still enjoyed a higher standard of living than the continental peasantry, despite the fact that industrialisation was depriving the farm workers of additional income derived from part-time weaving and spinning. Nor were arguments in defence of the Speenhamland system lacking: Canning maintained that the supplementation of wages discouraged rioting during a period of political as well as social conflict. But by 1818 £8,000,000 were being spent on outdoor poor relief.

The war years were profitable for the landed gentry. Their standard of living was high, and the war was a remote struggle in far-away countries. It was followed with much the same sort of interest as a sporting encounter. A son might serve under Wellington or make the Royal Navy his career, but the majority of gentlemen contented themselves with their duties in the militia. Wellington's army was recruited from the outcasts and ne'er do wells of society, the Duke himself referring to his troops as the scum of the earth—though he had the grace to add that they made fine soldiers. The industrial classes did less well. Many of the factory owners had got on by their own resource and initiative, but if some made huge profits, others were ruined. And there was much envy and distrust between the traditional gentry and the new middle class. The industrialists had little use for the landed aristocracy. They regarded them as idle, overprivileged, reactionary and inefficient. In return they were despised as coarse, pushing, greedy and uncivilised. This clash of interests was entangled in the dispute over the Corn Laws. During the war the price of wheat had soared. In 1792 it had been 43s. a quarter: in 1812 it was 126s. When peace came and cheap grain could once again be imported from Europe many farmers were ruined. Falling prices meant that they could not pay the debts which they had acquired through their passion for improvement and enclosure. In 1815 the price of wheat fell to 65s. 7d. a quarter. The landed interest clamoured for protection. They had answered the call of duty during the war: they claimed security during the peace. The industrialists grumbled about any suggestion to keep the price of grain high. This would affect the standard of living of their workers, and if the price of bread rose it would be more difficult to keep wages low. All the experts agreed that rising labour costs would have grave consequences upon industrial expansion. But the Commons was predominantly an assembly of country gentlemen, and the alleged needs of the farming community made a more immediate impression than the complaints of remote urban factory owners. It was decided to prohibit the import of foreign wheat until the price of home-grown wheat exceeded 80s. a quarter. This was the famous Corn Law of 1815: again a traditional remedy, applied by men with little knowledge and less understanding of the changes which were taking place in the society in which they lived. But, like so many traditional answers during a period of revolution, the expedient did not work. The Corn Law did not give the farmer the security he desired, for the price of wheat continued to fluctuate. In 1816 it stood at 78s. 6d. a quarter. A year later it had risen to 96s. 11d. only to slip back to 67s. 10d. in 1820. In 1822 it fell to 44s. 7d. The Corn Law was unpopular in the towns: the price of bread was too high for the poor, and the intention of the landed gentry to keep the price of grain at an artificially high level was bitterly resented. Yet the farmers and gentry clung to the Corn Law as an insurance (albeit an illusory one) against further misfortune. Throughout the 1820s Lord Liverpool and his successors were embarrassed by the Corn Law controversy, which vitiated political discussion. In the 1840s the Anti-Corn Law League, skilfully organised and unscrupulously exploited by Cobden and Bright, thrust the issue to the fore, and then the Irish famine drove the government to face the predicament without temporising. The price of repeal was the destruction of Peel's Conservative party and the end of his own career. The price of continued protection had been social antagonism, intermittent agitation and the constant threat of unrest. The greatest tragedy of all was that the agricultural interest gained little from the law. Any profit which was made when the price of wheat rose could not compensate for the chronic instability and frustrating uncertainty which afflicted English farming. The abnormal conditions which had made war-time prosperity possible could not be arbitrarily perpetuated.

Post-war Recession

But agriculture was not alone in experiencing the harsh realities of the peace. Industry slumped badly. The end of government contracts threw many men out of work, particularly in the armaments, iron and steel, and copper industries, and the problem of unemployment was aggravated by the demobilisation of soldiers and sailors, 300,000 of whom were discharged by 1817, without either a pension or a gratuity for their services, or even a medal to commemorate the campaigns in which they had fought. The heavy burden of taxation was fiercely criticised, especially the varied imposts levied on an immense number of goods. Sydney Smith acidly described the extent and nature of government taxation:

'The schoolboy whips his taxed top, the beardless youth manages his taxed horse with a taxed bridle on a taxed road, and the dying Englishman, pouring his medicine which has paid seven per cent into a spoon that has paid fifteen per cent, flings himself back upon his chintz bed, which has paid twenty two per cent, and expires into the arms of an apothecary who has paid a licence of a hundred pounds for the privilege of putting him to death.'

The incidence of indirect taxation made life more difficult for those who were already badly hit by high prices, but the most unpopular tax of all was the income tax. And here the government was forced to give way to public opinion, abolishing the income tax in 1816, despite the convictions which Lord Liverpool, the Prime Minister, and Vansittart, the Chancellor of the Exchequer, both held as to the tax's fiscal advantages. Castlereagh despised what he accurately described as 'an ignorant impatience of taxation', but the Whigs had made much of the alleged connection between a standing army, high taxation and sinister threats to the constitution. Lord John Russell thought that there could be 'no more dreadful calamity' than the continuation of the income tax, for it would enable the Crown, with the assistance of the army, 'to erase even the vestiges of departing liberty'. But, by honouring the war-time promise to abolish the income tax as soon as possible, the government could be accused of pandering to the wishes of the property-owning sections of society: the weight of indirect taxation still pressed down on the working classes. But how was the government to evade the harsh necessity of high taxation, when the National Debt stood at £861,000,000? Liverpool was also under constant pressure to restore the gold standard, for it was claimed that paper money intensified inflation. In 1810 the government had ignored the advice of a Select Committee of the Commons that a return to the gold standard was necessary, but once the war was over it was increasingly difficult to reject similar demands. In 1819 Peel's Committee of Inquiry recommended a gradual return to the gold standard, and this was accomplished over the next four years. But even here the Liverpool ministry was criticised. Both industrialists and agriculturalists blamed the restoration for the fall of prices in the early 1820s. At the same time the gold standard benefited Britain's position with respect to foreign exchange. Both those who advocated paper money and those who defended the traditional system overstated their case. Neither the suspension of cash payments nor their resumption were as decisive as various commentators maintained.

The far-reaching changes in industry and agriculture, the emergence of new towns, the growth in population, the problems of unemployment, finance and the transition to a peace-time economy would have been more than enough for any administration. But Liverpool, Sidmouth, Castlereagh and Eldon were anxious for yet another reason. The unrest which was so widespread among working people seemed to indicate that there was a real danger of revolution. Ignorant as they were of the true nature of the social forces which were revolutionising society, the ministry saw problems of agitation, radicalism and demands for reform too much in terms of the French Revolution of their youth. And here they were doing what many of the agitators themselves mistakenly did. Not until the failure of the Cato Street Conspiracy in 1820 did the Jacobinical element in agitation finally give way to the school of thought which emphasised parliamentary reform as the cure for the nation's ills. There was little unity within the ranks of the agitators, and less consistency in their various panaceas for the ills of society. If Liverpool and his colleagues lacked a profound comprehension of the deep-rooted causes of discontent, so did their most vociferous critics.

Radical Critics

William Cobbett typified all the bluff virtues of the English yeoman. He had once been a patriotic anti-Jacobin: now he was a no less patriotic Radical, bringing Tom Paine's ashes home for interment in English soil. But for all his worth—his warm humanity, his compassion, his flashes of insight—Cobbett was blinded by prejudice. Because he hated the new urban industries, the new gentry, the new nobility and the new property classes, he idealised the England of his youth. His highly individual brand of Tory Democracy tells us more about his own personality than the condition of England. He called for parliamentary reform because the existing Parliament had allowed old England to be traduced, exploited and destroyed. As a journalist he stirred men's feelings against the injustices of the age, and his boldness necessitated flight to America to escape the law. He loved justice and fair play and hated cant and humbug, but the intensity with which he held his own beliefs led him to dismiss Dissenters as rogues and Evangelicals as hypocrites—a judgment which was as unfair as it was extravagant. He detested formal education, and praised the value of learning country skills in traditional ways. He loathed those whom he described as 'feelosophers', pouring scorn on Ricardo and Malthus, and venting his spleen on Jews, foreigners and all whom he thought guilty of 'un-English activities'. But for all his enthusiasm, Cobbett was the panegyrist of a vanished society, not the prophet of a new order. He could describe, with imagination, vigour, exaggeration and grief, the passing of the old way of life. He was incapable of pointing the way to new forms of social order.

There were other Radicals whose personalities and assorted ideals caught the imagination of the angry, the bewildered and the perplexed. Old Major Cartwright, with a lifetime of agitation behind him, stumped the country, advocating parliamentary reform and manhood suffrage, organising his Hampden Clubs as the means whereby agitation was to be disciplined, and counselling good behaviour and a respect for the law to all who impatiently hankered after revolution. Cartwright was an eccentric, with a touching fidelity to parliamentary institutions, however much he called for their renovation. He stuck to his opinions in season and out of season. During the grim 1790s Horne Tooke confessed that he thought the cause of parliamentary reform dead and buried. Cartwright's response was to affirm his belief in the resurrection. The Major was a living link with the old days, when the Yorkshire Association had urged moderate reform and when Pitt himself had tried to abolish the worst excesses of the electoral system. Far different was Henry Hunt, whose gift for invective earned him the nickname 'Orator', and whose tall white hat attracted attention at any demonstration. Hunt was vain, fickle, unreliable and self-centred. He lacked Cartwright's honesty and integrity, but his demagogic talents were undeniable. Then there were the Spencean Philanthropists, who were obsessed with the nationalisation of land, a hatred of aristocrats and a Jacobinical solution to political problems. Of these the most famous was to be Arthur Thistlewood, the ringleader in the Cato Street Conspiracy.

But though these were the figures who monopolised contemporary fear or admiration, two less-flamboyant characters were to have a more durable influence. Jeremy Bentham, the sage of utilitarianism and the high priest of the pleasure principle, became a Radical towards the end of his long life only because he despaired of his ideas ever being implemented without the reform of the system of representation. Bentham distrusted all government. He tended to think of society as little more than the aggregate of individual needs and desires, and much English political theory in the nineteenth century was an attempt to remedy deficiencies in his thought. Men were under the sway of two masters, pain and pleasure. Happiness consisted in the freedom from pain and the enjoyment of as much pleasure as possible. Pleasure included experiences as diverse as push-pin and poetry, and it was for the individual to decide which he preferred. It was the duty of governments so to regulate society that this principle was given the necessary room in which to operate. The primary function of government was to secure the greatest happiness of the greatest number, and this was to be accomplished by eliminating all traditional obstacles to the pleasure principle. Bentham claimed to be the Newton of the social sciences, an ambition which many other nineteenth-century theorists later shared. His principle, worked out with arid logic, was as true as the law of gravity. (He never answered the question as to how and why so much contrary legislation and custom had thereby come about in the first place.) Bentham did not believe in absolute *laissez-faire*. The government would have to ensure that the balance between the needs of the individual and society was struck, and conduct which was socially beneficial would have to be encouraged by rewards and punishments. But Bentham certainly regarded eighteenth-century governments as obscurantist, inefficient and corrupt, possibly because his hopes that enlightened despots would adopt his own ideas had been disappointed. At the same time he had a genuine concern for the liberty of the individual, and with all his faults it was difficult to transform him into an apologist for tyranny. His books were not widely read in his lifetime, but a circle of influential and able disciples gathered round him, imbibing his ideas and applying them to a variety of topics, such as legal reform, prison conditions, the poor law, sanitation and public health. With its impatience of traditional forms of governmental control and its cult of the individual as the best judge of his own interest, his outlook chimed in nicely with the convictions and desires (many of them unconscious) of the new middle classes who had made their own way in the world and who were seeking political and social recognition.

Similarly, Robert Owen, the doyen of English Socialists, whose memory has been hallowed in innumerable eulogies, was another characteristic product of an age of self-made men. He was born in humble circumstances, did well in business, married the daughter of his employer and eventually proved that it was possible to combine a handsome profit with humanitarian principles and conduct. The mills at New Lanark became a legend in his own lifetime. Like Bentham, he had an eighteenth-century confidence in the essential goodness of man and his ultimate perfectibility. For Owen environment was the greatest factor in formulating character. If men were brought up in healthy surroundings, with plenty of opportunity for exercise, education and recreation, all would be well. Owen's ideas were given a sympathetic hearing until his less-successful experiments in communal living, his ambitious and premature indulgence in trade unionism, and his religious scepticism and anti-clericalism offended the suscepti-bilities and aroused the suspicion of the middle classes. In the hard struggle for existence and the tough fight for reform after Waterloo, Owen meant much less to unemployed factory workers than either Orator Hunt or King Ludd. His educational ideas, his desire to promote working-class organisation and his concern for the provision of adequate houses for the workers, congenial surroundings for their daily labour and a healthy upbringing for their children held out little prospect of that dramatic revolution which so many artisans desired during the post-war recession. They wanted an immediate transformation of society. Owen's approach to their problems, far-sighted as it was in some respects, needed time, patience and discipline. Furthermore, he never lost a taint of self-satisfaction, an aroma of priggery, which isolated him from those he wished to serve, and his virtues did not always commend him to his colleagues and rivals. Despite their merits, it is easy to overestimate the practicability of his projects. Although Owen's preoccupation with social conditions and economic justice was in advance of the narrow concern for political objec-tives which hindered so many of the Radicals, a thoroughgoing social revolution could not be carried through without first of all capturing political power and reforming the electoral system.

The Unreformed Electoral System

For, though the Radicals expected too much from the reform of Parliament, it was unlikely that the existing representative structure would ever facilitate long-term changes. At a period when the industrial middle class was becoming increasingly powerful the Lords and Commons remained the preserve of the landed interest. It has been said that in the early nineteenth century Parliament no longer represented the constituencies, and that the constituencies did not represent the nation. In the boroughs the franchise was chaotic. In some towns, such as Preston, the vote was given to every man who spent the night before the election within the borough. In others the franchise was limited to freemen, or to members of the corporation, or to the owners and occupiers of certain pieces of property. In some places every man who was not in receipt of alms, or who paid taxes such as 'scot and lot', or who boiled his own pot on his own hearth, had the right to vote. Many towns had been enfranchised long ago in Tudor and Stuart times. Some of these had disappeared, while others had declined into tiny villages, neglected and virtually deserted. Of these the most famous was Old Sarum, which had had the distinction of sending the elder Pitt to the House of Commons. The south-east and far west were grotesquely over-represented. The boroughs of Wiltshire and Cornwall returned as many members as those of eight northern counties. The north of England—especially those areas which were the main centres of new and flourishing industries—was under-represented. Manchester, Sheffield and Leeds had no representatives. Where the electorate was small an enterprising landlord or business man could control the election of M.P.s. These were the famous pocket boroughs, where nomination was habitual and genuine election an impossibility. Where direct control was impracticable a relatively small number of electors held themselves open for bribes from the rival candidates. These were the rotten boroughs, and the size of electorate was a more significant factor in their constitution than whether the local franchise was oligarchic or democratic. Local interests had to be courted, and the promise of contracts for regional industries, or of improved amenities in the town, could sway the decision for one candidate as against another. Elections were costly and troublesome. Though the franchise in the counties was uniform, the 40s. freeholder having the right to vote, the same practices were in operation. Local loyalties and patriotisms, and the ambitions of wealthy or influential families

1 GEORGE III in later life.

2 George IV

3 WILLIAM IV

4 QUEEN VICTORIA as a young woman.

5 WILLIAM PITT

whose sons were contemplating a political career or the enviable social prestige of the House of Commons, counted for much more than the remote generalities of national politics. Contested elections were the exception not the rule, for interested parties preferred to come to some amicable arrangement in order to avoid the expense of an election campaign. Parties might be built up in the corridors of power at Westminster, but the labels Whig and Tory had no precise meaning in distant counties or thriving boroughs. The confused and haphazard electoral system made any equivalent to a modern party—with a national organisation, a defined policy and a disciplined following—impossible and irrelevant. The organisations which pressed for the abolition of slavery, or the reform of Parliament, or the repeal of the Corn Laws, had more in common with the political parties of the future than had the aristocratic cliques at Westminster. Even then the nineteenth century was more than half over before politics assumed anything like their present shape, or party evolved into something recognisably like what is implied by the term today.

The Professions and Education

The responsibilities of the national government were circumscribed: finance, defence, foreign policy, the decisions of war or peace—these were the tasks of government. The distribution of national wealth, the provision of educational and health services, housing, the cost of living and the problems of recession or inflation all lay beyond the scope of the administrators at Whitehall. The traditional Elizabethan laws which had sought to regulate the economic life of the community had long been rendered obsolete by the pace of change. They were now formally repealed. But even if the government had wanted to extend its control of affairs it lacked the administrative machinery to do so, for the civil service was small, and in any case it was recruited by the time-honoured methods of patronage and influence. Nor were the professions equipped to take the lead in solving the problems of a new society. The Inns of Court had fallen into decline during the eighteenth century, and the greatest obstacle to the reform of English law was the lawyers—often ignorant, invariably pedantic

E

and usually blindly devoted to the preservation of outmoded traditions. Until the 1830s the medical profession also remained listless and indolent, with little encouragement for research from bodies such as the Royal College of Physicians. The less-glamorous apothecary was to be transformed into the general practitioner during the next generation. And despite Britain's initiative in industry and commerce, there was little provision for formal technical education, although the Institute of Civil Engineers was founded in 1818.

In fact, the country was poorly educated. Scotsmen boasted of their superiority in this respect. Probably between a half and a third of the population of England was illiterate. The upper classes sent their sons to the ancient public schools, where their boys were flogged through an ill-taught syllabus of Latin and Greek. Discipline was often ferocious, but there was much bullying, rebellion and unrest. The more discriminating preferred to keep their children at home, employing a private tutor for their sons' education. The Dissenters, who represented the new middle classes, had introduced the study of modern subjects such as chemistry and geology, and of modern languages instead of the classics, in their academies, but they were still excluded from Oxford and Cambridge, where learning still slumbered in eighteenth-century gentility. The Dissenters and Radicals sought to remedy this by the foundation of London University in 1827. No religious tests were to be imposed; no theology was to be taught; and the emphasis was to be put on modern studies and the natural sciences. Sunday Schools and Dames Schools sufficed for the poor, but here the struggle for education was complicated by the bitter conflict between Anglicanism and Dissent. The Nonconformists organised the British and Foreign School Society, which sought to meet the need for religious instruction by undenominational Bible teaching. It was assumed that the scriptures themselves would breed Dissenters. The Anglicans replied by forming the National Society for the Education of the Poor, which inculcated the doctrines of the established Church. But a more hopeful sign than either of these movements was the foundation of Mechanics Institutes, which originated in Scotland, and which became increasingly popular during the 1820s and 1830s. The artisans coveted education as the means to a fuller life and the more effective defence of working-class interests. Self-help was the surest way: in 1824 the *Mechanics Magazine* sold 16,000 copies and 1,500 workers each subscribed a guinea to the London Mechanics Institute. Perhaps the best education in England at this time was to be had in the better country grammar schools, but the greatest single incentive towards literacy was the enthusiastic commendation of daily Bible reading by both Church and Chapel: this habit was the most formative cultural influence on the middle and working classes.

Religious Attitudes

Few institutions have been so unfairly criticised as the Church of England in the eighteenth century. If there was much graft, indifference and worldliness, there were also faithful ministers— often the poorest paid and the worst provided for—who served their people in humble devotion to their calling. Attempts were made to meet the challenge of the prevailing rational temper, and however superficial and arid eighteenth-century apologetics seem today, they were nevertheless an honest effort to restate the faith in comprehensible terms. The Dissenting Churches suffered from the same faults as the Establishment, as the fervour and bitterness of the seventeenth century gave way to a more polite and less revolutionary creed, but it would be foolish to exaggerate the complacency of either Anglicanism or Dissent. Traditional Calvinism had hardened into unimaginative orthodoxy, but many Dissenters went even further than the Anglican clergy in their anxiety to speak the language of the age: English Presbyterianism soon became Unitarian. The Methodist and Evangelical revivals have been thrown into greater relief by the unashamed misrepresentation of the religious situation from which they sprang. Too much has been written of eighteenth-century clerics who were allegedly 'the stern foes of all enthusiasm in religion'; not enough is said of Watts or Doddridge or Butler. If the light of inspiration burned dim at times, it never lacked devoted spirits to keep the flame alive. The Methodist and Evangelical movements brought welcome vigour and fresh intensity into English religion, but although they were parallel developments, they were not identical. The Anglican Evangelicals were Calvinists: John Wesley was a forthright Arminian. The tactlessness of unsympathetic bishops pushed Wesley towards independence, but the rigid Calvinism of the Evangelicals played almost as great a part in converting Methodism into another species of nonconformity, instead of allowing it to remain a valuable dynamic within the existing order. Nor should it be forgotten that Wesley was in origin a High Churchman, a Tory and very much an autocrat. He organised his society on authoritarian lines, and he would almost certainly have disapproved of the increasingly democratic spirit which permeated Methodism after 1800. Wilberforce and Simeon are particularly associated with the revival within the Church of England, while George Whitefield—the most eloquent preacher of them all— invigorated the older Dissenting Churches, as well as co-operating with Wesley until the familiar controversy over Arminianism made further collaboration impossible. It is often said that Methodism saved England from revolution; be that as it may, Christianity was certainly taken to masses of people who were untouched by the remote generalities of eighteenth-century religion, especially in those industrial areas where the traditional forms of ecclesiastical organisation had broken down and where a brutal paganism flourished amidst squalor and vice. The religious reawakening also stimulated a more sensitive awareness to social problems, and whatever their differences, the disciples of Wesley, Whitefield and Simeon humanised the society of their day. Religious conviction inspired the reformation of manners, as well as the renovation of institutions. In their hymns the Methodists showed that common folk could express their faith in joyous song, and their unflinching emphasis on personal responsibility did much to create that close relationship between radicalism and nonconformity which has been so distinctive and so fortunate a feature of English politics. Methodism was a greater force for change than Karl Marx.

The greatest weakness of English Protestantism in the first quarter of the nineteenth century was its lack of preparedness for the shocks which were to be administered through German scholarship. The reappraisal of the Bible was to be a greater problem than Darwinism, for it struck even more ruthlessly at the infallibility of scripture, and only when an intelligent interpretation of the Bible was formulated did it become possible to answer the questions raised by geology and biology. Too many men panicked, some into a blind and obscurantist fundamentalism, others into a fickle and unstable modernism, or the fanciful reconstruction of medieval dogma. But this was another generation's battle: the years following Waterloo gave little indication of the precise trials which the churches had to face in the none-too-distant future. The religious paradox of the time perfectly mirrors the puzzling contradiction of Regency England: certainty keeping company with doubt, confidence poised unhappily on the verge of fear, frustration and anger rubbing shoulders with hope. The ambivalence of the post-war period was reflected in the personalities and outlook of the Liverpool ministry, which lacked the ability to give articulate expression to perplexities which were intuitively perceived. The magnitude of the tasks confronting them is a salutary warning of the demands which an extraordinary fate makes upon ordinary mortals. For too long Liverpool, Castlereagh and Sidmouth were decried as harsh and unbending, as wilful opponents of the self-evident spirit of enlightenment. Placed as they were, in the difficult position of governing a nation which was finding the problems of peace more intractable than the tribulations of war, they deserve justice, not abuse. Grievous as many of their errors were, these are additional testimony to the agonies endured by a people whose mode of life was changing at a pace unequalled in any former social revolution.

4 : The Age of Liverpool
(1815-27)

Liverpool and his Colleagues

LORD LIVERPOOL and his colleagues have had much scorn and
derision heaped upon their heads. Abused for many years as
reactionaries, or despised as mediocrities, they have only recently
received anything but scant justice from historians. The picture
of unrelieved reaction is misleading: it is easy to forget that
Liverpool's ministry was an assortment of various Tory groups,
with nothing like the cohesion and unanimity associated with a
modern administration, and with a great deal of divergence in
political outlook and patterns of thought. Even the famous
transition to liberal Toryism, conventionally dated from Castlereagh's suicide in 1822, was more gradual and less obviously
perceptible than has often been supposed. Although increasing
prosperity in the 1820s, with its mitigating effects on the unrest
which had provoked fears of Jacobinical revolution, coincided
with Huskisson's free trade policy and Peel's enlightened reform
of the penal code, Liverpool himself had always been sympathetic
to new ideas in economic theory, however disturbed he had been
by anything savouring of political revolution. As early as 1812 he
was convinced that the less commerce and manufacturers were
meddled with, the more they were likely to prosper—a sentiment
which would have done credit to Jeremy Bentham himself—and
eight years later he was of the opinion that if the people of the
world were poor 'no legislative interposition can make them do
that which they would do if they were rich'. Similarly, Canning's
foreign policy can be seen as a development, rather than rejection,
of that pursued so ably by Castlereagh: here again a less-dramatic
interpretation can be put on events. In some ways the years of
Liverpool's premiership illustrate how the ministry won its way

through to a greater confidence in ideas which many of its members had held for some time, and how these new policies were applied with increasing assurance.

Liverpool himself had had ample administrative experience. After his years at Oxford he had gone abroad in the usual eighteenth-century manner, and had been present at the fall of the Bastille. He never possessed any profound insight into its long-term significance, but he never forgot the grim spectacle of a mob in revolt. In the 1790s he soon achieved minor government office, once he had entered politics, and his ascent up the ministerial ladder was assured. Like his father before him, he was a sound and reliable administrator. Soon he became Foreign Secretary under Addington, and when Pitt returned to office he moved to the Secretaryship for Home Affairs. After Pitt's death he had a short spell out of office, but once the Talents were destroyed by the death of Fox and the Catholic question, he returned to the Home Office under Portland. In 1809 he became Secretary for War and the Colonies: it is often overlooked that Liverpool played a valuable part in supplying Wellington during the Peninsular campaigns. When Spencer Perceval was assassinated in 1812 Liverpool became the Chief Minister, a post which he was to hold without interruption for fifteen years. Yet, despite all his experience, he was deficient in initiative. He accepted conventional thinking too readily and too uncritically, and even when he did respond to original ideas he was cautious in applying his new-fangled doctrines. He shunned innovation even in the routine of departmental administration. Yet his narrowness of mind has been exaggerated. It is unjust to say that had he been present on the day of creation he would have implored God to preserve Chaos. He was patient in negotiation and tactful in Cabinet consultations. His modesty and common sense endeared him to his colleagues. He was respected for his honesty and integrity, for his justice and kindliness. His views on constitutional procedure were a mixture of eighteenth-century platitude and the acceptance of new conventions. Ambivalent and uncertain, he was far from the iron reactionary of legend.

His colleagues were as varied as the ideas which jostled for the mastery in Liverpool's own mind. Eldon, the Lord Chancellor, who had won all the usual distinctions of a legal career, was the most unyielding member of the government. He was opposed to any mitigation of the savage penal code, advocated capital punishment and rigidly resisted emancipation for the Catholics and full citizenship for the Dissenters. Yet he was affectionate and loyal, and not entirely devoid of sympathy and imagination. Sidmouth, likewise, was committed to the unenterprising defence of the *status quo*. (He was to make his last speech in the Lords in opposition to Catholic emancipation, while his last vote was to be cast against the 1832 Reform Bill.) He has usually been identified with the repressive policies of the government after Waterloo, with all the sinister paraphernalia of spies and *agents provocateurs*. Yet it is more accurate to see him as a well-meaning, but rather bewildered, country gentleman, getting on in years, and easily ruffled by tales of unrest and disorder, rather than a ruthless oppressor of the people. Both Liverpool and Sidmouth responded to the situation by applying the traditional remedies. They simply strengthened the powers of the local magistrates. They were unable to devise any more sophisticated method of maintaining public order. Castlereagh was the most distinguished member of the Cabinet. Handsome and imposing in appearance, and skilful in the wearisome technicalities of diplomacy, he was a poor speaker, whose shyness and reserve in dealing with the Commons passed for arrogance and disdain. He supported repressive legislation, and as Leader of the House of Commons had the duty of intro-ducing it, but his mind was on other matters, and it is often forgotten that in his youth he had flirted—like many other Ulstermen—with the new ideas from Paris. Because he was the most upright and honourable of men he accepted his share of the responsibility without complaint, despite the abuse which was hurled at him. The lewd rhymes of Byron and Shelley, gross, vicious and ignorant as they were, have led to a monstrous mis-understanding of Castlereagh's personality and outlook. No man drove himself harder, and the tragedy of his suicide in 1822, when his mind broke down under the strain of office and of a particularly lurid piece of contrived blackmail, casts a sombre shadow over his career. Wellington joined the government in 1818, but his high Tory opinions, expressed in the most forthright language, were moderated by a keen eye for realities and a selfless devotion to what he considered the King's service. Unfortunately the demands of party and of political conduct were as foreign to Wellington as military strategy was to the other members of the administration.

In addition to these established men, there were several other figures, some on the fringe of power, or on the threshold of long political careers. George Canning was the most brilliant, and the most unstable, of Pitt's disciples. His acid tongue, whose wit stung too deeply, earned him distrust and hostility, while his ambition added to the anxieties of his contemporaries. After his duel with Castlereagh he spent some years in the political wilderness, but in 1816 he accepted the Presidency of the Board of Control. He abounded in all the talents which Castlereagh lacked: spell-binding oratory, a flair for publicity, the ability to seize upon and exploit the feelings of the hour. The liberalism of his foreign policy has blinded historians to his conceit, his provocative self-assurance, his wilful individualism and the strong vein of chauvinism which gave so many of his speeches their appeal. Nor was he more liberal in domestic affairs than the older Tories. He defended the conduct of the magistrates at Peterloo and he was opposed to parliamentary reform. Even his support of Catholic emancipation was less consistent than that of the much maligned Castlereagh. Canning had to contend with a certain amount of social prejudice—his mother had been an actress—but the failings of his character contributed to the disappointments of his career.

Of those whom Liverpool had welcomed into minor office, and whom he encouraged to stay in politics, showing a shrewd appreciation of their qualities, the most outstanding was Robert Peel, the son of a Lancashire mill owner. Peel had a precise, lucid mind, which was admirably fitted to minister to his absorbing interest in good administration and in pragmatic reform. As Under-Secretary for War and the Colonies he had learned the complexities of politics. As Chief Secretary for Ireland he experienced their brutalities and intransigent enmities. Young Palmerston, too, was gaining ministerial experience at the War Office, while Huskisson, whose ideas on trade were very close to those of Liverpool himself, was biding his time, acting as colonial agent for Ceylon. In 1823 he became President of the Board of Trade, and within a few years he was to demonstrate the efficacy of his economic ideas. Liverpool's ministry was a compound of age and youth. As the initial fears of the post-war years died away, the more forward-looking elements gained the upper hand.

Liverpool's long tenure of power cannot be explained as the consequence of an unchallenged control of the Commons. His majority was as uncertain as all majorities before the advent of party, and he lacked some of the resources of patronage which had been available to his predecessors. The ministry did not provide its supporters in the Commons with convincing leadership. Castlereagh, the government's principal representative, was a poor debater, whose involved sentences and mixed metaphors baffled or amused, but rarely impressed. It will be recalled that the government was defeated over the income tax in 1816, and the need to conciliate the landed interest, as well as all who felt that property was being menaced by revolutionary conspiracies, could never be absent from Liverpool's mind. Although he occasionally complained of the independence of the Commons and the unpredictability of their ways, hankering for that weight and influence which he thought every government ought to possess, Liverpool never sought to tighten up discipline. All he asked of his supporters was a 'generally favourable disposition', for he had no desire to interfere with the individual M.P.'s right to vote as he thought best on any particular question.

Similarly, within the Cabinet, Liverpool presided with the benevolence of a reasonable man. He rivalled Baldwin in his lethargic mastery of business. He respected the opinions of his colleagues, and he refrained from imposing any point of view upon them. The Catholic issue remained an open question throughout Liverpool's ministry. As soon as he was removed from the scene it assumed the proportions of a major crisis. Of course it was increasingly difficult to defer the solution of this problem, and the situation in Ireland was enough to make a decision imperative, but that such a significant difference of opinion within the Cabinet could be tolerated for so long illustrates the relationship which Liverpool fostered between himself and his ministers. But, although George IV lamented in 1823 that the government was too much a government of departments, Cabinet responsibility was evolving nevertheless. Liverpool knew that if he was dismissed his colleagues would not stay behind to form the nucleus of a new administration. This was a break with eighteenth-century practice, and it partly explains why George IV's capricious and frequently objectionable behaviour never had the consequences which his father's prejudices had had upon the constitution and stability of ministries. Liverpool could not force his colleagues to adopt one line of approach to a political problem, but he could rely on their loyalty, and this strengthened his position when dealing with the unpredictable and unreliable George IV.

Liverpool was helped by the fact that the Whig opposition was in turmoil and confusion. For many years it lacked a recognised or respected leader. Grey had retired to his estates, playing only a spasmodic part in high politics. Neither Ponsonby nor Tierney had been impressive in leading the party in the Commons, while the most gifted of the younger Whigs, Brougham, was as distrusted on the opposition side of the House as Canning was amidst the government benches. Brougham was a brilliant lawyer, an enthusiastic and resourceful controversialist, a forceful and compelling speaker. But he was crudely and voraciously ambitious, unscrupulous and deceitful. It would be incorrect to think of anything resembling a two-party system at this period. The Whig aristocrats were divided on the major issues of the day, and they were no more disposed to treat agitation leniently than their Tory counterparts. The majority of M.P.s were still independent country gentlemen, more interested in the Corn Law or the property tax than any more abstruse political problem. They were concerned to defend their interests, and whatever labels men liked to use, the oligarchic structure of politics remained more or less intact. The Radicals—of whom the economist, Ricardo, was one—were gradually infiltrating into the traditional centres of power, but they were far from being what we should understand today as a third party. The deaths of Liverpool and Canning, and the renewed demand for emancipation by the Catholics of Ireland, finally shook the political kaleidoscope, but when Grey returned to office the administration over which he presided was yet another alliance of groups, not a closely integrated ministry in the twentieth-century sense.

Agitation and Unrest

Was there any real danger of revolution in England after 1815? The upper classes undoubtedly thought so. Tales of machine breaking in the Midlands, or dark rumours of workmen drilling in para-military formations or supplying themselves with firearms or pikes, together with the extravagant language of many of the agitators, reminded the aristocrats and the prosperous bourgeoisie of Jacobinism. But the degree of organisation among the working men was exaggerated. Many of the more extreme 'revolutionaries' were ill-educated men, with only the vaguest notions of what the successful overthrow of established authority would mean. For many of the more desperate spirits in Nottingham it was associated with free beer and jolly trips down the Trent. The image in the minds of the organisers of unrest was an unsophisticated return to the legendary good old days. There was no clear plan whereby the new republic was to be inaugurated. The spasmodic outbreak of disturbances, the ease with which they were suppressed and the pathetic futility which dogged their course indicate that though there was hardship, suffering, anger and frustration in abundance, there was little foresight and less genuine political consciousness. Dreams of direct action, of dramatic deeds which would restore vanished happiness, appealed to men to whom the more solemn arguments in favour of constitutional reform seemed cold and distant. Only as the more violent became discredited by the fury of their schemes, and by the naïve innocence which betrayed them into the traps laid by plausible *agents provocateurs*, did parliamentary reform become the watchword of the working classes. Some historians have deemed the Peterloo affair as the moment when the reform movement came of age, putting its Jacobinical past behind it in order to pursue a more disciplined path to a more practical goal. Others have pointed out that there were outbursts of rioting and frame-breaking in the 1820s, that even the cause of parliamentary reform itself was closely related to booms and slumps, and that it was primarily the political expression of social discontent and economic privation.

It would therefore be misleading to look for any single cause or factor linking or explaining all the diverse expressions of dissatisfaction and unrest during the post-war years. Often the recession experienced by a local industry, or the failure of a traditional craft, had more to do with a particular outbreak of disorder than any national issue. And while the agitators cannot be credited with any overall plan of campaign, Sidmouth himself had no strategic concept either. Living on memories of the past and fears for the future, without an adequate system of police, and dependent for his information on professional informers, irresponsible spies and agile rogues, he was out of touch with the realities of the situation. So much has been heard of the repression of the post-Waterloo period that Liverpool and his colleagues have been credited with a greater degree of energy and ruthlessness than they possessed, and certainly with more than they desired. Although they tightened up the law governing public meetings, newspapers and libel, the application of the law was in the hands of the J.P.s. This was no intensive reign of terror, backed by all the resources of the modern state. Rather it was a muddled attempt to solve the problems of a nascent industrial society by dutifully invoking the customary methods employed in the village and the parish. Both the agitators and the government fell back on habits of thought appropriate to a bygone era.

There were many events which frightened their lordships, but not only Tories feared for their heads. In 1819 Grey confessed that the leaders of the popular party—the Mob—wanted 'not Reform but Revolution' and went on to say that 'if a convulsion follows their attempts to work upon the minds of the people, inflamed as they are by distress, for which your Reform would afford a very inadequate remedy, I shall not precede you many months on the scaffold.' Even those who sympathised with the poor and the destitute had little idea what to do about it. Indeed, the best authorities were agreed that probably the best thing was to do nothing. Liverpool was as much under the sway of the new economists as any man, and the bleak science deserved its name at the beginning of the nineteenth century. Malthus and Ricardo might dispute the merits of protection for agriculture, but they were agreed in emphasising the dangers of an expanding population; the risk of starvation where the food supply expanded only in arithmetic progression as compared to the population's geometric increase; the salutary regulation of the economy by death, poverty and disease; the iron law of wages; the irresistible dominion of supply and demand. Humanitarian sentiments disturbed the natural laws of social and economic development, and therefore led to greater distress and more widespread suffering. 'The increasing wealth of the nation,' wrote Malthus in 1798, 'has had little or no tendency to better the conditions of the poor.' Although the economists did not advocate absolute *laissez-faire*—they were prepared to concede that the government had a certain limited role in securing an atmosphere in which the laws of the economy could operate without hindrance—the idea that political action could alleviate hardship was particularly dangerous. It was even thought that there was no connection between the two. 'Whatever might be the circumstances of that distress,' commented Lord Liverpool with respect to the instances of disorder in 1819, 'it was not connected with political causes.' But though Liverpool was right in seeing that more than the enunciation of selected political principles and objectives was behind the agitation, he thought that the government was as powerless to regulate the vagaries of economic development as the workers themselves. When Samuel Bamford appeared before the Privy Council in 1816 he was surprised at the kindliness of Liverpool and Castlereagh, but he was also given the advice to wait and see. Things were bad: their lordships fully sympathised with working men such as Bamford, but all they could do was to counsel patience. The government could not alter the laws of economics. Any effort to alleviate distress was left to voluntary organisations, such as Wilberforce's Association for the Relief of the Manufacturing and Labouring Poor, or provided by the building of churches and the opening of soup kitchens.

Several incidents caught the attention of contemporaries, as the more spectacular symptoms of unrest if not revolution. In 1816 a meeting at Spa Fields, London, degenerated into a riot. A gun-shop was broken into and a spectator wounded, while the more hardy souls decided to march on the Tower. The crowd was finally dispersed, but it had been an ugly business. In the winter of 1816–17, when Manchester was badly hit by a recession, a number of artisans left for London, where they hoped to plead their case. Each bore a blanket to provide him with some comfort on the journey, and this gave them the name of Blanketeers. But their hopes came to nothing. Some got as far as Stockport, others Macclesfield, but the magistrates, calling in the cavalry to help them, successfully snuffed the movement out. In 1817 there was a futile rising in the Midlands. In reply the government suspended Habeas Corpus, and tightened up the law governing public meetings. When Sidmouth tried to convict several newspaper men on charges of seditious libel and blasphemy he failed, and the knowledge that he was employing spies and *agents provocateurs* was not to his advantage. A better summer and a good harvest in 1817 meant that agitation damped down, but in 1819 discontent revived. There were meetings of protest in Birmingham in July, and on August 16th a vast crowd of fifty or sixty thousand people gathered at St Peter's Fields, Manchester, to hear Orator Hunt speak on parliamentary reform. They assembled in good order, marching in companies with flags flying. The magistrates panicked, attempting to arrest Hunt and calling on the incompetent yeomanry to scatter the crowd. The job was bungled, and by the time the regular soldiery were called in confusion and bloodshed had ensued. Nine men and two women were killed, and about four hundred other people were wounded. Within days the bitter nickname Peterloo had been invented. Although the Prince Regent congratulated the magistrates on their prompt action, the upper classes were uneasy. Fitzwilliam, the Lord Lieutenant of the West Riding, attended a protest meeting and was dismissed in consequence. In London the Common Council expressed its indignation. Meanwhile the Radicals writhed in horror, disgust and fury.

The government replied by passing the notorious Six Acts. Heavy penalties were imposed on all persons who were caught drilling, who used firearms illegally, who indulged in seditious libel or who distributed blasphemous publications. All meetings called for the purpose of drawing up petitions were limited to the inhabitants of the parish in which the meeting took place. Additional stamp duties were placed on newspapers and periodicals of the more popular sort. Liverpool complacently assured his colleagues that parish meetings would fall flat. The next few years saw a diminution of agitation and unrest. But the credit for this ought to go to commerce and industry, not the antiquated methods typified in the Six Acts. In 1820 prices were already rising, and a year later prosperity had already been achieved: soon Manchester, Birmingham and the Black Country were too busy making money to worry about insurrection and revolution. Liverpool and Sidmouth felt that their trust in the economy, and in the patience of the workers, had been justified by events. But one sensational incident reminded men of the passions which had all too recently been roused, and which still smouldered in many breasts.

Arthur Thistlewood had been among the more fanatical revolutionaries involved in the Spa Fields riot. After paying for his enthusiasm with a spell in prison, he returned to civilian life in a vindictive mood. The Peterloo massacre stirred him to contemplate a savage revenge. Knowing that the Cabinet were to dine at Lord Harrowby's on February 23rd, 1820, he and two dozen accomplices plotted to slay them all. Once the deed had taken place, a republic would be proclaimed. All this savoured very much of Paris in the 1790s, and the conspiracy was a grotesque mixture of the ludicrous and atrocious. But Thistlewood was betrayed, and the gang were arrested by the police as they made their preparations at a house in Cato Street. Thistlewood and several of his cronies were executed, and with their failure the Jacobinical illusion passes from English history. The future lay, not with the brutal advocates of crime, but with Francis Place, Robert Owen and the more sober-minded of the artisans. As trade improved men were more disposed to think in terms of gradual and lasting reform, rather than abrupt revolution. With employ-

6 LORD LIVERPOOL

ment high, and wages steadily going up, men turned their minds to parliamentary reform, as the first step to more far-reaching change. Rudimentary trade unions, still officially banned by the Anti-Combination laws, also flourished. They were often badly organised and poorly led. Their discipline was weak, but their appeal was strong. On the other hand, some of the more radical politicians, whose faith in the laws of economics was unshaken, thought that by permitting the men to combine the futility of trying to interfere with wage-rates would be demonstrated. In 1824 two Radicals, Hume and Place, succeeded in persuading a Select Committee of the House of Commons to recommend the repeal of the Combination Act of 1800. Both Hume and Place were skilled in the arts of political manipulation, and Parliament followed the Committee's advice with little understanding of what was implied. Soon trade unions sprang up overnight. Strikes occurred in the cotton mills, wool factories and coal-mines. There were instances of intimidation, of physical violence, even of murder. The government and middle classes were shocked. Only Place's energy and devotion saved the workers from feeling the full brunt of the law. In 1825 a frightened legislature passed a new Act, restoring the prohibition governing secret societies and combinations, but making an exception in respect of unions which were concerned only with the regulation of wages and working hours. The artisans could act together to ask for better wages, but their right to strike was severely curtailed. Liverpool admitted that he had not been aware of the extent of the 1824 Act, and that until it came into operation he had been ignorant of its provisions. The victory of 1824 had been rendered of no avail because of the impatience and indiscipline of the unions. A long and weary battle lay ahead before they were fully accepted and their rights recognised in law.

George IV and Queen Caroline

On January 29th, 1820, George III died. For ten years he had lived in a world of fantasy, chattering incessantly to himself, strumming his harpsichord in sad frustration, dreaming all the while of the days of his youth and the ghosts of men who were

F

long ago dead and gone. Although he was mad and blind, the old King's constitution was strong, but now he turned his face to the wall, murmured 'Poor Tom's a-cold!', and died. His death reminded his older subjects of Pitt and Fox, of North and Burke. His courage, honesty and obstinate English prejudices had won him the affection of his people. But his death made little difference to the real world he had left behind him a decade before. The Prince Regent became King George IV. Yet this was to embarrass the ministry, for the accession of the new monarch provoked a controversy over the rights of the Queen. George had married Caroline of Brunswick in 1795. He did so in a spirit of indifferent acquiescence to his father's wishes. Unfortunately the Princess was eccentric, plain and none too fond of soap and water. She lacked both the physical graces and the intellectual gifts to win George's devotion from Mrs Fitzherbert, whom he had illegally married ten years before. The Prince of Wales had asked for brandy on meeting his bride, and he spent his wedding night drunk in the fireplace. Within a year Caroline gave birth to Princess Charlotte, and once he had done his duty in providing for the succession, George left his wife. He pursued his own pleasures in his own company: the cranky Caroline was allowed to go her own way. Soon her behaviour became notorious. She consorted with Italian adventurers, toured Europe in a variety of questionable circumstances and surrounded by a motley collection of rascals, and offended almost every canon of taste and decorum. Rumour told of her adultery, and in 1805 the government had instituted a curious inquiry known as the 'Delicate Investigation': its findings were inconclusive but discreditable. Since the end of the war Caroline's case had been taken up by Brougham, who saw how useful it could be in embarrassing the ministry. Because the Prince Regent was so unpopular, feeling rallied round his wife. Cries of 'George—where's your wife!' greeted him at the theatre, and soon Caroline was the epitome of a wronged woman, despite her own excesses. The death of Princess Charlotte in 1817 won even more sympathy for Caroline, and the situation was made all the more difficult by Brougham's deceitful conduct of negotiations on her behalf.

But George IV was determined to divorce his wife: he had no wish to share his throne with the woman he loathed. He even postponed his coronation, on which he had lavished his aesthetic attention, in the hope that by the time he was crowned he would be a free man. Liverpool and his colleagues were more cautious than their volatile and selfish master. They knew how easily the divorce proceedings could be exploited by the opposition, and they were sensitive to the King's own indiscretions. Reluctantly they introduced a 'Bill of Pains and Penalties' to deprive the Queen of her title and rights, and to dissolve her marriage. While the Bill was before the Lords Caroline was received by cheering crowds. The peers became hesitant. Finally, after a fortnight during which the nation wallowed in the evidence purporting to prove the Queen's guilt, Liverpool withdrew the Bill. The King and the ministry were humiliated. London went wild with delight. But soon popular feeling turned against the Queen. In January 1821 she accepted a pension from the government. To the Radicals she was an apostate and as her political utility vanished her private life ceased to entertain. When she tried to force her way into the Abbey during the coronation service she was thwarted. In August 1821 she died. The government had survived, despite all the ingenuity of the opposition in exploiting the unhappy Caroline for their own purposes. And, far from being at the end of its tether, the Liverpool ministry took on a new lease of life.

Castlereagh's Foreign Policy

While his colleagues had been grappling with domestic problems Castlereagh had been directing the country's foreign policy. It was, above all else, a policy of conciliation and moderation. At Vienna Castlereagh had been concerned to procure a settlement which would provide adequate safeguards against a renewal of French aggression, but he had also prevented the Prussians from imposing a harsh and vindictive peace, and in collusion with France and Austria he had stopped Russia and Prussia from becoming too powerful. His aim was to establish a genuine balance of power in Europe. He looked forward to continued co-operation between the victorious allies as the best means of securing the peace of Europe and of protecting the interests of the Powers themselves. In December 1815 he outlined the principal considerations governing his policy:

> 'In the present state of Europe it is the province of Great Britain to turn the confidence she has inspired to the account of peace, by exercising a conciliatory influence between the Powers, rather than put herself at the head of any combination of Courts to keep others in check. . . . It is not my wish to encourage on the part of this country, an unnecessary interference in the ordinary affairs of the Continent.'

He was no idealist. He had no desire for the alliance to become 'a union for the government of the world or for the superintendence of the internal affairs of other states'; this was where he parted company with Metternich and the Tsar. Castlereagh wanted to create a true concert of Europe. By meeting regularly the Powers would compose their differences and take any steps necessary for preventing the outbreak of war or for containing revolution. At the same time the breach with the Holy Alliance was there from the beginning. Castlereagh was always of the opinion that if his allies were determined to be 'theorists' England would have to act in separation. Perhaps Castlereagh can be accused of wishing to save the *status quo* without being prepared to will the necessary means: the Austrian ambassador once described him as a great lover of music who found himself in church and who wished to applaud without daring to do so. But Castlereagh was more interested in international stability than in perpetuating any particular form of polity, and the years saw the disappointment of his hope that collaboration between those who had vanquished Napoleon would facilitate international order. The sixth article of the treaty of alliance which the Powers had signed in 1815 had pledged the allies to renew their meetings at regular intervals, for the purpose of consulting upon common interests and upon any measures necessary for the maintenance of the peace of Europe. For Castlereagh this was a practical precaution; for Metternich it was the opportunity for systematic repression. Of course Castlereagh distrusted liberalism and nationalism, on one occasion confessing that he liked to see evil germs destroyed even when he could not give open approbation. But he disliked them chiefly because he thought they would lead to war. Similarly, the distinction which he made between the purely internal affairs of a country, in which intervention was unjustifiable, and a threat to the peace of Europe, which rendered precautions imperative, was not clear, or even desirable, to those with whom he sought to co-operate. Consequently, England came to play an ever more isolated role in European diplomacy, especially after Talleyrand ceased to be in charge of French foreign policy.

The Congress of Aix-la-Chapelle (1818) was devoted to the settlement of French affairs. The reprobate was ready to return to the fold. She had paid her debts. The armies of occupation were ready to withdraw. Louis XVIII could take his rightful place amidst the defenders of the rights of legitimate princes. Castlereagh was able to foil the Tsar's scheme to inaugurate a league of monarchs, each guaranteeing the other's rights and territories and committed to the doctrine of intervention, and he gained another concession in that periodic meetings for the discussion of mutual interests were approved. But the implied conflict became increasingly intractable. In 1820 the Spaniards forced the vicious and reactionary Ferdinand VII to accept the constitution he had promised to promulgate as long ago as 1812. Immediately Ferdinand appealed to his fellow princes for help. Castlereagh found himself at odds with Metternich. He disapproved of revolution, but he did not think that insurrection in Spain threatened the safety of any of the Powers. The conditions in which military intervention would have to take place made him pessimistic about the outcome. He saw the danger to the rights of smaller states—indeed, to all states—if the doctrine of intervention was conceded. He intended to combat 'the notion, but too perceptibly prevalent, that whenever any great political event shall occur, as in Spain, pregnant perhaps with future danger, it is to be regarded almost as a matter of course that it belongs to the Allies to charge themselves collectively with the responsibility of exercising some jurisdiction concerning such possible eventual danger'. Castlereagh was prepared to exercise reasonable doubt. Unless the internal convulsions in any country could be conclusively proved to threaten the security of its neighbours, then intervention was illegitimate and unwarranted.

But new revolutions made it more difficult for him to hold to this point of view, without destroying the Concert of Powers upon which he had pinned so many hopes for the future stability of Europe. In 1820 it could be claimed that the example of Spain was catching: revolutions broke out in Portugal, Naples and Piedmont. But with that obstinate fidelity which was so distinguished a part of his character, Castlereagh did not flinch. He saw no need for the combined might of the Powers to be applied in every country which happened to suffer from 'domestic upsets'. There was to be no joint intervention. He would not oppose intervention in Naples by Austria alone, but he would not take part in any organised scheme. When the Tsar pleaded his case for a visionary alliance Castlereagh was unshaken: 'the more Russia wishes to transport us to the heights the further we must descend to the plain'. But his allies were becoming more 'theoretical' not less so, and the ties which gave the Quintuple Alliance whatever cohesion it possessed were under severe strain.

In the autumn of 1820 Castlereagh sent his half-brother, Lord Stewart, as an observer to the Congress which assembled at Troppau. The Holy Alliance drew up a protocol, affirming their right to intervene in the domestic affairs of any country, as the need arose, and arguing that the articles of the Quintuple Alliance gave them this privilege. Castlereagh protested: general interference would 'destroy all wholesome national energy and all independent action, more especially within the smaller states'. The man who was so suspicious of the diabolical tendencies inherent in nationalism and liberalism was defending the rights normally claimed by sovereign states against the unrestricted discretionary powers demanded by his allies. He announced that Britain would not charge herself, as a member of the alliance, with 'the moral responsibility of administering a general European Police'. When the Powers met again at Laibach (1821–2) the rift widened. The Greek revolt fanned British fears of Russia. Castlereagh had seen his conception perverted, and like his mentor, Pitt, he valued a real liberty more than a theoretical one. At every meeting of the

Powers his allies were preoccupied with dabbling in the domestic policies of other countries, instead of enhancing the pacific settlement of disputes between states. The tensions between the allies became tighter and more fragile. Another Congress was arranged for Verona in October 1822, but before it met Castlereagh was dead. In an age when the Foreign Office was badly staffed and incompetently administered he had driven himself mercilessly. Despite his reserve, he had been deeply hurt by the ignorant and insulting abuse hurled at him from every side. His allies were wrecking the Concert of Europe in the sense in which he understood the term. His countrymen were incapable of perceiving the mainsprings of his policy. His colleagues were unable to share the burden with him. Although he had once lightly claimed that he had known both popularity and unpopularity, and that of the two unpopularity was by far the more preferable and gentlemanlike, he was a sensitive man, acutely conscious of his loneliness and profoundly distressed by the misrepresentation he encountered at every turn. His mind broke under the strain. He was also the victim of a cruel and unscrupulous plot to ruin his character and reputation. Throughout the summer he became more depressed. His self-control was shattered. He found himself bursting into tears, and confessing strange and incoherent fears to his friends. On August 12th, 1822, he cut his throat.

Sidmouth had resigned in the previous year, and Liverpool was now compelled to carry out a more drastic remodelling of his administration. Canning was waiting to go to India, where he was to take up the post of Governor-General. Now he accepted the offer of the Foreign Secretaryship: since he also became Leader of the House of Commons he entered fully into his old rival's inheritance. Six months earlier Peel had succeeded Sidmouth at the Home Office, and in January 1823 Robinson replaced Vansittart as Chancellor of the Exchequer, while Huskisson took over at the Board of Trade. These were the men most closely identified with what looked like new policies in foreign affairs, commerce and the law. Canning fired the imagination of his countrymen, blinding many of them to the fact that he was carrying on where Castlereagh had left off. Peel worked patiently at the colossal task of

bringing some sort of rationality and order to the chaotic criminal code. Huskisson proved that free-trade ideas were as profitable in practice as they had been attractive in theory. Yet without an improving economy not even Canning's gift for spectacular publicity would have lulled the working classes into oblivious indifference to reform, and Peel's work at the Home Office could not have taken place at a time when the upper and middle classes lived in constant fear of insurrection and unrest.

Peel and Huskisson

Although Canning made the more immediate impact on the consciousness of the age, Peel's achievement was the m re impressive and the more lasting. The confusion and severit ᶠ the English legal code ᵥ ᵤre notorious. There were well over two hundred capit. offences on the statute book, for during the eighteenth centu y deficiencies in the prevention and detection of crime were allegedly made good by extending the death penalty to a multitude of minor offences. Death was thought an appropriate punishment for one who impersonated a Chelsea pensioner or who defaced Westminster Bridge, as ll ng inflicted for any theft involving article or t i ve shillings. But the very ferocity t a. as g atest drawback in the punishment of ff ers. Juries often preferred to bring in verdicts of not guilty ather than exposing some unfortunate to the sentence of death: the leniency of the juries offset the harshness of the law and the sternness of the judges, but it hardly contributed to the regular administration of justice. Even if the death penalty was not imposed imprisonment was arbitrary, and the prisons themselves were in an appalling condition. They were overcrowded, insanitary and all too often corruptly managed. Instead of reforming the criminal they hardened him in his ways. Brutality and vice were common. While methods of punishment were unpredictable and intuitive, there was no adequate machinery for the maintenance of public order. The government had relied, as governments had relied from time immemorial, upon the local magistrates and yeomanry. Yet these were demonstrably inefficient, and men were coming to see the need for a more effective instru-

ment for the prevention of crime. But there was a considerable prejudice against the formation of anything resembling a police force. Men preferred to put up with the inconveniences of freedom rather than risk any diminution of the Englishman's traditional liberties. Peel was emphatic in pleading the case for a regular police force. In June 1822 he told the Commons, 'God forbid that he should mean to countenance a system of espionage; but a vigorous preventive police, consistent with the free principles of our free constitution, was an object which he did not despair of seeing accomplished'.

Peel owed much to those who had advocated the necessity of legal a⸱ ⸱ pen⸱l reform: R⸱⸱⸱⸱ly, Mackintosh, John Howard, Elizabet⸱ ⸱ ⸱⸱ ⸱ le⸱ ⸱⸱⸱ ⸱⸱ham. Both evan⸱elicals and radical utilita⸱⸱ ⸱⸱ ⸱⸱ ⸱⸱ a common hur⸱⸱⸱ it⸱rianism in pressing fo⸱ a ⸱ ⸱rm of th⸱ 1 code and the mo⸱ ⸱⸱⸱ane treatment of offenders. In 1819 (the year of Peterloo) a C⸱ ⸱ns' Committee f Inquiry was set up, and three recommenda⸱ ⸱ were ultimately made: the repeal of obsolete and redundant st⸱ ⸱s, the abolition of the death pen⸱ ⸱ty f⸱ ⸱⸱⸱ classes of theft ⸱d the reform of the ⸱rgery laws. In 1823 five Acts of Parliame⸱t p⸱t many of the ref⸱ners' dem⸱⸱ ⸱s into practice, and in 1⸱⸱ ⸱ d 1827 the work of simplifying ⸱⸱ ⸱ al code w⸱⸱ ⸱⸱ ⸱rther. Peel swept away many of the old capita⸱ o⸱er⸱⸱⸱ ⸱⸱efit of clergy was abolished. The ancient practice of burying s⸱⸱cides at cross-roads with a stake through the heart was officially terminated. Judges were permitted to withhold the formal sentence of death in all capital convictions except murder. In 1828 Peel consolidated the law governing offences against the person and tightened up the law of evidence. Except where a felony was specifically stated to be a capital crime, it was to carry anything between two years' imprisonment and seven years' transportation. Peel confessed that it was his legitimate ambition to leave behind 'some record of the trust I have held, which may outlive the fleeting discharge of the mere duties of ordinary routine, and that may perhaps confer some distinction on my name, by connecting it with permanent improvements in the judicial institutions of the country'. At the same time he had to proceed cautiously. He was no advocate for capital punishments, but he warned the House of Commons of the danger of moving too rapidly. If they did so 'a strong prejudice might arise in the country against measures that were intended for the public good; and thus the great object of justice and humanity might be defeated'. Peel could proudly point out that there had been less executions during the 1820s than during the previous decade. As the old savageries were being abolished, the need for ferocity was passing away.

But Peel did not content himself with pruning the law. He also turned his attention to the prisons. In 1823 the Gaols Act established common gaols in every county or riding, in London and Westminster, and in seventeen other towns. These were to be administered by the local magistrates, inspected three times a quarter and made the subject of an annual report to the Home Office. Peel attempted to speed up the devious process of the Court of Chancery, but with little success, and radical reform had to wait until after 1830. His attention was increasingly devoted to the problem of an efficient police force: however picturesque the Bow Street runners and gentlemen of the Watch may have been, they were of limited utility. Peel was acutely conscious of contemporary anomalies, expressing himself forcefully to the Duke of Wellington: 'Just conceive the state of one parish, in which there are eighteen different local boards for the management of the Watch, each acting without concert with the others! . . . Think of the state of Brentford and Deptford, with no sort of police by night! I really think I need trouble you with no further proof of putting an end to such a state of things.' In 1826 Peel gave notice of an inquiry into the police forces of London, but Liverpool's stroke and Canning's death compelled him to postpone his plans. In 1828 another inquiry was instituted, and in June 1829 the Metropolitan Police Act was passed. A regular force of 1,000 men— later to be augmented to 3,000—was established, under the direction of a commissioner and assistant commissioner, with headquarters at Scotland Yard. A new police rate was levied to pay for the force, and every attempt was made to minimise any resemblance between the constabulary and the military. The constables were not equipped with firearms, and their blue uniforms gave them as civilian an appearance as possible. Old suspicions died hard, but gradually the experiment proved its worth. The force became the envy of the country, and a respectable and worthy career had been opened up for many working men. There were early difficulties in recruitment, and Peel had to check his subordinates for officious behaviour, but a satisfactory solution to public order had at last been found.

Huskisson wasted little time in reducing customs duties, once he had settled at the Board of Trade. He was a convinced free trader. As long ago as 1810 he had published a pamphlet arguing that the interests of every country were 'most effectually consulted by leaving . . . every part of the world to raise those productions for which soil and climate were best adapted'. He had defended the Corn Law in 1815, on conventional grounds, but he was now much less sympathetic to the demands of the landed interest. In any case Huskisson represented the viewpoint of the overwhelming majority of British merchants. In 1820 the wholesale traders of London had petitioned in favour of free imports, and they were supported by the merchants of Manchester and Glasgow. They were confident that in a free market they could outstrip and outsell their foreign competitors. They relied on their superiority in equipment and organisation. The industrialists also desired free trade, for this would mean that they would obtain the raw materials which they needed more cheaply. Political expediency might be cited as a partial justification for the regulation of trade by the government, but there was no doubt where the sentiments of the commercial and manufacturing classes lay. The working men saw the Corn Laws as an artificial means of keeping the price of bread high, so they, too, favoured a drastic reduction in tariffs. Only the country gentry and the farmers were suspicious. In 1826 it was rumoured that Huskisson had told an election meeting in Liverpool that trade in corn was to be free. At once there was a storm of controversy. Huskisson claimed that he had been misquoted, that he had not said what was attributed to him. Whatever the truth of the matter he never regained the confidence of the landed interest, who regarded him as the agent of the sinister school of political economists.

Nevertheless, the 1820s saw an impressive reduction in tariffs, especially since the government depended, in the absence of an income tax, upon indirect duties for so much of its revenue. In 1822 Robinson tampered with the Navigation Acts to facilitate trade with the rebellious Spanish colonies in South America, as well as with Canada and the West Indies. Huskisson relaxed the Acts still further in order to stimulate trade between Britain, the colonies and Europe. In 1823 the Reciprocity of Duties Act authorised the government to negotiate commercial treaties with foreign states, and within the next three years reciprocity treaties were concluded with Prussia, Sweden, Denmark, Brazil and Colombia. Huskisson slashed the duties on silk, wool and rum in 1824, and in 1825 he extended his reductions to linen, cotton, china, copper, lead, iron, zinc, glass and books. He cut the duty on general manufactures (that is to say, goods which were not liable for a specific tariff) from 50 to 20 per cent. He abolished many of the trade restrictions between Britain and Ireland, and permitted gold to be exported. In 1827 he attempted to modify the Corn Laws by introducing a sliding scale. This proposal was defeated, but he was successful a year later, when a graded set of duties was imposed on foreign corn, the price of 60s. a quarter being taken as the norm.

Huskisson had his critics. When the boom ended in 1825 his experiments were blamed for the slump, despite the fact that many of his innovations did not take effect until 1826. Also his failure to achieve free trade in corn lost him some favour among the industrialists, just as his sliding scale further embittered the farming community. But his achievement was a considerable contribution to the prosperity and welfare of England during the last years of Liverpool's premiership. He was no doctrinaire: he had his convictions, but he was always sensitive to what was practicable and acceptable. He typified that sober common sense which was so necessary during a time of violent change and intensive competition.

Canning at the Foreign Office

But however valuable the reforms of Peel and Huskisson appear to posterity, for contemporaries the political scene after the death of Castlereagh was dominated by the brilliant and controversial figure of George Canning. At last the most wayward of Pitt's disciples had come into his own, and he soon showed that he preferred flamboyant gestures to the staid methods which had been usual under Castlereagh. Canning's policy was wilful, opportunist, paradoxical, difficult to interpret with any consistency. Like Castlereagh, he disapproved of the Holy Alliance and of Metternich's policy of intervention. Unlike Castlereagh he was prepared to intervene on the other side, provided that this could be accomplished with the least danger and the maximum drama. Even if Castlereagh had been compelled to resist Metternich more actively, he would not have relished performing a task which Canning so obviously enjoyed. Before he had been at the Foreign Office three months Canning was gaily confessing, 'for *Europe* I shall be desirous *now* and *then* to read *England*'. Castlereagh had had a concept of the Concert of Europe, limited and moderate as it was. In reaction against Metternich's own interpretation of this idea, Canning swung to a more insular and unblushingly nationalistic line. He refused to take into account 'the wishes of any other sovereign, the feelings of any other government, or the interests of any other people, except in so far as those wishes, those feelings, and those interests may, or might, concur with the just interests of England'. He was lucky in that British sea-power enabled him to get away with it, for he was pursuing a policy which was irresponsible and which contained within itself the seeds of disaster. He was a practised and inveterate exponent of brinkmanship. Though he encountered frustrations and disappointments, he was able to carry them off (as Palmerston was to do) because of the resilience of his personality. Castlereagh represented the professional eighteenth-century diplomat: indifferent to public opinion, sceptical of nationalism, preoccupied with restraint and order. He had seen diplomacy primarily in terms of conciliation and co-operation between mature states, each of which was to act with a sense of responsibility appropriate to its power. It was no mean tradition. Canning, on the other hand, saw foreign policy as a bright essay in competition, in which risk possessed additional glamour. His was an adolescent conception. If it looked to the future it lacked coherence. He cheerfully exploited public opinion (at times he created it) and fanned the flames of nationalist or liberal feeling whenever he thought that British interests would benefit. Yet he had no desire to promote revolution. He was no crusader for moral causes: 'Let us not, in the foolish spirit of romance, suppose that we alone could regenerate Europe.' He was capable of admonishing the French ambassador after the success of French intervention in Spain—'Be yours the glory of a victory followed by disaster and ruin, be ours the inglorious traffic of industry and ever increasing prosperity'—but he could hardly be surprised if the European Powers saw his policy in a much more sensational light. It was a continuous improvisation, a policy of confusion, not stability. Only a single Power could hope to carry it off. Even Canning's cult of liberal movements abroad looks questionable nowadays: was he trying to distract attention from necessary reforms at home, by indulging in an exciting foreign policy to the accompaniment of liberal slogans? There was much force in Wellington's charge that Canning was continually 'upsetting all our foreign policy', and his comment in 1823—'There are some people who like to fish in troubled waters and Mr C. is one of them'—was just.

The greatest contrast between Castlereagh and Canning lay not in what the new Foreign Secretary did, but in what he was. The withdrawal of Wellington from the congress of Verona, in protest against the proposed intervention in Spain, had already been prefigured in the disillusionment of Castlereagh's last years. Continuity can be discerned: Canning's objection to the domination of Europe by the Holy Alliance was not new. But what gave British foreign policy a new flavour was his unpredictable and highly individual personality. He was not applying a more enlightened concept. He simply saw his first loyalty as being to British interests, rather than to the diplomatic abstraction known as Europe. It was no accident that he had not been involved in the peace settlement, for he did not think in the terms which had been common to Castlereagh, Talleyrand and Metternich. Canning's self-reliant optimism, his brisk self-confidence and his disregard of conventional attitudes of mind were characteristic of a new England, whose industrial supremacy gave her an unshakable belief in her superiority to the nations of the continent. Economic advancement enabled isolation to be safe, prosperous and splendid. It did not induce a respect for the traditional niceties of diplomacy.

Canning was not content with verbal condemnation of the policy approved by the Holy Alliance. Like many Englishmen, he was disappointed when the Bourbons achieved what had eluded Napoleon—a sharp campaign to restore tranquillity to the Iberian peninsula. But Canning's retort has become the most famous example of his conduct of affairs. He strengthened the navy, announced that Britain would not permit the occupation or annexation of any part of the Spanish dominions and finally recognised the independence of the South American republics. He had resolved that if France had Spain it should not be Spain with the Indies—'I called a New World into existence to redress the balance of the Old.' Although the United States did not prove as co-operative as Canning hoped, and although the Monroe Doctrine could be interpreted in an anti-British as well as an anti-French or anti-Spanish sense, the American government's determination not to permit European intervention in the affairs of the western hemisphere was a further vindication of Canning's policy. In 1825 he recognised the independence of Brazil, and in the following year he sent a fleet to Lisbon to protect the Portuguese from the Spaniards, who had been dabbling in the domestic squabble between the absolutist and constitutionalist factions in the Portuguese royal family.

The situation in the Near East was more complex. Although the Ottoman Empire could be regarded as the legitimate authority in the Balkans, sympathy for the Greek Christians, and the fear of Russian designs on Constantinople, made it impossible for any lucid policy to be formulated. The Russians had been given a vague status as protectors of the Christian subjects of the Sultan by the treaty of Kutchuk Kainardji in 1774, and this could be made the pretext for intervention on the part of the Tsar. In 1821 the Greeks rebelled against the Turks, and in January 1822 they proclaimed their independence. At once there was a great outburst of sympathy for the rebels. Liberals saw them as a people rightly struggling to be free. Romantic poets dreamed of that brighter Hellas which seemed about to arise. Devout Christians identified themselves with their co-religionists embattled against the Turk. The savage peasantry of the Morea were represented as descendants of the ancient Greeks, nobly seeking to restore lost glories. Nothing could have been more ridiculous, but when Byron left his haven in Italy to die amidst the swamps of Missolonghi the Greek cause was hallowed by one of the most romantic of martyrdoms. Unfortunately the diplomats could not see events in literary terms. Theirs was a more exhausting task—to discover the political realities which lurked beneath grandiose gestures and poetic fancies. Metternich knew his duty. The Austrian Empire was as vulnerable as the Ottoman to the disrupting effects of nationalism. He therefore exerted all his influence to persuade his fellow diplomats to treat the Sultan exactly the same as any other legitimate ruler. But it became increasingly difficult for the Powers to stand idly by when the energetic and reforming Sultan, Mahmud II, came near to crushing the insurgents. The rebels had already fallen out among themselves, murdering each other with the same zeal with which they attacked the Turks. Atrocities on both sides were bloody and outrageous. The Patriarch and three other bishops of the Orthodox Church were slaughtered by the Sultan: the Greeks replied by taking no prisoners. By brutal reprisals, and systematic terror, Mahmud II succeeded in limiting the scope of the insurrection to the Morea, and when he called in the ruthless Pasha of Egypt, Mehemet Ali, to his aid, the cause of the Greeks seemed doomed. In 1825 Mehemet's son, Ibrahim Pasha, landed in the Morea. Two years later his savage policy of depopulation had almost annihilated the rebels.

The reverses endured by the Greeks were even more serious than their initial successes. The Tsar could not allow Orthodox Christians to be butchered. His moral sense and his ambitions for a port in the Mediterranean went hand in hand. He proposed that three Greek republics should be set up, under nominal allegiance to the Sultan. The other Powers resisted this suggestion. Metternich and Canning both distrusted the plan. The Greeks, now fighting for their lives, interpreted it as betrayal. They appealed to Canning for help: he offered mediation. He had no desire to become too involved in the Greek struggle. Though he had recognised the Greeks as belligerents in 1823 his motives had been mixed. He had wanted to secure British trading interests in the eastern Mediterranean. He sympathised with the Greeks, but he was suspicious of the Russians, and he had no intention of helping Russian designs on Constantinople by weakening the Turks too much. He was sceptical of the philhellene case: Britain had no reason for going to war for 'Epaminondas or St Paul'. The death of Alexander in December 1825 changed the situation. His successor, Nicholas I, was a soldier, free from the idealistic yearnings which had so beset his brother, who saw his duty in the simplest terms. Canning felt that the only way of moderating the Tsar's policy was by co-operating with him. In 1826 Wellington went to St Petersburg. The two Powers agreed to insist that some measure of independence should be given to the Greeks. The French—who were determined not to be left out of any settlement —supported Russia and Britain, and the treaty of London was signed in July 1827. Prussia and Austria remained aloof and ill at ease.

Canning had been pushed into intervention. It seemed to be the only method by which Russian aggrandisement could be checked and the Turkish Empire sustained. The three Powers sent their fleets to the eastern Mediterranean. The Turks refused to accept an armistice, and their fleet was sunk at the battle of Navarino (October 1827). The news threw the British government into confusion, for Codrington, the English Admiral, had gone far beyond his instructions. Even more confusing was the fact that Canning had died in August, leaving behind a policy which was tentative and uncertain. Wellington tartly described Navarino as 'an untoward event', and the King's speech in January 1828 bewailed the clash with an ancient ally. When the Russians picked a quarrel with the Turks over the Danubian principalities and

G

marched on Adrianople Wellington feared for the existence of Turkey, which he thought essential for the preservation of the balance of power. In September 1829 Mahmud II was forced to accept the treaty of Adrianople, which yielded the Danube delta to the Russians and allowed them to garrison the principalities for five years. Meanwhile the French had rescued the Greeks in the Morea. Wellington saw that it was impossible to do more than limit the losses which were to be inflicted on Turkey. The Powers decided to set up a completely independent Greece, but the new state was severely restricted in extent. It did not include Thessaly or Crete. France and Britain thought that a small Greece would be a less dangerous pawn in the hands of Russia, and that Turkey would not be too gravely weakened. The Greeks grumbled, but finally gave way, and in February 1830 they formally gained their independence. In the following year, after the assassination of Capo d'Istria, the throne was offered to Otto of Bavaria, who accepted it. But the eastern question was far from settled. Turkey was still in decline, Russian designs were unabated, while the Greeks hankered after a fuller recognition of their status and the acquisition of new territories.

The year 1827, the date of Liverpool's stroke and Canning's death, forms a watershed in English history. The trials of the post-war years had been overcome, however great the cost. Moderate reforms had been carried out. But the old order was soon to face two new challenges, both of which shattered what was left of its structure: Catholic emancipation and parliamentary reform. Not that a new order was achieved overnight. Old modes of thought, established political habits, conventional assumptions still lingered, but despite all the tenacity which they showed in resisting new ideas and modern methods, they were no more than tough remnants from the eighteenth century. The decisive battle had already been lost. Catholic emancipation and parliamentary reform were closely linked. Without the first it may be doubted whether the second could have been accomplished in 1832. The Catholic issue wrecked Wellington's ministry, just as the retirement of Liverpool and the death of Canning threw political life into confusion. Liverpool and his colleagues were men of the old order. They governed in traditional style. But they were remarkably successful in dealing with the vast problems which faced them. No other government of the time was as successful in combining public order with necessary change. The age of Liverpool was not an age of black reaction. It was a period of cautious advance, of careful adjustment, of distinct, if circumscribed, achievement. Despite their timidity, some credit for this must be given to Liverpool and his colleagues. Liverpool was no genius. He could neither arouse the imagination of men nor inspire them to acts of daring. His course was orderly, his decisions predictable. But he created a foundation on which others—more original in thought, more diverse in their gifts, more spectacular in their accomplishments—could build. The full measure of his worth is shown in the crisis which followed his retirement. Without his steadying influence it was as if chaos had come again into the enclosed and fluctuating world of high politics.

5 : Catholic Emancipation and Parliamentary Reform

Canning's Ministry and Death

On February 17th, 1827, Lord Liverpool suffered an apoplectic stroke. Though he did not die until the following year, it soon became evident that he would never be able to return to political life. But finding a successor was no easy task. No one had Liverpool's ability to preserve that delicate alliance between conservative and liberal Tories which had been the secret of his success. It was well known that the King had long harboured a grudge against Canning, and that the Foreign Secretary was unpopular with the more reactionary members of the Cabinet. Yet despite this, there seemed little choice in the matter. Canning was the most brilliant of the Tories. His colourful personality and astonishing gift for capturing the national imagination had endeared him to the public, just his adventurous policy and spectacular gestures had appalled Wellington and the conservatives. For a month George IV hesitated, artfully enjoying the sense of power which his procrastination gave him. But he knew well enough to whom he had to look to carry on the government. He put his old prejudice behind him and asked Canning to take over. But although Canning was admired by the people, he experienced acute embarrassment in forming his ministry. Without Liverpool the old Tory party splintered into fragments. There were murmurs and fears over Catholic emancipation, which Liverpool had tactfully allowed to remain an open question for so long. Wellington had no desire to serve under Canning, and Peel's convictions on the Catholic issue drove him to resignation. Among the Tory backbenchers Canning was regarded with suspicion and foreboding. He was compelled to seek support in other quarters. His ministry was a curious coalition of liberal Tories and moderate

Whigs. Grey shared Wellington's aristocratic disdain for the new Premier and held aloof, but several Whigs, including Melbourne and Stanley, accepted office, while of the Tories Huskisson, Robinson and Palmerston remained. The varied composition of Canning's ministry is a reminder of the looseness of 'party' in the early nineteenth century, and of the way in which eighteenth-century attitudes to the formation of a new government still lingered. His difficulties underline the skill and tact which had enabled Liverpool to preserve the illusion of Tory unanimity for so long.

The new ministry faced ugly problems. The Corn Laws were a constant headache: we have already noted the opposition which Huskisson encountered in applying his policy of a sliding scale. Canning's foreign policy seemed to many men to be no more than an exciting sequence of dangerous and irresponsible adventures. More serious still, the Catholic problem, which had lurked in the background of English politics for almost forty years, threatened to push itself to the fore. But Canning was not spared to grapple with these grave and momentous issues. His triumph was short-lived. For some time he had been overworking, and he had also complained of ill health. Attacks of gout became more frequent, undermining his strength. Already in January 1827 he had been seriously ill. He had scarcely installed himself in office when he fell ill once more. He died on August 8th, in the same house in Chiswick in which Charles James Fox had died in 1806. A similar irony can be discerned in the way in which Canning, like Fox, was struck down within months of attaining the office which he had coveted through many weary years. The frail coalition of Canningite Tories and aristocratic Whigs dissolved without Canning's force and charm. The King asked Lord Goderich (as Robinson had now become) to assume the responsibilities of presiding over the ministry. For an agonising half year Goderich endured the anxieties of office, casting this way and that for an opportunity to end his worries. He shrank from decision, yet he could not bring himself to resign. His premiership was no more than a desperate and fussy interlude. Not even the tears and protestations of the King could keep Goderich at his post. In

January 1828 he surrendered the seals: he had not even met Parliament.

Wellington Prime Minister

George IV did the only possible thing. He asked the Duke of Wellington to form a ministry. It was hoped that the victor of Waterloo would provide the firm hand which was needed to restore stability to English politics. Wellington had a high sense of duty, and a dedicated devotion to the nation's welfare, but his political experience was limited and his vision narrow. He had a haughty distaste for the necessary compromises of political life, and he had little understanding of the nature of the relationship between the head of a ministry and his colleagues. He was said to possess a social contempt for his intellectual equals, and an intellectual contempt for his social equals. His dealings with quarrelsome and fickle Spanish politicians during his Peninsular campaigns had left him with a keen suspicion of all who professed to be expert in the science of government. He despised ideologues as windbags and demagogues as unscrupulous charlatans. He had criticised Canning's foreign policy—with much justification—and as an Anglo-Irish aristocrat he had little sympathy for Catholic emancipation. He thought the English constitution perfect, and dismissed pleas for parliamentary reform as little more than devious manoeuvres on the part of ambitious rogues who sought power. His speeches were those of a High Tory. Yet he never shrank from changing his policy in order to bring it into line with a new situation. For all his stubborn insolence, he retained the tactical sense of a general. He valued political peace more than intellectual consistency. His unbending attitude provoked Radicals to wrath, but he always knew when the time had come to give way. Perhaps only someone as indifferent to the conventional acclamations of politics could have survived so many political retreats. But Wellington was unfitted to be Premier. Though he included the Canningites in his ministry, he did not disguise his distaste for their policies. When Huskisson offered to resign after a dispute over parliamentary reform Wellington surprised everyone by accepting it. The Canningites left the administration. It seemed that the Duke would have to rely on the more conservative Tories if his ministry was to last. Yet soon he was taking the lead in solving the Catholic problem, and any unity which the remnants of Liverpool's Tory party shared in common was wrecked by the bitter dispute over Catholic relief. It was this, rather than any nation-wide agitation, which eventually made it possible for Grey to come to power and for the Reform Bill to be introduced. It was no accident that the Old Order should be broken as the result of a wrangle in high politics. It was not surprising that parliamentary reform followed so swiftly upon the emancipation of the Catholics. Peel and Wellington had both opposed relief. Though they believed that their tactics saved Ireland from civil war, they earned the undying hatred of the older Tories for the way in which they abandoned the opinions of a lifetime. And however justifiable their opportunism was, it earned them no gratitude from the Irish.

The Emancipation Controversy

It is easy to guy the anti-Catholic viewpoint. It can be denounced as nothing more than an obscurantist resistance to the march of progress. But to men reared in the eighteenth century the supremacy of the Anglican Church was more than an ecclesiastical preference. The Protestant ascendancy was part of the Constitution: one might say that without it the Constitution would never have existed. The Coronation Oath pledged the monarch to maintain the Protestant religion as by law established, while the Act of Settlement ensured a Protestant succession. Both the landed gentry and the commercial classes—as well as the urban mob— believed that if the Protestant ascendancy went the gates were open to unimaginable horrors. It should be remembered that at this time the Catholic population of England was negligible. Catholics numbered no more than 60,000, and the faith was the religion of a handful of old families, most of whom had been Jacobite in sympathy, and who lived in quiet retirement. Only as Irish immigration gained momentum in the 1840s did the Catholic population of the cities swell. And this was the crux of the matter. When Englishmen thought of Catholicism they called to mind the peasants of Ireland—ignorant, brutalised, superstitious, disloyal.

The long history of conquest, atrocity and massacre made it impossible for either side to come to an objective judgment. If men looked farther afield than Ireland the Church of Rome was associated with the Spanish Inquisition, French despotism, Papal tyranny and black superstition. Those who knew some history recalled the fires of Smithfield and the reign of Good Queen Bess, or the Seven Bishops and the Glorious Revolution. There were no doubts that the Church of England was a Protestant Church. The old Constitution had given the country a century and a half of civil peace, but, once it had been altered in so important a particular, where would innovation end? The Catholic claim to full citizenship would mean the disturbance of that magical balance in Church and State which had proved its worth. Faithful Anglicans such as Robert Peel were simply and sincerely convinced on this point. Peel and Wellington changed their minds because that civil peace which they valued so highly was more threatened by the stubborn refusal to grant emancipation than by its accomplishment. This does not mean that they should be condemned for not changing their minds earlier. It is unjust to decry men simply for being on the losing side. It might be claimed that if emancipation had formed part of an overall settlement of the Irish problem— as Pitt had hoped—then the bitterness of the 1820s would have been averted. But the fact that Peel and Wellington lost does not prove that they did not have a case, however remote its assumptions seem today. The arguments on the other side were clear. The age of religious strife was over. The distrust of Catholics as potential traitors was outmoded. The Irish problem could not be solved without emancipation: even the Union was the first step towards a solution on these terms. Fears of the domination of the United Kingdom by the Irish Catholics were unfounded, for they would be swamped in the imperial Parliament. Yet it could also be asserted that emancipation would result in the destruction, not the stabilisation, of the Union, and whatever the rights and wrongs of the question, events showed that the misgivings of the Tories were not without foundation. Emancipation was just and necessary, but men who thought that the established Constitution in Church and State was the greatest bulwark of order in an increasingly unstable world were not entirely unjustified in claiming that to tamper with the Old Order in one respect was to expose it to more far-reaching attacks.

The Struggle for Catholic Emancipation

The prelude to emancipation was the repeal of the Test and Corporation Acts with respect to the Protestant Dissenters in February 1828. It was now all the more illogical to resist a similar concession to the Catholics, though before his death Canning had opposed relief for the Dissenters because he thought it would prejudice the Catholic cause. Though the Anglican supremacy made sense on its own terms, the first breach had been made. The Protestant cause was being weakened by the ineluctable ravages of time. Many of its supporters retired from politics. Others died. Younger men had less sympathy with the refusal to give civil equality to the Catholics. In 1821 and 1825 private members' Bills favouring emancipation had passed the Commons, only to be thrown out in the Lords. In May 1828 a pro-Catholic motion was passed in the Commons and, although the Lords came to the rescue by rejecting it, the first alarm had been sounded. More serious still, in Ireland the redoubtable Daniel O'Connell had organised his Catholic Association to press for relief. In close co-operation with the priesthood he won the devotion of the Irish peasants. His supporters dutifully paid the Catholic Rent of one shilling a year to aid him in his fight. Public meetings were arranged and propaganda distributed. The Irish did not doubt that emancipation was only a beginning: Home Rule was the ultimate goal. In 1825 the Catholic Association was outlawed, but this made little difference to O'Connell. The Order of Liberation carried on the same work in the same way. O'Connell wisely refused to contemplate illegality or crime. By keeping within the law he strengthened his own position.

In the spring of 1828 Wellington appointed Vesey Fitzgerald, the member for County Clare, to the Presidency of the Board of Trade. Fitzgerald was a popular landlord and a renowned Protestant champion of Catholic claims. In obedience to the custom of the time, he resigned his seat on his appointment as a minister of the Crown, and stood at the by-election. But now O'Connell intervened. Though he was initially hesitant, he decided to exploit the situation. Catholics were excluded from the Commons, but Catholic freeholders had the vote: why not stand as a candidate, despite the law, relying on the certainty that the Catholic freeholders, under the guidance of their priests, would cast their votes for a Catholic candidate? Although he would not be able to take his seat in the House, O'Connell knew that success in the by-election would revive and invigorate the Catholic controversy. A defeat for the government would be nothing less than a humiliation, and the knowledge that Vesey Fitzgerald was himself sympathetic to emancipation would emphasise that the patience of the Catholics was exhausted. Previously O'Connell had been content with procuring the return of well-disposed Protestants, but victory at Clare could be followed up by the wholesale election of Catholics at a general election. With the masses behind him, he could threaten to throw the whole country into turmoil. The by-election was a triumph. The peasants marched to the polls with their priests at their head, and on the fifth day of the contest Fitzgerald conceded victory to his opponent. It seemed that Ireland was on the verge of revolution, for O'Connell's victory inspired the Irish with new hope and new determination. They were demanding emancipation as the price of peace.

Wellington temporised. He despised the Irish peasants and loathed all the arts of demagogy which O'Connell practised so ably, but he had no wish to see the country engulfed in civil war: 'I have passed a longer period of my life in war than most men, and principally in civil war, and I must say this, that if I could avert by any sacrifice even one month's civil war in the country to which I am attached, I would give my life to do it.' Wellington had never committed himself to the extreme Protestant position. Though he wished to preserve the ascendancy, he realised that there were limits which bound this desire. With aristocratic pessimism he was prepared to give way. Peel was in a more embarrassing position. His opposition to emancipation had been consistent and honourable. His position had been carefully thought out, and he had defended it on many occasions with skill and courage. He was generally regarded as the most able of the Protestants, and was held in especial esteem by his constituents at Oxford. But he, too, was prepared to bow to events. He wanted to go out of office, in order to allow emancipation to be carried by others who supported it from conviction, rather than necessity, but when it became clear that Wellington would find it difficult to carry the Bill without his support, he consented to remain. All the ferocity of the Tories was turned on him. Previously Peel's opposition to relief had earned him the nickname 'Orange Peel': now this was transformed into 'Lemon Peel'. The joke went about that he had changed his name from R. Peel to Repeal. When he resigned his seat, in order to allow his constituents to judge his action, he was rejected at the polls. Wellington secured his honour by fighting a duel with Lord Winchelsea. But however much the Protestant Tories fumed, the government's Emancipation Bill was passed with Whig support. In April 1829 it became law. Catholics were to be eligible for most public offices, though no Catholic could hold the Lord Chancellorship in England or the Lord Lieutenancy in Ireland. An attempt was made to moderate the extent of the Catholic victory by putting up the franchise qualification in Ireland to £10 a year. Many of those who had played so decisive a part in O'Connell's campaign now found that they would not, after all, be able to vote for a Catholic. This new piece of crude Machiavellianism only confirmed the suspicions which the Irish still nursed: to the majority the English had once more broken faith.

But though they had averted chaos in Ireland, Wellington and his colleagues had offended both sections of the Tory party. The Canningites could not forgive the Duke for his hostility to their master's foreign policy and the eagerness with which he had accepted Huskisson's resignation. The conservatives saw him as an apostate who had given way, not so much to the inevitable, as to the worst sort of popular agitation. Nor did the government have the consolation of moving into quieter times. The year 1830 was packed with dramatic events. Revolutions in France, Poland, Belgium, Germany, Italy and Portugal gave a breathless, expectant, nervous quality to political life. And at home Wellington's ministry experienced additional shocks.

The Accession of William IV

George IV died in June. He had been a wayward and capricious monarch, whose vices and extravagance had confirmed his unpopularity. Only in Scotland and Ireland, where his flair for public occasions and his flattery of national pride and sentiment endeared him to his Celtic subjects, did he find that popularity which he desired so passionately. His selfishness remained to the end, as did his love of petty intrigue, which pandered to his pathetic delusion that he was as powerful as he imagined himself to be. He had resisted Catholic emancipation to the uttermost, much as his father had done, but he had given way with flamboyant ill-grace. His death brought his brother, the Duke of Clarence, to the throne as William IV. The new King was well meaning and good natured, but he never lost the eccentricities of behaviour which he had picked up during his naval career. The habits of the quarter-deck were displayed on formal occasions, and one wag commented, 'It is a good sovereign, but it is a little cracked.' William tried to be a constitutional monarch. He wanted to be the King of the nation, not just the King of a faction. But his limited intellectual capacity, and his habitual indiscretions, were grave handicaps. In his younger days he had opposed the abolition of the Slave Trade with more enthusiasm than sense, and a similar combination of qualities characterised his performance of his royal duties.

More serious for Wellington was the general election which followed the accession of a new King. The election of 1830 was fought along traditional lines, only a quarter of the seats being contested. Local issues and regional loyalties counted for much more than any obsession with revolution in Europe or reform at home. But the result was unfavourable to the Duke. The extreme Tories were the most bitter of his enemies, and they did not spare themselves to do all they could to weaken his position. When the new Parliament met Wellington found himself in an awkward predicament. Though his supporters were in a minority this was not necessarily the end, but he was incapable of wooing and placating the various groups in the House. Having offended both sections of the Tory party, he proceeded to rebuff the Radicals and the Whigs by asserting that the system of representation was as perfect as any that could be devised, and that as long as he had any responsibility for the nation's affairs there would be no tampering with the electoral structure. His remarks were all the more unfortunate, since they followed a restrained speech by Grey. Perhaps Wellington was making a crude bid for the support of that section of the Tories whose confidence he had lost by his acquiescence in Catholic emancipation. If so, he failed lamentably. The Tories had heard him make similar statements before, only to see them forgotten in the hour of crisis. The Duke had antagonised every political faction, and a fortnight after he made his comment on the inadvisability of parliamentary reform the ministry was defeated in the Commons on a motion calling for a Select Committee to look into the Civil List accounts.

The majority against them was no more than twenty-nine, but Peel and Wellington had had enough. They were weary of warding off attacks from both right and left. They had forfeited the allegiance of the country gentlemen without winning over the liberals, and they saw little prospect of achieving greater stability. Their personal relations, which had been polite without being cordial, were also under strain. When they resigned on November 22nd it was with pardonable relief. William IV, who did not share his brother's perverse dislike for Grey, turned to the leader of the Whigs. Yet Grey lacked a disciplined party in the Commons, and it cannot be said that he was swept into power on a wave of popular enthusiasm. His ministry was a combination of Whigs, Radicals and Canningites, with a good deal of dissension within its ranks, and without an agreed and coherent policy covering the whole range of national affairs. It was, in fact, very much on the old pattern. Yet it was this ministry which followed up the emancipation of the Catholics with the reform of Parliament.

Grey's Character and Outlook

Grey himself was an ageing aristocrat. In his youth he had been a breezy reformer, campaigning with Fox and Sheridan against Pitt and Grenville, and earning for himself something of a reputation as a firebrand. But his passion for reform had cooled with the years. He was now thoroughly respectable, and his motives for reform were conservative, not revolutionary. He feared democracy and had no wish to bring in 'popular' government. He wanted to preserve the national heritage. Although he hated the new world of industrialists and factories, he thought that by admitting new forms of property within the pale of the constitution the traditional structure would be safeguarded. He despised the more plebeian advocates of reform: 'Is there one among them with whom you would trust yourself in the dark? Look at them, at their characters, at their conduct. What is there more base and more detestable, more at variance with all tact and decency, as well as morality, truth, and honour? A cause so supported cannot be a good cause.' Such were his feelings in 1819. There had been times when reform had seemed the prelude to bloody revolution, and he looked out upon the frightening new world with all the languid hauteur and unconcealed distaste of the old aristocracy.

The Debate on Parliamentary Reform

Yet men were clamouring for change—inarticulately and eloquently, inconsistently and relentlessly, above all, impatiently. Intellectuals such as Bentham poured scorn on the existing methods of parliamentary representation. Radicals read their copies of Tom Paine and applied the lesson of common sense. Rotten boroughs and pocket boroughs, the supremacy of the landed interest, the predominance of the south and the neglect of the thriving and populous north, where new industries and new wealth abounded—all of these anomalies seemed worthless to prosperous industrialists, intellectual radicals and unemployed artisans. With Peterloo and the failure of the Cato Street Conspiracy the Jacobinical solution gave way to the Parliamentary one. As the old-fashioned advocates of direct action were discredited, exaggerated hopes were pinned on electoral reform, and the slumps of the mid-twenties gave the reform movement added stimulus. The middle and lower classes were agreed on the inadequacy of the existing political structure, but their conflicting motives, confused expectations and ill-defined idealism ensured later disillusionment. Yet in the 1820s this diversity gave reform a great appeal, although the full force of popular agitation was felt only when Grey and his Cabinet were locked in conflict with the House of Lords. It was during that tense and protracted struggle that the mass organisations came into their own.

But the debate over parliamentary reform must be put into perspective. It is wrong to imagine that those who supported reform were necessarily progressives, while those who resisted it were reactionaries. Both Whigs and Tories loathed popular agitation and mob-rule, and both suspected democracy of being no more than legalised licence in which all property would be exposed to assault. For the Whigs reform was not the first step towards some democratic ideal. Rather it was the final renovation of a political edifice which was basically sound. Grey was not alone in regarding the more fanatical reformers as dangerous men, indifferent to morality and patriotism alike. Property was the key to the Whig interpretation. They admitted—often with considerable reluctance—that new forms of property had come into being. If the new property owners were unrepresented they would be tempted to ally themselves with the masses, thus endangering the foundations of society. But if the industrial middle classes were given the political recognition which they sought they would prove a valuable barrier to further change. It was not surprising that during the debates on the Reform Bill Whig spokesmen constantly emphasised the moderate nature of the proposed reforms. They seized every opportunity of reminding their hearers of the wisdom of giving way to popular demands, while those demands could still be met without resorting to extreme measures. During the second reading of the Bill Melbourne warned the Lords of the necessity for listening to the popular outcry:

'All experience proves, when the wishes of the people are founded on reason and justice and when they are consistent with the fundamental principles of the constitution, that there must come a time when both the legislative and executive powers must yield to the popular voice or be annihilated. ... When your lordships see that on every occasion of public calamity and distress, from whatever cause arising, the people call for an alteration in the representation, and that the call is accompanied with a deep, rankling sense of injustice suffered, and of rights withheld, can your lordships suppose that an opinion so continually revived has not some deep-seated foundation, and can you be insensible to the danger of continuing a permanent cause for angry and discontented feelings to be revived and renewed at every period of public distress and public calamity?'

The Whigs, then, were opportunistic in inspiration. They thought of themselves as practical men, engaged in the task of bringing the constitution to completion, rather than initiating the process which would culminate in democracy. Had they seen the consequences of reform, in the political structure of the late nineteenth or early twentieth century, they would have been aghast. As far as its advocates were concerned, the first Reform Bill was no leap in the dark. It was more in the nature of a gentlemanly and restrained piece of repair work. It was not surprising that many of the Radicals were disappointed with the outcome.

The Tory case was an impressive one, and some recent authorities have gone so far as to say that in terms of insight and prophecy it was wholly justified by events. This is not the same thing as saying that it was politically wise or politically advisable. The Tories can be divided into two groups: those who opposed reform simply because it was reform, on the assumption that all change must be for the worse, and those who opposed this particular reform because of its implications. The Tories feared the people. The populace was too easily swayed by unscrupulous agitators and wild demagogues. What was popular was not necessarily right. It was the duty of the country's rulers to govern justly, and it would be derogatory to the national interest if they pandered to ignorant prejudices in order to stay in power, while refusing to take steps which were necessary but unpalatable. The Tories had no doubt that democracy would ruin government, and that any tampering with the representative system would prepare the way for nothing less than a fully fledged democratic state. Since the Bill would inevitably have this result, they could not accept it. Peel said that he was unwilling to open a door which he saw no prospect of being able to close, and this accurately reflected the genuine apprehension which was felt by thoughtful and responsible Tories. Of course, unpopular policies are not undeniably right, any more than popular ones are, but men who were primarily interested in preserving social order were acutely aware of the theoretical limitations of popular rule. They also feared that the balance of the constitution would be disturbed. Again this was pure eighteenth century, resting as it did upon the assumption that King, Lords and Commons existed in a delicate equipoise, in which the virtues of each countered the failings of the others. But the Tories were right when they claimed that a lower House elected on a popular franchise would assume the dominant role in the state, even though the 1832 Act did not bring about such a situation. They also maintained that the conflict between the landed and industrial interest would be heightened as a result of reform, and that the landed interest would be exploited by the commercial classes. Here they were on less satisfactory ground, for the industrialists complained that under the existing state of affairs the landed interest exploited the urban and commercial interests. But perhaps the most grievous of all their charges was the assertion that parliamentary reform would expose all property to attack. One of their spokesmen warned his fellow countrymen of the dire future which lay in store for them:

'Take away the influence . . . possessed by the great masses of property. . . . The consequences are certain. . . . Prepare for similar spoliations to those which have recently been witnessed in a neighbouring country, where property bereft of its influence lost its right, and only served to mark out its possessors to certain destruction.'

Both Whigs and Tories were especially anxious for the security of property. The former claimed that the Reform Bill would safeguard it, the latter that by preparing the way for the rule of mere numbers, it would subject property to the greedy mercies of the avaricious and the needy. Whatever their differences, both Whigs and Tories disapproved of those long-term consequences of the Reform Bill which are usually taken for granted today. They were united in condemning those aspects of reform which liberals and democrats regard as the most convincing and most admirable. The Whigs were inferior prophets. If they had seen the future more

H

clearly most of them would have been Tories, too; but they were right when they claimed that new forms of property needed recognition, and that reform was a practical necessity. From the twentieth-century viewpoint they were right for the wrong reasons, just as it might be said that the Tories were wrong for the right reasons.

The Passing of the First Reform Bill

In March 1831 Lord John Russell introduced the first version of the Reform Bill in the Commons. Though the Whigs had pledged themselves to reform, their notions were ambiguous and vague, and Grey admitted that he had no formulated pattern of reform. Several ugly instances of agrarian disorder jolted the government along the road to reform. The ministers sought to make an example of the offenders, but reform became more attractive as a means of placating distress. The Bill seemed to go further than the Tories had originally anticipated, and when they succeeded in inflicting a reverse upon the government in committee the Cabinet decided to go to the country, in order to seek a mandate for their proposals. At first William IV refused a dissolution, but eventually he gave way, and in the ensuing election the ministry gained a more comfortable majority by winning some fifty or sixty seats. Russell then introduced another version of the Bill, but although its passage through the Commons was successful, it was rejected by the Lords on October 8th. The prospect of a dispute between the two Houses, and especially the possibility that the Bill would be mauled, or even killed, by the peers, inspired an outburst of rage (some of it well organised) among the Radicals. There were demonstrations and riots in London, Bristol, Birmingham and other large towns. Buildings were pillaged and set on fire. Angry crowds, often ominously big and vigorously led, paraded the streets, chanting the slogan 'The Bill, the whole Bill, and nothing but the Bill!' Peers who had voted against the Bill were jeered and hissed in the streets. Some were assaulted. An outbreak of cholera added to the prevailing fear and panic. The government brought in the Bill a third time. Once again it passed all stages in the Commons. In the Lords it was given a second reading, but the more extreme Tories mutilated the Bill in committee by post-poning some of the clauses disfranchising various of the rotten boroughs (May 7th, 1832).

Grey asked the King to create enough Whig peers to get the Bill through the Lords. William had been shocked by the fury of the mob, but he did not want to swamp the upper House. He floundered amidst conflicting advice. His wife told him to reject Grey's request, and although he sincerely wished to perform his constitutional duty, he could not make up his mind as to what it was. When he offered to create twenty new peers, Grey demanded fifty. Grey resigned and the King called on Wellington to form a Tory ministry. The Duke tried—and failed. The King was thrown back on Grey and the Whigs. After much heart-searching William gave Grey the required promise: if the Lords threw out the Bill he he would create a sufficient number of Whig peers to make its passage certain. At the end of May the Bill went up to the House of Lords. The Lords had been made aware of the King's promise, and in order to relieve their sovereign of the responsibility, as well as securing the privileges of the House, Wellington and a hundred other Tories left their seats, thus allowing the Bill to pass by a majority of eighty-four. Three days later, on June 7th, 1832, the Bill received the royal assent, though William declined to come to the Lords to signify his good pleasure in person.

The Significance of the 1832 Act

The nation gave itself up to noisy celebration. Bonfires were lit and windows illuminated. Toasts were drunk and endless speeches delivered to enthusiastic audiences. But what did the Act—which had provoked so much disturbance, which had thrust the King into a position of acute embarrassment and which had embittered relations between Lords and Commons—achieve? It hardly lived up to all the fine boasts and dark prophecies which it had inspired. First of all it redistributed 143 seats. Fifty-six boroughs of less than 2,000 people lost both M.P.s. Thirty-one, with between 2,000 and 4,000 people, lost one M.P. Of these seats, sixty-five were given to the counties, which were still thought to represent the pure and untainted element in the Commons, while seventy-eight were given to boroughs which had previously been without representation. The newly enfranchised boroughs included several of the large industrial towns, such as Birmingham, Leeds, Manchester and Sheffield, as well as older boroughs such as Lambeth, Greenwich and Marylebone. The Act also standardised the franchise. In the boroughs the vote was given to all resident occupiers of premises worth £10 a year. In the counties the 40s. freeholders kept their votes, but all £10 copyholders, £10 long leaseholders, £50 short leaseholders and tenants-at-will paying a rent of £50 a year were enfranchised. The electorate increased by just under 50 per cent to about 652,000.

The results of these changes were much less dramatic than the Radicals had hoped, or the Tories feared. Those who were qualified to vote under the old franchises did not lose their privileges immediately, but the franchise died with them. Some franchises, such as that at Preston, where everyone who spent the night before the election in the town could cast a vote, disappeared at once. But even with the redistribution of seats the south retained its predominance in the Commons. A hundred and twenty M.P.s came from north of the Wash and the Severn: 371 were returned for the counties and boroughs to the south of that line. About one Englishman in thirty had the vote, but proportions ranged from one in four in some of the smaller boroughs to one in thirty-seven in Lancashire, one in thirty-nine in Middlesex and one in forty-five in some of the manufacturing towns.

Similarly, bribery and corruption, influence and patronage, remained prevalent, and in some places they were rampant. (It is often forgotten that Dickens's famous description of an election in *Pickwick Papers* refers to a post-1832 contest.) Many Radicals were disgusted that the ballot had not been introduced: open voting continued on the traditional hustings. The enfranchisement of tenants-at-will in the counties strengthened the influence of the landlords. In the parish of Rattery in South Devon twenty out of twenty-one electors were tenants of Sir Walter Carew. In 1832 Sir Walter voted Whig: all his tenants did the same. Three years later he transferred his allegiance to the Tories. With one exception his tenants followed his example. In 1841 the Duke of Westminster made no secret of the fact that he regarded Gladstone's canvass of the electors of Flintshire as an 'interference between a landlord and his tenants . . . not justifiable according to those laws of delicacy and propriety . . . considered binding in such cases'. Delicacy and propriety—as understood by his Grace—were to play a great part in elections for many years to come.

The size of the electorate—not the franchise qualification—determined the extent of bribery and influence. In towns where the electorate was still small all the traditional arts were carefully cultivated and enthusiastically practised. Between 1832 and 1852 the 200 voters of St Albans absorbed £24,000 during elections: they were finally disfranchised for their pains. Ipswich grew steadily more corrupt after 1832. In 1841 as much as twenty or thirty pounds were offered openly for a single vote. Some boroughs which had previously been categorised as open or independent now acquired the habits of corruption. In some cases the influence of a family became predominant—as at Leominster in the 1840s, where the Arkwright family built up effective control of the borough's elections. Yet before the Reform Act Leominster had been regarded as above reproach. While some families were extending their influence in boroughs which had previously been independent, others were perpetuating their ascendancy in traditional centres. In 1832 Reigate lost one of its M.P.s, but for another twenty years Earl Somers procured the election of an acceptable relation. In 1832 and 1837 his eldest son was returned unopposed, and in 1835 and 1841 he was elected by comfortable majorities. In 1847 and 1852 another member of the family, a Mr Thomas Cocks, was returned. Almost fifty boroughs depended on the influence of great peers or landowners. Forty peers could virtually nominate a representative in the House of Commons. At Chester the influence of the Grosvenor family was unchecked between 1832 and 1869. The Duke of Richmond saw that a Lennox was returned for Chichester at every election between 1832 and 1852. At Calne the Lansdowne interest was maintained during the same period—without a contest on any of seven occasions. The old practice of compromise elections continued, such as those at Northampton in 1832 and Harwich and Nottingham in 1842.

The social composition of the House of Commons was relatively unchanged. A handful of industrialists—a Cobden or a Bright—came to represent the towns of the north, but in 1865 there were 180 sons of peers or baronets in the Commons, as compared with 217 in 1832, and 400 representatives of the landed interest instead of 500. Clearly there was no sudden or decisive alteration in the character of the House.

At one time it was thought that the Reform Act of 1832 was the decisive factor in stimulating the growth of party organisation in the constituencies. Registration of voters was called for by the Act, but it was up to those who thought themselves qualified for the franchise to see that their names were put on the roll. For this privilege they paid a fee of one shilling. Men were quick to see the potential value of registration societies in ensuring that the maximum use could be made of electoral support. In 1832 the recently founded Carlton Club began to scrutinise electoral registers. Three years later the Radicals opened a Registration office in Cleveland Row, and in 1838 the Reform Club undertook to do for the Radicals what the Carlton Club was already doing for the Tories. But it is possible to exaggerate the importance of these developments. Though Peel himself saw the registration of voters as 'a perfectly new element of political power . . . more powerful than either the sovereign or the House of Commons', party organisation in the House scarcely existed. It was not the case that two disciplined parties were ready to push down their roots in the constituencies. The registration societies were new agencies of corruption and influence, rather than the forerunners of modern party organisation. The judicious exploitation of a piece of pro-perty could provide a patron with an obedient body of voters, committed not to some party cause but to a family interest. Political agents multiplied leaseholds and small freeholdings. Dead men were registered. Forged receipts for rent were produced to support claims to be placed on the electoral roll. Hostile voters were disfranchised by the unscrupulous utilisation of legal ruses. (In the 1840s the Anti-Corn Law League became particularly adept at all these tactics.) Instead of marking the development of party, the post–1832 Parliaments were the heyday (if not the swan song) of the independent member. Peel's Conservative Party was a premature experiment, and in any event it was shattered by the Corn Law crisis. In the mid-nineteenth century politics were still dominated by influence, regional loyalties, dynastic interests. We are still far from the world of the modern party.

In the short term the Reform Act did not institute a dangerously democratic political structure. It brought the upper middle classes into the established order, but by excluding artisans who would have possessed the vote under some of the old franchises it substituted a middle-class electorate for a mixed one. The old argument that all interests and classes were 'virtually' represented in the Commons could no longer be urged. Though more people had the right to vote, they came from a more limited sector of the community. With so many people either excluded from the franchise or increasingly conscious that the reformed political order did not give enough weight to their interests or to their point of view, demands for further change were inevitable. And once the initial breach with tradition had been made, it was more difficult to resist peremptory calls for the extension of the franchise and a more rational distribution of the constituencies. Disillusionment was widespread and bitter, and in one sense it is more surprising that additional reform should be delayed until 1867 than that men should be so dissatisfied with what had been achieved in 1832. Yet, whatever its shortcomings, the Great Reform Bill gave England two generations of relative stability and civil peace. If the Tories could claim that they were justified in the long-run, the Whigs could point to immediate consequences which bore out their contention that only parliamentary reform could secure the confidence of the middle classes. And this, in itself, was no mean feat.

6 : The Rule of the Whigs and the Rise of Chartism

For nine years after the passing of the Great Reform Bill England was governed by a succession of Whig ministries. Yet there was no true continuity. There was one short break in 1834, when William IV called Peel and the Tories to his aid, and another in 1839, which has become famous for the Bedchamber Crisis. Nor were the Whigs a tightly knit party. Grey's ministry was a loose coalition of interests, and its composition was heavily aristocratic. When Grey went out of office in 1834 because he was in open disagreement with his colleagues over Irish affairs he was succeeded by Lord Melbourne, another peer whose outlook had been shaped by traditional patterns of thought. As time went on the ministry became more lethargic. Melbourne had little enthusiasm for the premiership, yet the longer he held the post, the more reluctant he became to give it up. Public issues occupied less and less of his attention, and his boredom with contemporary controversies was unashamed. When a young and inexperienced Queen ascended the throne in 1837 he found satisfaction in playing the role of an avuncular adviser to an immature girl, and his eighteenth-century charm and worldly wisdom admirably fitted him for such a task. But listless good breeding and a kindly cynicism were not the attributes best suited for tackling the problems of government in the impatient and raucous 1830s.

Yet the Whigs accomplished several far-reaching and much-needed reforms. A Cabinet of aristocrats listened to the cold wisdom of the intellectuals: the amateurs of politics sat at the feet of self-confident experts. It was a curious alliance, and one which amply illustrates the paradox of the time.

The New Poor Law

For contemporaries the most dramatic of the Whig reforms was the amendment of the Poor Law. The old Elizabethan code had broken down long ago, and the expedients applied since the Speenhamland experiment had increased the burden on the rates without solving the problem or ameliorating the incidence of distress. In the south of England the agricultural labourer had been degraded to the level of a pauper. By 1818 the cost of relief had climbed to £8,000,000, and although a committee had studied the matter, no constructive suggestions for reform had been made. Meanwhile the economists harped on the disastrous effects of outdoor relief. By contributing to the growth of population it threatened to engulf the nation's standard of living. By tampering with the sacred laws of political economy it made unhappiness and misery certain. While the advocates of efficiency demanded the abandonment of the system of poor relief it inspired indignation and disgust on the part of the older Radicals. Men such as Cobbett were roused to bitter wrath by the plight of the country poor and by the callous attitude which the respectable members of society so often adopted towards the victims of the blind forces of change. 'What is a pauper?' Cobbett demanded angrily. 'Only a very poor man!' But many of his contemporaries could not agree with him. Poverty was a grim spectre which everyone feared, and it was only too easy to assume that there was some connection between indigence and laziness, that the needy were suffering for their sins and that the cure lay in their own hands. Men who urged the virtues of thrift were not necessarily hypocrites. Many of them had risen from humble origins by practising the austere code which they preached so enthusiastically. They lacked the knowledge and insight which alone could have exposed the weaknesses of their position. They often appeared heartless and oppressive because they were blind and ignorant. They shrank from following their generous impulses because they believed that to do so would be to make catastrophe inevitable. Like the poor, they were lost and afraid.

The agrarian disturbances of 1830 frightened landowners and

aristocrats, whatever their political label or their opinions about parliamentary reform. The government was driven to act. In 1832 a Royal Commission was appointed to investigate the administration of poor relief. The Bishop of London acted as chairman, and Whigs, Tories and Benthamites were all represented. In March 1834 the Commission published its recommendations. Its primary concern was the termination of outdoor relief. This was stigmatised as the most grievous fault of the existing system. Any able-bodied paupers who desired or required public assistance would have to go into a workhouse in order to qualify. The other guiding principle was a determination to make the workhouse as unattractive as possible, for the reformers were convinced that every penny spent on making the condition of paupers more comfortable than that of the independent labourer was 'a bounty to indolence and vice'. The workhouse was not to be a happy refuge. It was to be an incentive to self-help. The Commission's major recommendations were put into effect by the Poor Law Amendment Act of 1834.

Soon the new workhouses became known as bastilles. Among the poor they were identified with humiliation, cruelty and the loss of self-respect. There was much inhumanity on the part of the overseers, and a harsh indifference to the feelings of those who had fallen on bad times through no fault of their own. The Commission had recommended that a separate workhouse should deal with each class of the poor—the elderly, the able-bodied, the sick, the lunatic, the young. But for reasons of economy this suggestion was not put into operation. All classes were thrown together, often in degrading conditions. The rules governing residence were brutal. Until 1842 married couples were not allowed to live together, and all meals were taken in silence. Smoking was prohibited and paupers could leave the workhouse only on certain occasions, such as when going to church or, in the case of children, when going to school. Edwin Chadwick, the dedicated, energetic and overbearing secretary of the Poor Law Commissioners, boasted that the new Poor Law was 'the first great piece of legislation based upon scientific or economical principles'; but to ordinary men and women who felt themselves threatened by a grim fate which they did not deserve it seemed a travesty of justice. Many who had toiled hard for years could be thrown out of work by a slump, by illness or by old age. In most cases penury stared them in the face. When this happened they were often thrust rudely into a workhouse, possibly separated from their families, and compelled to keep company with criminals, lunatics and, in the case of women, even with prostitutes.

The new law grouped parishes together in order to set up workhouses. By 1840 six-sevenths of England were covered by Poor Law Unions, and six years later over six hundred Unions had set up their own workhouses. A central Commission was set up to supervise the application of the Act, and this ended the traditional independence of the parish in matters of relief. Though each parish had still to bear the financial responsibility for providing for its poor, the ultimate decisions were now taken by others. In each parish Boards of Guardians were to be elected, but though they had the task of meeting the cost of looking after their own poor, they were under the authority of the Commissioners in London. The new dispensation was severe, but the old had been frustrating and disastrous. Despite its harshness, and the bitterness which it inspired, the new law halted the demoralisation of the rural poor. Perhaps its very strictness provoked a salutary reaction among the workers. The greatest opposition came from old-fashioned Tories and popular (as distinct from Benthamite) Radicals, who saw in the Poor Law another blow at what was left of Old England. The agricultural labourers were being deprived of their traditional rights. Yet the law was not fully adequate for the contemporary situation. Despite its vaunted modernity, it was a solution for rural, not for urban, poverty. It did little to meet the needs of the industrial towns. In the factories and mills of the north men experienced recurrent unemployment because of fluctuations in the market. It was both unpopular and impracticable to apply the workhouse test during these recessions. The imposition of the new Poor Law in districts where the Speenhamland system had never been in operation was only partially successful. Working men could hardly be expected to harken to cerebral pleas for that uniformity and efficiency which men such as Chadwick found so compelling. All they knew was that they were treated like outcasts whenever they were out of a job. This bitterness explains much of the appeal of Chartism. The unreasoning violence which was so much part of the Chartist movement, and which was also one of its gravest handicaps, was one legacy of the new Poor Law.

Factory Legislation

While the Poor Law set up a central authority to co-ordinate its application, another move towards central control—albeit a cautious one—can be detected in the Factory Act of 1833. Ashley (later Lord Shaftesbury), the evangelical campaigner for factory regulation, whose conscience was smitten with a burning zeal to combat the exploitation of children, was cruelly disappointed with the 1833 Act. He had hoped for an eight-hour day for children, but the Act contented itself with a nine-hour limitation. The Act applied to all textile factories, with the exception of some of the silk mills, and the employment of any child under the age of nine was forbidden. The nine-hour day, which was stipulated for children between the ages of nine and thirteen, had to be accommodated between five-thirty in the morning and eight-thirty at night. The working day for young people between the ages of thirteen and eighteen was limited to sixty-nine hours a week, with a daily maximum of twelve hours. An hour and a half a day was to be set aside for meals, while children were to go to school for two hours a day. Even more important was the provision for the appointment of inspectors to enforce these regulations. This was a crucial development. Previous factory acts had been easily evaded in the absence of any supervision. Now the rudiments of control were available, though evasion was still possible, and unscrupulous employers could deceive the inspectors by giving false information or by resorting to trickery or fraud; but after the registration of births, marriages and deaths was introduced in 1836 it became more difficult to elude the law or baffle the inspectors. At first the workers feared that the inspectors would favour the employers, and in some cases their anxieties were justified, but the reports of the factory inspectors helped to spread a fuller knowledge of working conditions, and by doing so they gave added impetus to the demand for reform. Meanwhile Ashley and his friends, despite disagreements among themselves and abuse and misrepresentation on the part of their opponents, carried on their fight for a ten-hour day for adults and an eight-hour day for children.

The Abolition of Slavery

For many years the evangelical party had been campaigning for the total abolition of slavery. The suppression of the Slave Trade within the British Empire inspired them to greater efforts. They subjected public opinion to a well-organised and untiring assault. They gained the reward for their labours when slavery was declared illegal throughout the British colonies in 1833. All slaves were to be given their freedom within a year, but were to serve apprenticeships to their former masters for either seven or five years. This was intended to prevent a sudden change of labour from crippling the economy of the West Indian plantations. It worked badly. The Radicals wanted to discredit it, while the planters and ex-slaves misunderstood its purpose. There were instances of cruelty and mismanagement, and the system was discontinued in 1838. The abolition of slavery brought no immediate paradise to the Negroes, and despite the payment of £20,000,000 compensation, the planters resented the interference of distant meddlers at Westminster. One great wrong had been righted, but much remained to be done. The Negro was illiterate and backward. He needed to be taught how to use his freedom.

Municipal Reform

In 1833 another Commission was set up to investigate the municipal corporations. Joseph Parkes, a vociferous and enthusiastic Radical, was its secretary. The old corporations were a strange and confusing assortment of privileged communities. Some were democratic, others oligarchic. Their standards of honesty and integrity were as various as the principles determining their composition. In some towns the city fathers shamelessly exploited endowments and charities for their own purposes. At election time these were often plundered to pay the expenses incurred by the favoured candidate. But in 1835 retribution struck in the shape of the Municipal Corporations Act, which was hailed by the gleeful Parkes as 'a smasher'. He welcomed a thorough purge of existing corporations and the institution of a uniform household suffrage. Over 200 of the old corporations were dissolved, and in their place 179 municipal boroughs were established. They were to be governed by elected councils. All ratepayers who had lived in a town for three years qualified for the local franchise. The corporation income was to be paid into a borough fund, and corporation accounts were to be audited. Town clerks and borough treasurers were to be public employees. Local loans needed the approval of the Treasury. The councils were empowered to draft by-laws, collect rates and organise police forces. But the 1835 Act did not inaugurate local government as we know it today. The functions of the town councils were strictly limited, and the responsibility for improving urban amenities lay with the Improvement Commissioners. In 1848 thirty councils lacked the authority to drain, clean and pave their public places and highways. Sixty-two towns were still without councils to perform such tasks, for the Act did not impose borough status. Unless towns belonged to the older class of corporations which had been reformed by the Act they had to apply for charters of incorporation. Many of the new towns remained unincorporated, though Birmingham and Manchester both received charters in 1838. As we have seen, Radicals such as Parkes were more concerned with household suffrage than with local government in the modern sense. Even so, privilege had taken another jolt. Democracy was a long way off, but tradition had been sapped where it meant most—in the locality. Enlightenment—the demand for standardisation and efficiency—had gained another victory.

Working-class Discontent

But this enlightenment was far from appreciating the sufferings and ambitions of the working class. The Whigs feared popular movements as much as the Tories, while the Benthamite Radicals had little time for organisations such as trades unions. The hour of danger to property had passed, but the fear of Jacobinism was not yet dead, astonishing though this seems to modern susceptibilities. This is another indication of the persistence of old ways of thought and of obsolescent social attitudes. The antagonism of the upper classes towards artisan movements was demonstrated in the famous trial of the Tolpuddle martyrs in 1834. Six Dorset labourers were found guilty of administering secret and illegal oaths, and were sentenced to seven years' transportation. Their trade union had been sober and, the oath-taking apart, law-abiding, and the men themselves were upright and sincere Methodists, whose Christian faith inspired them to work for the betterment of their fellows, but unfortunately they had devised an initiation ceremony, and this gave their society a sinister connotation in the eyes of the magistrates. The government, with Melbourne taking an active part for once, decided on a repressive policy. But even among the property-owning classes the sentences were recognised as excessive, and in 1836 the men were pardoned. Three years later they were repatriated at public expense. Five became farmers in Essex before emigrating to Canada; the other returned to Tolpuddle. Throughout their ordeal they had borne themselves with dignity and courage, and without bitterness. They had originally intended that their union should form part of Owen's Grand National Consolidated Trades Union. Owen intended to bring all occupations into one huge union, which would revolutionise society by running industry and commerce on co-operative and communal lines. But there were differences between Owen and his colleagues. James Morrison and J. E. Smith contemplated strike action—'a long strike, a strong strike, and a strike all together'—as a means of bringing in the new dispensation. Owen shrank from such a conflict, putting his faith in his schemes of regeneration rather than in acts of violence, but his quarrel with his friends reflected tensions between the various unions themselves. They lacked discipline, were often jealous of each other and were unwilling to accept external supervision. Though their aims were ambitious, their judgment was disastrous. They exhausted their energies in internecine feuds and futile strikes which dissipated their slender resources. Wild talk of direct action antagonised the middle classes. The trades-union leaders were too preoccupied with visions of the future to be successful negotiators in the less-Utopian present, and their lack of skill and discretion soon led the societies into a series of catastrophic disputes. Owen's project collapsed, and many of the smaller unions disintegrated amidst recrimination and disgust. But the government was on the alert. The Whigs had not forgotten the agrarian disorders of 1830. They detested anything which savoured of a conspiracy in restraint of trade, and the luckless Tolpuddle labourers bore the full fury of their anger. Once again the tale is of a social order in decline. The attitudes of mind on both sides were reminiscent of the old days of bread riots and of vague dreams of a speedy end to hardship. The place which the Tolpuddle martyrs have come to occupy in the history of trade unionism has obscured the fact that their sufferings were signs, not that a new era had arrived or even that the proletariat was on the march, but that an old way of life was passing away more slowly than has often been assumed. The new unionism was to be very different. Its aims were more modest and its leaders more responsible. Instead of seeking to overthrow the existing order, they contented themselves with improving wages and working conditions. Though they were inspired by the memory of Tolpuddle and all that it stood for, they wisely avoided the errors of the 1830s. This won them deserved success, and ultimately power.

Chartism

Yet the working classes needed a balm for their anguish and a ground for their hopes. Disappointed with the consequences of parliamentary reform, acutely conscious of the severity of the new Poor Law and angry at the lack of sympathy which the Whigs showed for their plight, the workers longed for a millennium. Economic distress and social discontent took a political form—Chartism, which was born in the 'thirties and nurtured on the anxieties and privation of those years, even though it gained its greatest notoriety in 1848, the year of revolutions. Yet modern research makes generalisation about the Chartists difficult. Misery, unemployment, and social insecurity were more important than ideology, and the wide variations in the character of the movement from area to area confound attempts to dovetail the

8 The Opening of the Stockton and Darlington Railway, 1825.

Chartists and their ideals into any simple pattern of class struggle. Chartism made a particularly strong appeal to disillusioned trades unionists, to radical artisans in some of the new industrial towns and to old-fashioned craftsmen—such as the handloom weavers —whose livelihood was jeopardised by new methods of production. On the other hand, it was weak in the older market towns and in the agricultural villages of the south and west.

Its roots lay in William Lovett's London Working Men's Association, and in 1838 Lovett and Place drew up the People's Charter, containing the famous six points: universal male suffrage, equal electoral districts, the abolition of the property qualification for M.P.s, the payment of M.P.s, the secret ballot and annual parliaments. These demands clearly illustrate the affinities which the movement had with traditional radicalism and with eighteenth-century reform societies. The disillusionment which had followed the passing of the Great Reform Bill had not sapped working-class faith in political institutions. It was still believed that the control of Parliament was the decisive factor in transforming society. The Chartists did not turn in disgust from parliamentary processes, but they were determined to reshape the national assembly in a more democratic mould, and this did most to antagonise the ruling classes. Both the aristocracy and the bourgeoisie shrank from democracy. Although five of the demands which the Chartists made have been conceded during the past hundred years, this consummation has been part of the development of democracy, and if annual elections had been granted the system of government would have been much more like direct democracy. Nor should it be forgotten that the Chartists wanted the whole of their programme to be put into practice without delay. The implementation of their principles, one by one over a period of time, deprived them of much of their revolutionary character.

Lovett was moderate and peaceable, but he was soon joined by other enthusiasts, not all of whom shared his respect for law and order. Agitation spread. In Birmingham Attwood refounded the Political Union and took up the cause of the People's Charter. Chartist propagandists and Chartist newspapers set about

I

diffusing their gospel. They had exaggerated notions of their power and status, and they underestimated the strength of their opponents. All that was necessary was to unite the people behind the Charter: then Whigs and Tories, and 'all dark and deceitful things' would flee away 'as shadows disappear before the rising sun'. The Chartists had a naïve confidence in the essential innocence of the common people. Only the stupidity and selfishness of the ruling classes prevented the bounties of Providence from being enjoyed in peace and contentment. Once the political institutions of the country represented the will of the majority the foolishness of the governing classes would be of no account. Nor did the Chartists possess any insight into the social and economic realities which lay behind political life. Though they might talk of the movement as 'a knife and fork question', their only answer to the problems of production, distribution and exchange was to toy with romantic schemes for land reform, modelled on mythical versions of the rural simplicities of an earlier age. When Fergus O'Connor came on the scene the movement became even more amenable to windy rhetoric and flamboyant posturings. O'Connor was an Irish landowner of Protestant stock. He had dabbled in Irish nationalism, but had fallen out with Daniel O'Connell, only to find in English radicalism the opportunities he sought for display and vainglory. He assumed control of the Leeds newspaper, the *Northern Star*, and soon he was exploiting it as the vehicle for savage attacks on the factory owners—the 'millocrats'—and the shopkeepers—the 'shopocrats'. On his conversion to the Chartist cause the *Northern Star* became one of the principal mouthpieces for Chartist propaganda, and at one stage it had a weekly circulation of 50,000 copies.

When a great public meeting was held in Birmingham in August 1838, O'Connor emerged as one of the most popular figures in the Chartist ranks. Unreliable and temperamentally unsound, he nevertheless had a fine flair for the more specious, but often singularly effective, forms of demagogy. He had a big voice and an imposing manner. Rude and overbearing, he welcomed disputations with hecklers. He exploited the feelings of his audiences without mercy and without restraint. His acid wit and mordant tongue whipped up all the bitterness which had been inspired by the Poor Law, and his gibes at the aristocracy won him the plaudits of the crowd. His journalistic gifts made him pre-eminently the organiser of propaganda and agitation in the northern towns. Other extremists—some of them much more in earnest than O'Connor when it came to physical conflict—gathered round him. Stephens, Bronterre O'Brien and Harney, who posed as an English Marat, were all active for the Charter, and in 1839 a National Convention was organised in London to present the first monster petition to Parliament.

But the delegates had no sooner arrived in London in February 1839 before they were engaged in quarrels and rivalries. Lovett, the most sincere of them all, advocated a policy of peaceful agitation, in which schemes of popular education were to play a prominent part. He had no desire to break the law, nor did he wish to offend the more sympathetic of the middle class. He wanted to win his case by appealing to reason, enlightenment and common sense, trusting that the inherent justice of his cause would ensure eventual triumph. He was interested less in immediate political advantage than in winning a lasting security for the working classes, and he saw his mission as one of civilisation and improvement, rather than as a political campaign. But O'Connor wanted speedy results. Soon he became the hero of the more violent Chartists, who were demanding a national strike as a way of bringing the government to their senses. Others were arguing that the Convention was more representative of the British people than the Parliament at Westminster, and that it should become a permanent assembly, acting over and against the Commons. Some delegates ranted in a style which roused the suspicions of the governing classes. One fanatic recommended that every man should carry a loaded bludgeon as nearly like a policeman's truncheon as possible. Another boasted that before the end of the year the people would have universal suffrage—or die in the attempt. Peace, law and order, these were Lovett's principles, but the Convention agreed to abide by them only 'so long as our oppressors shall act in the same spirit'. Attwood and the Birmingham delegation left in disgust, and J. P. Cobbett, the son of the great Radical, also withdrew. O'Connor had won the day, but at the cost of losing some of the movement's most valuable adherents. Lovett and the advocates of 'moral', as distinct from 'physical' force, stayed on, but the rift widened with every month that passed.

In May the Convention moved to Birmingham, for London had proved less congenial than had been anticipated, and during the 'forties support for Chartism in the capital declined still further. In July the first petition was presented to the Commons. The Chartists claimed that it bore over a million signatures, but the Commons were unimpressed and preferred to listen to Lord John Russell's warnings that the Charter would undermine all property. The petition was rejected. The Convention was indignant. There had already been scuffles with the authorities and now the advocates of physical force maintained that the time for action had come. Plans were made for a sacred month—that is, a general strike—which would humiliate the government and achieve final victory. But these projects ended in confusion. There were riots, fights, strikes and disturbances in various towns, but the government was unruffled. In the north of England General Napier, who sympathised with the workers and who blamed the troubles on Tory injustice and Whig imbecility, gave the local Chartist leaders a demonstration of the effectiveness of his artillery, and an additional lecture on how mobs could be controlled by small-arms fire and cavalry. This salutary lesson cooled the ardour of those who had envisaged a popular rising. Many of the Chartist leaders were flung into gaol as a precautionary measure. The Convention collapsed and Chartism was now thrust back on the ingenuity and resource of the local rank and file. Here the essential weakness of the movement became apparent, for there was no systematic discipline or oversight. Despite the payment of a national 'rent', the Chartists had no effective organisation; even the delegates to the Convention had in many cases been elected at noisy and turbulent public meetings, and the centrifugal forces within the movement began to pull it now this way, now that.

The extremists still longed for a last desperate throw. In Newport John Frost, an ex-Mayor and a member of the Convention, led four or five thousand Welsh miners in an armed uprising in protest against the arrest of a local Chartist leader. The pathetic little army was soon dispersed by the practised musketry of the regulars. Frost was arrested, and with his chief accomplices was sentenced to death, though these sentences were commuted to transportation. By the middle of 1840 almost every Chartist of any standing was in gaol. About five hundred had been apprehended, including O'Connor, O'Brien and Lovett. The movement was in dire straits, but the leaders were defiant.

Even while they were in prison they sought to remedy the deficiencies in organisation which had proved so disastrous. O'Connor founded the National Charter Association, which copied the Methodist practice of grouping supporters in wards and classes, and which also levied a subscription of a penny a week in imitation of the Dissenting sects. O'Connor now moved to the fore. His schemes (hazy though they were) were more attuned to the desires of his supporters than Lovett's educational projects. Soon O'Connor and Lovett were in violent competition. The aggressive, resourceful Irishman gained the upper hand. His personality and ideas stamped themselves indelibly upon the Chartist movement, and his rejection of any co-operation with middle-class movements, such as the Anti-Corn Law League, and his increasing preoccupation with land reform, had decisive effects on the outcome of the struggle for the Charter.

Yet the belief in the efficacy of petitioning still lingered. While O'Connor talked more and more extravagantly, the collection of signatures went on. In 1842 the second petition was presented. This time it was claimed that over three million people had signed it, and rumour asserted that when unwound it was over six miles long. But the Commons remained antagonistic. Roebuck a Radical, attacked O'Connor as a 'malignant and cowardly demagogue', while Macaulay reminded the House that universal suffrage would be fatal to good government, that it was utterly incompatible with the existence of civilisation and that capital and property would be placed absolutely at the foot of labour.

The rejection of the petition was followed by more riots and strikes, in Lancashire, Yorkshire and Staffordshire particularly.

The Chartists floundered. O'Connor had often talked in language which had encouraged direct action, but when faced with the brutal truth he hesitated. First of all he tried to evade responsibility for the strikes by blaming them on the Anti-Corn Law League (and there is some evidence to support his accusation); then he condemned them outright. When order was restored the Chartists found that their appeal had been eroded, and the movement's further decline was assisted by the animosities and dissensions among the leaders, by fierce competition from the more effectively organised Anti-Corn Law League, by the revival of moderate trades unionism and by the rise in wages and fall in unemployment during the 1840s. As the fortunes of the Chartists waned, so O'Connor's rose, and as time passed he became more unbalanced and unpredictable. He devoted more of his attention to his Land Plan—a scheme to escape from the evils of industrialism by providing clients with permanent small-holdings. Plots of land were to be bought out of subscriptions to his National Land Company, and the rents from those holdings which were let were to be used to acquire more land. This was merely a pathetic nostalgia for a legendary past. It shrank from the harsh realities of life, and it was part of the Chartist ideal of a nation of small masters and skilled craftsmen. Yet it was not socialist in the modern sense, for O'Connor had no truck with theories of land nationalisation. He had triumphed in his quest for power and glory, but under his wayward command Chartism withered away until the economic crisis of 1847 gave it a new lease of life.

A new Convention was summoned in London and a third petition was presented. Tremendous claims were made, and it was said that as many as six million names had been put to the petition. A great rally was planned on Kennington Common. The government, apprehensive lest this should lead to an English version of the revolutions which were sweeping the continent, called in the Duke of Wellington, who deftly hid additional contingents of troops behind barrack walls, while recruiting thousands of special constables, of whom the future Napoleon III, then a fugitive in London, was one. But the great demonstration was a fiasco, and when the petition was scrutinised it was discovered that many of the signatures were forged. Names as varied and as improbable as Victoria Regina, the Duke of Wellington, Mr Punch and Sir Robert Peel appeared, not once but many times. The petition was rejected, and the Chartists were covered in ridicule and scorn. O'Connor had flinched from a showdown with the authorities, and his discomfiture was complete when it was revealed that the National Land Company had no proper accounts. Although Chartism survived into the 'fifties and 'sixties, it was no longer of any significance. O'Connor ended his days in a lunatic asylum, and though Ernest Jones toiled bravely to keep the movement alive, his efforts were of no avail.

But it would be foolish to see Chartism as no more than a slightly comic failure. O'Connor's faults and eccentricities should not hide the more profound elements in the situation. Despite their failure, the Chartists were one of the most active forces at work in the England of the 1830s and 1840s. The movement's lively phases usually coincided with depression or unemployment, and in one sense it was a sensitive barometer registering the troubles of the working classes. It was a blind, tragic protest against the onward march of improvement. It represented the fears and anxieties of the little men to whom progress had brought bewilderment, anguish and despair. It mirrored the aspirations of the working classes, and the greater solidarity which was manifesting itself among working men. But some historians have preferred to stress the part which Chartism played in stimulating middle-class consciousness, rather than its role in formulating working-class ideals. Certainly its failure can be taken as an indication of the strength of the middle classes amidst the social turmoil of the age: when the dust had settled after the presentation of the third petition in 1848 Lady Palmerston confessed to Mrs Huskisson that it was 'very fortunate that the whole thing has occurred as it has shown the good spirit of our middle classes'.

The Chartists were never as strong as they had supposed. Their leaders were too willing to translate cheers at the hustings, or a rousing reception at a public meeting, as evidence of political might as distinct from popular sympathy. In looking back to 1832 many of them exaggerated the importance of popular demonstrations in pushing through the Great Reform Bill. It was too much to say, as one Chartist did in 1837, that 'in 1832 the working classes by their moral and physical organisation beat the Tories for the sake of the Whigs—by the same means they can . . . beat both the Whigs and Tories for the sake of themselves'. This overweening confidence led the movement into perilous paths. By denouncing both Whigs and Tories, by asserting that the House of Commons was an unrepresentative and venal body, and by insisting on all points of the Charter, instead of trying to win concessions one at a time, the Chartists threw away any advantage which they might have gained by their belief in the validity of political institutions. Here the paradox of the movement becomes apparent. Though it was fundamentally a means whereby the working classes could express their discontent with prevailing working and living conditions, the movement hinged on a political programme; yet its leaders neglected opportunities to use existing political machinery in making that programme effective. Such a task would not have been easy. In an era before party organisation the character of the assembly would have militated against their success. The Chartists would have been wiser if they had emulated the Anti-Corn Law League in securing the election of a sufficient number of spokesmen to ensure that their point of view was aired in the Commons. But even when O'Connor was elected to Parliament he failed to do what Cobden and Bright achieved so brilliantly. Instead of becoming the spokesmen for an extra-parliamentary movement, he spent most of his time expatiating on Irish affairs. Yet the faith which the working classes put in the Charter, as the instrument by which they would obtain justice, is a touching tribute to their trust in representative institutions. With better leadership the Chartists would not have antagonised the middle classes, but the wildness of O'Connor and his cronies made it difficult for respectable men to feel that the Charter did not constitute a threat to property.

Chartism was not a total failure, however. It was an impressive piece of working class self-help, and in quieter times its example gave impetus to the development of the trade unions. It drew attention to the hardships of the common people, and helped to promote a more perceptive awareness of social evils. Its errors of judgment and mistaken tactics were duly noted by the Anti-Corn Law League, which scrupulously avoided repeating them. Though the Chartists overestimated the immediate consequences of political reform, it remained true to say that such reform was beneficial and valuable, and that the improvement of factory conditions, housing standards and urban sanitation was dependent on political action and parliamentary legislation. Although no concessions were made along the lines of the Charter during the lifetime of the Chartist movement, the 1840s saw legislation dealing with conditions in the mines and factories and with public health, while the Poor Law was administered in a more humane fashion. The Whigs learned little from the Chartists, but Peel's determination to do something about the state of things in the mines and factories was stiffened by his awareness of Chartist agitation. The ultimate acceptance of five of the Charter's six points does not mean that the Chartist leaders were far-sighted, for the attainment of their goals did not transform society in the way in which they had hoped it would. There was no return to the pre-industrial era, nor did democracy take on a more direct character. (Like almost everyone else, the Chartists reckoned without the rise of modern party.) An inherent disillusionment was embedded in the Chartist mentality, for the wrong expectations were stubbornly associated with a precise and limited political programme. There is a wistful melancholy about Ernest Jones's lament in 1857 that there could be 'no doubt as to the wisdom of allying with the middle classes and their leaders if they offer such a measure of reform as we can be justified in accepting'. Regret for the errors of the past was no substitute for a contemporary policy, and the recognition of the strength of the middle class came too late to save Chartism. Even the lessons of 1832 had not been thoroughly assimilated, and instead of questioning the efficacy of Parliamentary reform in furthering their desired ends, the Chartists contented themselves with asking for more of it. The Chartist movement reflected the two nations of which Disraeli spoke, but it was infinitely more complex than any 'proletarian' interpretation of it would suggest. The confusions and contradictions in its history are reminders of how dangerous it is to see the past in terms of the present, and to look for the antecedents of modern movements in political organisations whose thinking and behaviour were wholly conditioned by the problems of a bygone age.

Irish Unrest

Chartism typified the restless, turbulent society which appalled and horrified the aristocratic statesmen of the time, but the stately game of politics was still played out in ways which were reminiscent of earlier contests for power and place. Even after the crisis of the Reform Bill had passed, the 1830s were full of incident. The baleful controversy which embittered English public life throughout the nineteenth century had already cast its shadow over the scene. Ireland and the Irish destroyed Grey's Cabinet, just as they destroyed Gladstone's many years later. O'Connell and the Irish members were allegedly in alliance with the Whigs, but Grey soon found that they were difficult associates to control. Argumentative and lively, and unpredictable in debate, they exploited the antagonisms and stalemates of English politics with a shrewd eye for their own advantage. The privileges of the Church of Ireland were bitterly resented by the Irish Catholics, the payment of tithe provoking intense anger and disgust. O'Connell now mounted an attack on the established Church with all his wonted skill. Soon the ministry felt compelled to act. But the Cabinet was divided. Some ministers were prepared to give way to the demands of the Irish, in the hope that this would solve the problem. Others were apprehensive about the threat to law and order, and sceptical about the contribution any concessions would make to a better understanding between the peoples. They favoured a policy of coercion and repression. The government tackled the problem in a gingerly fashion. They tried to soothe wounded feelings by moderate reform. The number of Protestant bishops was reduced. The Easter tax was abolished. Promises were made of grants towards Irish education. But it was necessary to introduce a Coercion Bill in 1833, for the country seemed to be on the verge of bloodshed and disorder. A disunited Cabinet strove to bring peace and justice to a divided country. Grey and Stanley supported stern measures to maintain civil security, but Russell, Durham and Althorp disagreed. Then in 1834 Lord John Russell, who made a habit of suddenly revealing the secrets of his heart in public, told the Commons that the riches of the Church of Ireland ought to be used for the general welfare of the Irish nation. This meant that he was converted to applying ecclesiastical revenues for secular purposes. Several members of the Cabinet resigned in protest, and when Grey found that many of his colleagues were doing all they could to frustrate the policy of coercion he resigned as well. He was weary of politics, and returned to his Northumbrian estates with undisguised relief. Lord Melbourne took over as head of the ministry, though he had little enthusiasm for the task.

Peel's First Ministry

Althorp had wanted to go into retirement in company with Grey, but Melbourne persuaded him to carry on as Chancellor of the Exchequer and Leader of the House of Commons. Then, in November 1834, Althorp succeeded his father as Earl Spencer, and his consequent elevation to the House of Lords precipitated a full-scale crisis. Melbourne had lost his ablest spokesman in the Commons, and the government desperately needed a new Leader of the House. Without Althorp Melbourne doubted whether he would be able to retain the support of the Irish and the Radicals. He suggested that Russell should suceed Althorp as Leader of the House of Commons, but he handled the affair ineptly, and made a scarcely veiled offer of resignation. William IV loathed Russell, and was determined not to tolerate his promotion. Like his father and eldest brother, he clung stubbornly to his right to choose his ministers. On occasion he became wildly excited on this point, and there were times when his rough tongue threatened his ministers with impeachment if they did not mend their ways. Determined as he was not to have Russell at any price, and suspicious as he had been of what his ministers were up to in Ireland, William avidly seized the opportunity offered by Melbourne's indecision, and asked the Tories to form a ministry. Peel was in

Italy, but he was soon hurrying home, and in the meantime Wellington set about providing the King with a government. The incident illustrates the traditional terms in which men were still thinking. Cabinet ministers regarded themselves as primarily the King's servants, and though William had acted hastily in getting rid of Melbourne, he had not acted unconstitutionally. Melbourne had lost confidence in the government's ability to control the Commons: the King had no confidence in the individual proposed as the new Leader of the House. William's action looked very much like dismissal, but Melbourne's willingness to go out of office was tantamount to advising the King to look elsewhere. That the episode smacked so strongly of the eighteenth century only shows that the 1830s were much nearer the world of Pitt and George III than has often been supposed. That it was the last time a monarch took such a high-handed line does not mean that William IV exceeded his rights. The lack of success which followed helped to discredit what the King had done, and to make such conduct unacceptable in the future, but it was William's political judgment which was at fault, not his understanding of constitutional conventions. Peel accepted his share of responsibility: 'I am by my acceptance of office responsible for the removal of the late government.' But if Peel felt that the change of ministry was the King's 'own immediate and exclusive Act', he also felt that the King was entitled to get rid of ministers whom he considered no longer capable of carrying on public affairs with advantage, and to call upon others who had his complete confidence. This echoed Pitt's outlook after George III's dismissal of the Fox–North coalition, and if Peel had repeated Pitt's success in the ensuing general election the interpretation usually put on the crisis of 1834 would have been very different. As it happened, although Peel made some gains, he could not command a majority in the new House of Commons. Despite their disagreements, the Whigs, Radicals and Irish were too strong for him, especially after February 1835, when Russell and O'Connell reached a new understanding—the Lichfield House compact—which meant that the Whigs and the Irish would act together against Peel. It was therefore no surprise when Peel maintained that his fall was the result of a conspiracy on the part of the Whigs and the Irish. But he waited until he had been beaten no less than six times in as many weeks before resigning—another indication of the attitude he adopted towards the appointment and dismissal of ministries, and the response of a government to a general election. The crisis is also noteworthy because of Peel's election address to his constituents at Tamworth—the Tamworth manifesto, as it has come to be called. Peel accepted the 1832 Reform Bill as 'the final and irrevocable settlement of a great constitutional question', and pledged the Conservative Party (a new name in politics and one which expressed the realignment of political forces which was taking place during this period) to those reforms which could be shown to be just and necessary and consistent with established rights. Later Peel proved himself as good as his word, not only during his great ministry of 1841–6 but also by his conduct of opposition during the Melbourne ministry. He shunned faction and judged each proposal on its merits. His maturity and responsibility won him respect and admiration, laying the foundations for his later success.

When Peel resigned in April 1835 Melbourne returned to office. The Irish received their reward in the Irish Tithe Act, which levied a charge on the income which landlords derived from their rents, instead of demanding the tithe from the peasants. This compromise was more acceptable to the Irish Catholics than a direct subsidy to the Church of Ireland. O'Connell still longed for disestablishment, but after this partial victory he turned his attention to campaigning for the repeal of the Act of Union.

Accession of Victoria: the 'Bedchamber' Crisis

In 1837 William IV died. With all his faults he had striven hard to be a good King. He was succeeded by his young niece, Victoria, the daughter of the Duke of Kent, who had died in 1820. The Princess, who had been brought up by her mother, was only eighteen years of age. She was immature and inexperienced, but she had a mind of her own and sincerely wished to perform her duties honourably and faithfully. Endowed as she was with her full share of Hanoverian obstinacy, she was capable of intense prejudices and strong antipathies. Her accession meant that Hanover was finally separated from Britain, for there the Salic Law prevailed, and Ernest, Duke of Cumberland, the most repulsive and reactionary of the Queen's uncles, became King. During her early years Victoria leaned heavily for guidance upon the cultured, kindly and urbane Melbourne. Some thought that her dependence upon the Prime Minister was morbid and unhealthy and politically dangerous, while others were convinced that the Queen was too much of a Whig. Certainly she saw politics in personal terms, and there were times when she believed that, come what may, the Whigs and even the Radicals could be relied upon to save her from the Tories. She did not know what to make of Peel—'such a cold, odd man'—and her emotional reliance upon Melbourne, and her stubborn determination to have her own way, were to provoke a political crisis.

When Melbourne resigned in 1839, after his majority in the Commons had shrunk to five, Peel was asked to take over. He demanded some change in the selection of the ladies of the royal household, as a sign of the Queen's confidence. This was the celebrated 'Bedchamber Question', and despite its ludicrous aspect, it was not without significance. Peel did not ask for the dismissal of all Whig ladies-in-waiting and their replacement by the wives of Tory peers, but, conscious as he was that the Queen was identified with the Whig interest, he wanted some changes in the household before accepting the Premiership. He knew his party's weakness in the Commons, and he needed some public acknowledgment of the Queen's support. With the experience of 1834 behind him he was not disposed to form another minority government, and when Victoria hedged he abandoned a thankless task. The Queen resented Peel's interference in her domestic affairs, and while his request was reasonable, he was not adept at humouring the capricious young Queen. Perhaps he was pleased when her conduct allowed him to decline the responsibilities of office at a time when he doubted the wisdom of accepting them. During the negotiations the Queen had turned to Melbourne for advice—a questionable proceeding—but soon another influence took control of her affections, one less fraught with political embarrassments, but equally important for her emotional and intellectual development. In 1840 Victoria married her cousin, Albert of Saxe-Coburg-Gotha, best known as the Prince Consort.

The Prince Consort

Although he was only twenty-one, Albert was mature, self-controlled and serious minded. He was sincerely fond of the arts, and genuinely interested in contemporary problems. This gave him a ready sympathy with new ideas, especially in education. His judgment was sound, and his advice invaluable, particularly in foreign affairs. He was rather priggish and over-earnest, but his services to the monarchy and the nation were outstanding. At first he was distrusted as a foreigner, the aristocrats being acutely antipathetic to his intellectual pursuits, his sober moral code, and his place in current politics. For many years the common people viewed him as a mysterious outsider exercising a sinister influence on national policy and harbouring all sorts of dangerous ambitions. But gradually his fine qualities and spotless integrity won him the respect—if not the popularity—he deserved, and when he died in 1861, the victim of an attack of typhoid fever which overwork had made him less able to resist, his presence was sadly missed. Soon men realised the magnitude of the nation's loss. Even the robust and breezy Palmerston broke down on hearing the news of the Prince Consort's death, referring to him (somewhat unhappily) as 'that perfect being'. The extravagance of the Queen's grief, and the cult of Albert the Good, had their ridiculous side, but they should not obscure the devotion, nobility and patience with which Albert served his wife and her people.

Colonial Affairs: Foreign Policy

Melbourne's ministry staggered on for two more years after the Bedchamber incident had prolonged its tenure of office. Few matters call for comment. Possibly the most important was the Durham Report of 1839, which recommended that the provinces of Lower and Upper Canada should be reunited, thus undoing the Canada Act of 1791, and that the colonists should be given a greater degree of responsible government. In 1837 rebellions had broken out in both provinces, and though they were put down without much difficulty, they drew the government's attention to the fears entertained by the French-Canadians that they were becoming subservient to the British, and the dissatisfaction felt by the majority of Canadians at the minor role which they played in the government of the colony. In 1840 the government fused the two provinces into one colony, as well as going some way towards responsible government by instituting a two-chamber legislature comprised of a nominated legislative council and an elective assembly. Russell, the Colonial Secretary, made it clear that members of the council should retire when this was expedient for the implementation of policy. Though the government was not technically responsible to the elected lower House, the tactful application of this principle meant that the administration was more sensitive to the feelings of the colonists.

Foreign policy was directed by the cocksure, truculent and irrepressible Palmerston. Like Canning, he was a stout defender of liberal régimes abroad, and his flamboyant and sometimes bellicose policy diverted attention from his growing conservatism at home. Palmerston was energetic and capable, with a capacity for hard work when the fit took him. His independence and impatience mirrored the irritation which a man who knew his own mind felt over the hesitations of his colleagues. He was confident that he was better informed than his fellow ministers and that it was often necessary to act promptly in the conduct of foreign policy. His notorious fondness for horses, and his ostentatious disdain for foreigners, won him the goodwill of the people. He had no rigid set of principles to guide him, and certainly no ideology. He was determined to secure British interests, and cheerfully used any means to attain this end. His greatest fame was won during the years when he dominated public life after the death of Peel, but the 1830s foreshadowed what was to come. In 1830 he supported the Orleans monarchy in France, and when the Belgians rose against the Dutch he took their part. Joint Franco-British action did much to secure Belgian independence, and the integrity and neutrality of Belgium were guaranteed by the Powers in 1839. Palmerston also sent help to the constitutional monarchs in Spain

10 The Opening of the Great Exhibition. 1851.

11 Sir Robert Peel

and Portugal when these were threatened by their more reactionary relatives. In the Far East the Opium War was fought to compel the Chinese to open their ports to British merchants (1839–41). In 1842 the Chinese signed the treaty of Nanking, by which they opened five ports to western trade, ceded Hong Kong to Britain and paid an indemnity of $21,000,000. It was discreditable that the war should be caused by a dispute over cargoes of opium, but this did not shake Palmerston's vigorous and unquestioning self-righteousness. He was convinced that Britain 'stood at the head of moral, social, and political civilisation' in her conflict with China: the development of the Chinese market was in itself a civilising mission.

More dramatic events centred round the restless and ambitious Pasha of Egypt, Mehemet Ali, who wanted to throw off the hazy sovereignty of the Sultan and to carve an empire for himself in Syria and Asia Minor. Palmerston took the side of the Sultan in this quarrel, for he feared that a weakened Turkish Empire would endanger the stability of the Middle East. He was also suspicious of Russian designs in the Balkans, especially after the treaty of Unkiar Skelessi (1833) had pledged Russia and Turkey to give each other mutual help, and to consult on common interests; worse still, the Turks undertook to close the Dardanelles to foreign warships when asked to do so by the Russians. Palmerston interpreted this as a plot by the Tsar to install himself as the Protector of the Ottoman Empire and to gain control of the Straits. When Mehemet Ali and the Sultan clashed in Syria Palmerston's distrust of the Russians urged him to intervene on the Sultan's behalf. British forces bombarded and took Acre and Sidon, and Mehemet Ali was compelled to give way. Although he was recognised as the hereditary (and virtually independent) ruler of Egypt, he had to return Crete, Arabia and Syria to the Sultan. Unfortunately, while achieving his object of strengthening the Turkish Empire, Palmerston had come into conflict with his French allies. Louis Philippe and his advisers had looked favourably upon the ambitions of the Pasha of Egypt, for they assumed that Mehemet Ali would prove a powerful friend of France in the Levant. When they realised that they were alone in supporting

K

him they felt betrayed. The weakness of the Franco–British *entente* was exposed, and relations between the two countries worsened. Palmerston had transferred much of his distrust to Louis Philippe: 'one must admit in one's own mind that if he had been a very straightforward, scrupulous, and high-minded man, he would not now have been sitting on the French throne.' In the last resort Palmerston sought Russian co-operation in reaching agreement about the Straits, and in July 1841 the Powers— including France—declared that they would abide by the old convention, which closed the Dardanelles to the warships of all nations while Turkey was at peace. Palmerston knew that if he had collaborated with the French in destroying Turkey in order to set up a strong puppet state in Egypt and Syria he would have forced the Tsar to intervene. It was wiser to prop up an existing state (however weak) than to attempt to create a new one. Besides, at their meeting at Münchengrätz in 1833, the Tsar and the Austrian Emperor had agreed to uphold the integrity of Turkey. But there were good reasons for Palmerston's misgivings over Russia, even when he saw the utility of co-operating with her, for the Tsar was soon disillusioned with the diplomatic rewards of protecting the Ottomans, and reverted to his earlier policy of anticipating and preparing for the downfall and break-up of the Turkish Empire. The eastern question resumed its original form. Palmerston had gained an impressive tactical victory, but the strategic problem remained.

But within two months of the signing of the Straits Convention the Whigs fell from power. At the general election of 1841 Peel gained a comfortable majority, and it seemed that the revivified Conservative Party, under its great leader, was entering on a long period of supremacy. The story of how those expectations were disproved by events must be told in another chapter.

7 : Peel and the Corn Laws

Peel's Personality and Position

THE politics of the 'forties were dominated by the austere and imperturbable figure of Sir Robert Peel. No other statesman possessed his wide experience both of office and opposition, or his masterful command of the essentials of government. He combined a discerning interest in commerce and finance with a willingness to reform proved abuses, yet he was conservative by temperament. He distrusted the spirit of innovation, and despised metaphysical speculation divorced from practical experience. He thought it both impossible and undesirable to seek to create a new society from first principles, and while he respected the opinions of the experts, he did not trust himself absolutely to their guidance. His readiness to accept new ideas made him peculiarly fitted to guide the nation through a period of social upheaval, but this very sensitivity made him a poor party man, as well as laying him open to the charge of hypocrisy. In the past he had changed his mind over Catholic emancipation, because he was convinced that the measure was a political necessity, and although he had opposed parliamentary reform, he had come to acquiesce in it. Similarly, his conversion to Free Trade was a gradual one, based on his understanding of the facts of the case. He found it easier to apply new policies in particular instances, rather than to reshape the framework of his political thinking. His earlier reforms in connection with the legal code were empirical in inspiration, and this was true of all that he accomplished during his great ministry.

Despite his achievement in forming a new Conservative Party out of the shattered remnants of the Toryism which had seemed wrecked by the controversy over the Reform Bill, Peel did not doubt where his primary responsibility lay, should party loyalty and national duty clash. It was ironic that Peel, the son of a mill-owner, who never lost traces of his Lancashire accent, should lead a party which was representative of the landed interest above all else. Yet to suggest that his tragedy stemmed from the choice of the wrong party smacks too much of the false line of descent usually drawn for the Liberal and Conservative parties of the time of Gladstone and Disraeli. Peel himself was of the Pittite tradition, and before the Liberal party could be brought into existence the Peelites had to coalesce with the Whigs and Radicals. This could not have been foreseen when Peel entered politics in 1809. The spirit of Victorian Liberalism owed as much to Pitt and Peel as to Fox and Grey, despite the highly edited versions of history propagated at Holland House, and it was no accident that Gladstone, the greatest of the Liberals, was also the greatest of Peel's disciples. In thinking of himself as a minister of the Crown whose allegiance belonged to his monarch and his country rather than to any party, Peel placed himself unambiguously in the traditional camp, and to condemn him for betraying his party— whether over Catholic emancipation or the Corn Laws—is to ignore the difference between party in the early nineteenth century and party after the Second Reform Bill. Today it is impossible to think of politics without organised parties; in Peel's time there were no organised parties, and though men were using registration societies to aid their electoral battles, there was no parallel in early Victorian England to the modern party, with its central headquarters and its regional branches, committed to a definite programme and a doctrinaire policy.

Within the Cabinet Peel exercised a predominance which was unequalled by any other Victorian Prime Minister. As one of his ablest colleagues, Sir James Graham, put it: 'We never had a Minister who was so truly a first Minister as he is. He makes himself felt in every department, and is really cognisant of the affairs of each. Lord Grey could not master such an amount of business. Canning could not do it . . .' Peel controlled every department, and liked to be kept fully informed about what was going on. Even foreign affairs—not usually associated with him— did not escape his meticulous attention. Gladstone himself bore witness to the fact that Peel's government had been carried on not so much by a Cabinet as by the heads of departments each in communication with Peel himself. Peel was too fond of commanding his subordinates, rather than persuading them, and he assumed too readily that they would always follow where he himself led. He preferred to introduce his own budgets, and he did not permit any doubts as to where the supreme responsibilities lay. Ashley complained that the ministry was no more than 'a Cabinet of Peel's dolls', and the very supremacy which Peel had wielded made the tragedy of the Corn Laws all the more bitter.

Peel was a shy, withdrawn man, though on occasion he could display a peppery temper, and contemporaries described him as a prig and an iceberg. Yet he won the devotion, even the affection, of his colleagues. After his death the Duke of Newcastle confessed, 'I never take a step in public life without reflecting, how *he* would have thought of it.' He was rather humourless, and O'Connell once referred to his smile as reminiscent of the silver plate on a coffin lid. But most of those who were initially repelled by his aloof self-control were finally lost in admiration. Even Victoria, who had been hostile when Peel replaced her charming counsellor, Melbourne, was brought round, possibly because Albert was sympathetic to Peel's personality and political aims. When Peel died in 1850, as the result of a fall from his horse, many working men contributed to funds to raise statues to his memory. The gibes of Disraeli, and the breach with his party over protection, did not besmirch his reputation for honesty, patriotism and integrity. If anything, he was probably more universally respected after his fall than ever before, and few men doubted that he was the greatest statesman of the age.

Peel's Financial and Commercial Policies

The Whigs had managed the national finances badly, and Peel soon applied himself to balancing the budget and stimulating trade. Boldly, he reduced the customs duties on numerous articles. In 1842 he cut the duties on 750 articles: two years later the annual deficit of £2,000,000 which he had inherited from the Whigs had been converted into a surplus. In 1845 he abolished the duties on over 400 articles, and reduced them on many other goods. He was particularly anxious to reduce the tax on raw materials, which were so necessary for British industry. Of course the immediate loss to the Exchequer had to be met, and Peel unhesitatingly adopted an income tax of sevenpence in the pound. When he imposed the tax in his 1842 budget he promised to abolish it after five years. But since that date no Chancellor of the Exchequer has dared to dispense with so profitable a tax. Indeed, Peel himself asked the Commons to renew it for another three years in 1845, and before it came up for renewal he was out of office. Despite the grumbles of the middle classes, the income tax was neither excessive nor arduous, while the reduction of duties was of immeasurable benefit to the working classes, as well as encouraging industry. Peel's fiscal policies were crowned with success, and in 1842 he amended the sliding scale on imported corn so as to reduce prices during periods of high demand and inadequate supply. He had taken the country a good way along the road to Free Trade. Later, the process was to be completed in the 1860s, during Gladstone's term of office at the Exchequer.

Peel also set up district courts to deal with bankruptcy, and swept away the old practice of imprisoning men for debt, except in cases where the sum owed was more than £20. (Debtors' prisons did not vanish altogether until 1869.) Another cause of financial embarrassment, especially for business men, was the unreliability of many banks. Recessions were invariably accompanied by the collapse of small, provincial banks which had issued notes far in excess of their limited resources. The Whigs had tried to deal with the situation by passing a Bank Charter Act in 1833, but further crises occurred in the late 'thirties, and Peel decided to take further steps to meet the problem. Most men were aware of the need for action, and in 1844 the Bank Charter Act passed the Commons with little debate. Peel made the Bank of England responsible for the issue of any new notes, and imposed certain restrictions on this privilege. The Bank of England could issue notes backed by government securities—the fiduciary issue—to the worth of £14,000,000, but any paper money issued in excess of that figure had to be backed by gold. Peel thus concentrated the manipulation of the nation's currency in the hands of the Bank of

England, and successfully controlled the circulation of paper notes. He hoped that the problem of inflation would thereby be solved, and that the dangerous and irresponsible issue of notes by small and insecure banks would cease, but he recognised that in special circumstances, the provisions of the Act might have to be suspended. (In fact, the Act was temporarily annulled three times during the next twenty-two years.)

Just as unreliable banks had caused much financial loss, so the proliferation of minor companies, often deliberately floated by racketeers and rogues, was the curse of an age which urgently required new instruments of commercial expansion. Peel had every sympathy with those who sought a due reward for industry and initiative, but he was resolved to curb reckless speculation, and the fruits of this determination were embodied in the Companies Act of 1844, which was a companion piece to the Bank Charter Act of the same year. All companies were required to be registered and to publish their accounts. By doing so their status was assured. They could sue and be sued in their corporate capacity, but their shareholders were denied the advantages of limited liability for another twelve years. Of course, these measures did not ensure the disappearance of fraud, but they did much to build up the confidence of the middle classes at a time when insecurity threatened the means whereby necessary developments could be financed.

Ashley and Factory Legislation

Peel's achievement was not confined to matters of cash and profit, for his ministry saw new advances in the protection of women and children in the mines and factories; but here the principal credit belongs to Ashley, who had devoted himself to the improvement of the working conditions of the factory hands, and who was especially concerned for the plight of pauper children. Ashley epitomised all that was best in contemporary evangelicalism. His religious faith—intense, unshakable, all-consuming—inspired him to serve his less fortunate fellows. It is cheap and foolish to praise his philanthropic activities while sneering at his religion, for without his religious faith Ashley would not have been a reformer. Victorian religion cannot be judged by the standards of a secular age: whatever its intellectual short-comings, it demands the respect, not the supercilious disdain, of posterity. In the person of a man like Ashley the overpowering sense of the mercies and power of God was the mightiest energising force in giving his life purpose and effect. Though men's con-sciences were insensitive to many of the hardships and injustices of industrialism, the greatest single factor in awakening men to their humanitarian responsibilities was the Christian faith. This is not to deny that Victorian Christianity could be complacent, self-righteous and hypocritical on occasion. nor does it condone the short-sightedness of too many devout but narrow-minded men. But it is impossible to understand the Victorian mind without taking into account the sincerity, strength and variety of religious belief. Certainly the moral feelings of the nation were outraged by the revelations contained in the report of the Royal Commission on the coal-mines, published in 1842. What seems like indifference to suffering was in reality ignorance, and the presentation of a vast weight of irrefutable evidence, which told of children of five years of age spending long hours down a mine attending ventilating doors, or of women employed in tasks as degrading and exhausting as dragging coal-trucks like beasts of burden, shocked and alarmed the public. Its peace of mind was also disturbed by tales of brutal immorality and gross vice, which had often been un-checked in the appalling conditions in which women and young girls worked. Ashley and his friends pressed for further legislative action. They met with misrepresentation from their opponents, many of whom believed that the prosperity of the country de-pended on the free operation of the laws of supply and demand. The suggestion that hours of labour should be restricted more severely was denounced as a threat to the nation's economic welfare. It was said that all profit was earned in the last two hours of the working day. All this puzzles us today. Many of the men who attacked Ashley so pompously and so unfairly were defending their own interests, but many of them genuinely believed that what he was advocating would threaten the well-being of the workers themselves. Psychologists might talk of rationalisation; ardent progressives of hypocrisy. The historian can only point to the baffling mixture of human motives, the obstinacy with which men cling to their shibboleths, the slow progress of compassion, wisdom and enlightenment.

The government shuffled uneasily through the controversy. Graham, the Home Secretary, amended Ashley's proposals, and the reformers were disappointed by the provisions of the Mines Act of 1842 and of the Factory Act of 1844. Yet their value must be recognised. The Mines Act prohibited the employment underground of women and girls, and of boys under the age of ten, and set up an inspectorate to enforce the new regulations. The Factory Act limited the hours of work for women to twelve hours a day, while children between eight and thirteen were not to work for more than six and a half hours daily. An effort was made to forestall evasion of these requirements by insisting that all workers should start the day's shift at the same time. It was also laid down that machinery was to be fenced off, chiefly to prevent the skirts of women and girl workers from being entangled in the machines. This rudimentary safety precaution was a great innovation at the time. Ashley had eloquently pleaded for a ten-hour day for all workers in mills and factories, but this objective was not realised until Fielden's Bill was passed in 1847. A more serious deficiency was the failure of the 1844 Act to improve educational facilities for factory children. The government had wanted either the morning or the afternoon to be left free for the children to attend grant-aided schools, but the Dissenters were roused to wrath by the prospect of the Church of England having a bigger say in the training of the young. Although the government tried to reach some agreement on the vexed problem of religious instruction, Graham was compelled to give way: concessions to the Dissenters only angered the Church party. This virulent sectarian dispute held up the cause of public education for a generation, and the problem of religious teaching in state schools still bedevilled English education at the end of the nineteenth century. The controversy is a reminder of the passion surrounding religious allegiance, and while the outcome can be deplored, to contemporaries the quarrel was not an insignificant one. Both the Church and Dissent felt that great principles were at stake. While the Anglicans feared national apostasy, the Dissenters saw themselves as defending religious freedom. Neither cause was trivial, but neither was blameless.

Irish Troubles

Peel was also troubled by Irish affairs. O'Connell and his supporters were still carrying on their agitation for the repeal of the Act of Union, but new ideas were in the air. Young Irishmen found it hard to resist the appeal of a more romantic brand of patriotism which sought to revive the heroic days of 1798. Under the guidance of firebrands such as Smith O'Brien and Gavan Duffy, the 'Young Ireland' movement existed to give practical expression to its motto, that England's extremity was Ireland's opportunity. Unlike O'Connell, the Young Irishmen countenanced the use of force, and when the great liberator was discredited in 1843 more Irishmen turned to the extremist movement. O'Connell addressed several large meetings in 1843, the sequence culminating in a vast gathering of several hundred thousand Irish patriots at Tara, the seat of the ancient Irish Kings. O'Connell rashly promised his hearers a parliament of their own on College Green within a year. He was then arrested for sedition, and though he was formally acquitted, his magical hold over his followers was broken. This was the troubled background to the Irish famine of 1845–6—the famine which made the repeal of the Corn Laws imperative and which brought about the break-up of Peel's ministry. Yet, while he was just as determined as ever he had been to maintain law and order in Ireland, Peel was eager to win the favour of the Irish. In 1845 he gave a grant of £30,000 to the Catholic college at Maynooth, and he also tried to improve Irish education by establishing three additional colleges in the north, south and west. But both Protestants and Catholics resented Peel's efforts at conciliation, and in England his actions earned him distrust and hostility. His record on the Catholic question counted against him. He was forced to withdraw a Bill which would have compensated Irish tenants for any improvements carried out on their farms. The Conservative party was divided, and dissension over Irish policy foreshadowed that over the Corn Laws.

Peel's Foreign Policy

Peel's foreign policy was nicely balanced between moderation and firmness. The old frontier quarrel with the United States was settled amicably, the 49th Parallel being taken as the boundary between Canada and the United States from the Great Lakes to the Pacific. Relations with France were less happy. The *entente* had already been strained by the controversies provoked by Mehemet Ali's high-handed conduct in the Near East. It was virtually destroyed by a dispute over Tahiti—in which the French contented themselves with a protectorate instead of outright annexation after they had seized the island and insulted the British consul—and by Louis Philippe's devious and unscrupulous behaviour over the Spanish marriages. The crafty old King had his eyes on the revival of French influence beyond the Pyrenees, and became increasingly attracted to the thought of an Orleanist Prince sharing the Spanish throne. Aberdeen, Peel's Foreign Secretary, and Guizot, the French King's minister, carried on rambling and inconclusive negotiations on the problem of possible husbands for Queen Isabella of Spain, but the question came to a head in the summer of 1846, shortly after Peel's fall. Louis Philippe, impatient with the pattern of negotiations, and infuriated by Palmerston's bluff and bluster, resorted to a policy which he had previously thought dishonourable. He announced the betrothal of one of his sons, the Duke of Montpensier, to the younger sister of Queen Isabella, and the simultaneous betrothal of the Queen of Spain to her cousin, the Duke of Cadiz, who was commonly thought to be impotent. In this way the Spanish throne would ultimately come to Montpensier's wife, for Isabella would be childless. But events soon thrust the Spanish marriages out of men's minds. Within two years Louis Philippe was a refugee in England, France having become a republic again. In any event, Isabella of Spain did have children, though gossip suggested that they were not begotten by her husband. But Englishmen were more worried by the controversy over the Corn Laws and Free Trade than about the sordid intrigues which were so diligently pursued within the Spanish royal family.

The Corn Laws and the Anti-Corn Law League

The controversy over the Corn Laws reflected the antagonisms within English society. To the landed interest the Corn Laws were the last security against ruin. To the industrial classes they were the means of keeping the price of food artificially high, and the symbol of the unfair predominance of the agricultural, as distinct from the manufacturing, community. Throughout the 1840s the controversy was given ample publicity through the activities of the Anti-Corn Law League.

The League has been the subject of much adulation and much abuse. For many years historians represented it as an idealistic and humanitarian organisation, dedicated to a noble cause and distinguished by high-minded and disinterested leadership. In recent years this interpretation has been sharply questioned. The League has been denounced as a selfish instrument of capitalist exploitation, ruthlessly controlled by avaricious manufacturers, who were seeking an excuse to keep wages down, and who therefore campaigned for cheaper food prices. The tactics adopted by the League have also been scrutinised in detail. They seem to have been distinguished by extreme skill in the deft manipulation of all the conventional weapons of influence and corruption, rather than by scrupulous honesty. The truth is that while the League had its selfish as well as its idealistic aspects, it cannot be written off as little more than a capitalist plot. Cobden and Bright were convinced that the Free Trade cause was just, though they also knew that the industrialists would benefit from it. Free Trade promised peace and international understanding, in addition to material prosperity, and if this seems naïve today it does not mean that men who were otherwise fully aware of the realities of politics did not sincerely believe in the gospel which they preached so uncompromisingly. The ruthless tactics employed by the League remind us that men who were dedicated to what they thought was a noble cause stooped to less-noble methods in order to win the day. For every idealist who supported the League there were many men of the world. The cruelty and unfairness of its propaganda, the violence and intimidation which were often used to silence opponents, most of all the gross lampoons which were pelted at Ashley—all these leave a sour taste in the mouth.

Yet the League remains important as the most significant piece of political organisation undertaken by the industrialists of the north, who never forgot that Parliament was dominated by the landed interest, and that they themselves were excluded from effective participation in the government of the country. The League helped to formulate that middle-class consciousness which was so decisive a factor in the defeat of the Chartists, while its organisation and tactics prepared the way for later party developments. It is to the League, rather than to the registration societies, that one must look for the origins of what is now understood by party structure. It was significant because of its exploitation of parliamentary representation, as well as extra-parliamentary agitation. It was one of the most effective, as it was also one of the first, of pressure groups. During elections it sought to induce or compel candidates to pledge themselves to Free Trade and the repeal of the Corn Laws. However underhand some of its methods were, the League always tried to appear respectable, and although it was predominantly middle class, it never gave up courting the working classes, and the attempt to convert them to the cause of cheap bread and the big loaf. Though the Irish potato famine finally forced the government to repeal the Corn Laws, without the relentless and skilful campaign which the League had carried on against the notorious duties men would not have been ready to revoke the laws which had protected English agriculture for so long.

The League was founded in 1839, but it had its origins in the Manchester Anti-Corn Law Association, which had carried on propaganda against the Corn Laws throughout the previous winter. The League was not a democratic organisation. Though control was vested in a Council of Subscribers, each subscription of £50 carried a vote. The policies of the League were directed by men who had contributed most lavishly to League funds. The headquarters of the League were in Manchester, and despite efforts to strengthen its membership in London, the League never lost its northern character. Local associations sprang up in Leeds,

Blackburn, Bradford, Huddersfield, Preston and Birmingham. In the local elections which followed the granting of a charter to Manchester, the Free Traders were successful, and within the Commons C. P. Villiers, the M.P. for Wolverhampton, took up the cause of repeal. The League dedicated itself to repealing the Corn Laws, to the exclusion of all other considerations. It did not become involved in a complicated and extensive programme of political reform—unlike the Chartists. Its faith was neatly summarised in one simple and unambiguous article of belief. Yet the initial propaganda campaigns were disastrous. Conflicts broke out between the League's lecturers and Chartist agitators. The League suffered because the antics of the Chartists had antagonised the middle classes. Lecturers were given rowdy hearings, and were implicated in scuffles with the authorities. No impact was made on agricultural areas, and the expense of the propaganda tours almost brought the League to ruin. Support in London was disappointingly weak, and statesmen such as Russell and Wellington refused to receive deputations from the League's London Conference. In the Commons the Free Traders were trounced in debate by Peel. The year 1840 was as depressing as 1839.

With the failure of the second and more ambitious of the propaganda campaigns Richard Cobden emerged as the most perceptive of the League's leaders. He had always advocated the League's entry into the political arena, and he had never disguised his scepticism for propaganda divorced from political activity. The defeat of further efforts to reform Parliament meant that the League would have to work within the existing political structure. Cobden had no illusions about what lay ahead: 'The people should be told that the country's salvation must be worked out at the hustings and in the polling booths.' Unless more effective representation in the Commons was achieved, the League would not be able to secure justice. Therefore from September 1840 Cobden concentrated all his energies on procuring the election of Free Trade candidates in constituencies which were amenable to Radical influence. He told Francis Place of the methods he proposed to use:

'We have determined upon a plan for influencing the electoral bodies. As soon as the registries are revised by the barristers, we shall obtain copies of them in all the boroughs in which we intend to operate. We shall then send circulars, calling a meeting of voters to meet a Deputation of the League to confer with them upon the question of the Corn Law—we shall separate the question entirely from *party* politics, and induce as many electors as possible to associate themselves together to form a body pledged only to the abolition of the Corn Law.'

Such were the priorities which governed the League's policy. Propaganda and pamphleteering still continued, and every means was used to keep the Corn Law issue before the public, but the League's political activities became increasingly important. When a by-election at Walsall demonstrated the extent of the pressure which could be put on voters, all resources were diverted to influencing electoral behaviour. The Free Traders did not shrink from the more questionable practices of the time. Dead men were registered. Voters were intimidated or impersonated. Tories were carried off to taverns, where they were detained in a drunken stupor until the poll was over. Opponents were struck off the registers. Bribery and corruption, treating and influence—all were exploited by the League with enthusiasm and judgment. In the 1841 general election several representatives of the League were returned, including Cobden himself for Stockport, and though there were several disappointments, the League was now an effective political machine—perhaps the most efficient in contemporary politics. Cobden's election confirmed his pre-eminence. He was the leader of the movement within Parliament as well as in the country.

These successes were followed by renewed efforts to set up branches of the Anti-Corn Law League in towns which had previously resisted the League's blandishments, and within existing branches organisation was improved. Every town was divided into sections, each with its own affiliated association and its own officers. The League did all that it could to ensure the support of Dissent. The pulpit was still a potent political weapon, and the leaders of the League realised the advantages of a Nonconformity preaching the good news of Free Trade as well as the gospel of

Jesus Christ. Immense efforts were also made to win the support of O'Connell and the Irish, whose goodwill was particularly valuable in the thriving towns of the north-west, where Irish immigration had swelled the population. Thus, although the League remained committed to one ideal, it succeeded in uniting several diverse interests in campaigning for that ideal—an achievement which had eluded the Chartists.

But there were still difficulties to be surmounted and crises to be overcome. Differences between the more militant of the League's supporters, led by John Bright, and the moderates, led by Cobden, became acute in 1841–2, when Bright advocated closing the factories as a means of forcing the government's hand. Cobden insisted on political, as distinct from direct, action, and the failure of the strikes of 1842—inspired partly by a trading recession, partly by Chartist agitators and partly by the more impatient Free Traders—emphasised the wisdom of his policy. Cobden's regard for legality and unceasing devotion to restraint earned a handsome dividend. Soon the League's financial worries were over. It had a small, but vocal, spearhead in the Commons, supported by an effective organisation in the country, and its Parliamentary representation became even more active after Bright entered the Commons in 1843. In 1842 Cobden admitted that after four years of agitation the League had 'got a pretty strong hold of public opinion', and he was confident that the Free Trade party was gaining ground more rapidly than at any former period. The future filled him with jubilation: 'There is no earthly doubt now of the ultimate triumph of our cause. It is merely a question of *time.*'

Cobden and Bright had their eyes on the general election which was due in 1848. They embarked on another campaign to collect funds for the League, and they also engaged in propaganda tours, instead of employing paid agents to do the job for them. In 1843 they moved the League's headquarters to London, a sign of the close link between the League's parliamentary leadership and its non-parliamentary activities. They lobbied M.P.s—Macaulay among them—in the hope of inducing them to adhere to the Free Trade cause. They sent emissaries into agricultural areas in another

12 Lord Palmerston

13 The Blessings of Peace or the Curse of the Corn Bill. A cartoon by Cruikshank, 1815

THE PENNY POST · 153

attempt to convince the farmers of the deficiencies of protection. They took full advantage of the penny post, which had been introduced on the advice of Sir Rowland Hill in 1840, to distribute their tracts and to maintain a tight liaison between Westminster and the local branches of the League. The final crisis over the Corn Laws justified Cobden's conviction that the matter would be decided in Parliament, but without its national organisation the League would not have carried the weight it did within Parliament.

Two oversimplifications about the events of 1845-6 need correction. It is not true to suggest that the League was solely responsible for the repeal of the Corn Laws. Neither Cobden nor Bright could be expected to foresee the Irish potato famine, which rendered all previous political calculations obsolete. Despite its successes, the League was not powerful enough to carry repeal against the opposition of a united landed interest, and without the Irish potato famine the landed interest—and inevitably the Conservative party—would not have been split so dramatically. Even when due allowance is made for the tremendous efforts which the League was making in preparation for the 1848 general election it is unlikely that it would have done more than substantially increase its Parliamentary representation. It could hardly have gained an overall majority. At the best, it could only hope to form a stronger pressure group. Yet it is equally unsatisfactory to claim that without the potato shortage the Corn Laws would not have been repealed. Peel was convinced of the need to repeal the Corn Laws before the onset of the Irish crisis, and in part this was the result of the League's work. The amended Sliding Scale, and the revision of customs duties, indicated a move towards Free Trade. Peel had hoped that the Corn Laws could be repealed—or amended out of existence—after the beneficial effects of his commercial policies were obvious to all and when the fears of the agriculturalists had thereby been assuaged. Instead he was driven to choose between serving the national interest or preserving the unity of his party. It was a cruel choice, but Peel's tragedy should not obscure the part played by the League in disseminating Free Trade ideas and in transforming his own thinking. The blight

L

which ruined the Irish potato crop compelled Peel to act before he had expected it would be necessary to do so, and in circumstances far different from those he had anticipated. But it did not revolutionise his outlook; this had already been modified. Cobden's own words come nearest the truth: 'The League would not have carried the repeal of the Corn Laws when it did, had it not been for the Irish famine and the circumstance that we had a Minister who thought more of the lives of the people than his own continuance in power . . .'

But the League's importance is not limited to the Corn Law controversy. As the franchise was extended, so the organisation, local structure and propaganda techniques of the Anti-Corn Law League were imitated and reflected in the nascent political parties which sought to control the new mass electorate. The apparent success of the League gave its methods a powerful appeal, and the League has a distinguished, perhaps a decisive, place in the growth of modern political parties. Many of its supporters stayed in politics after the repeal of the Corn Laws, and their experiences during the Free Trade agitation equipped them to fight other political battles, often using similar tactics and strategy. The history of the League is a revealing commentary on electoral practices after the first Reform Bill, and a foretaste of those which followed the passing of the second.

The Corn Law Crisis and the Fall of Peel

The Irish crisis took everyone by surprise. Too high a proportion of the population depended on the potato for their staple diet, and when the crop failed in the autumn of 1845 the gaunt spectre of starvation stalked the land. The corn harvest in England was also poor, and the Irish had the grim experience of seeing corn exported to England from Ireland at a time when they themselves were starving. The corn merchants were reluctant to lose the English market, and the government did not think it proper to interfere with the regular habits of trade. But the catastrophe demanded action. As the fields blackened the peasants starved, and the horrors of the mid-'forties left an indelible impression on the imaginative and emotional Irish mind. Peel tried to meet the need by importing maize from America. This was sensible, but the unfamiliar corn was unpopular, and the desperate peasantry gave it the bitter nickname of Peel's brimstone. The remedy required time. Only the suspension or repeal of the Corn Laws would allow foreign grain to be imported quickly enough at prices the poor could afford, but Peel knew that many of his supporters still revered the Corn Laws as a solemn pledge to the farming community. When he suggested that the Corn Laws should be suspended several members of his Cabinet resigned. Meanwhile Lord John Russell, the leader of the Whigs, announced his conversion to Free Trade in his famous Edinburgh letter. Peel saw what had to be done, but, as in the Catholic crisis eighteen years earlier, he did not think he was the man to do it. He resigned and Russell tried to form a government. But now the rivalries within the Whig ranks wrecked the chances of a Whig ministry. Grey refused to serve if Palmerston was Foreign Secretary. Palmerston declined to hold any other office. Russell abandoned the task, and Peel returned, conscious of where his duty lay, conscious, too, of the price which had to be paid.

The division between Free Traders and Protectionists within the Conservative party was a painful one. Memories of previous collaboration heightened the sense of betrayal. When several of Peel's friends resigned their seats, as was customary when accepting ministerial office, in order to present themselves for re-election, borough-mongers such as Richmond, Buckingham and Marlborough told them to look elsewhere. The Duke of Newcastle turned Gladstone out of Newark. Within the Commons the opposition to repeal was led by Benjamin Disraeli and Lord George Bentinck. Disraeli was a brilliant, ambitious man of letters, whose cultivated dandyism and flamboyant dress had earned him the suspicions of his colleagues. His intellectual gifts did nothing to diminish this distrust. He had expected office in 1841, but had been disappointed. Now he avidly seized the opportunity to become the leader of an interest which had contemned him for too long, and whose mentality he secretly despised. Men who had questioned his sincerity welcomed him as the dazzling spokesman for the inarticulate. He pleaded the claims of party and of the landowning classes with an eloquence which was enthusiastically applauded by his less-fluent supporters. He maintained that only loyalty to one's party made parliamentary government possible, and that by breaking with his party and deserting the interest which he had been elected to safeguard Peel was indulging in conduct which must prove fatal to civilised politics. The other leader of the Protectionists, Lord George Bentinck—a son of the Duke of Portland—was fonder of the racecourse than of politics, and had refused office because he was unwilling to give up the necessary time from his favourite sport. Less interested than Disraeli in the niceties of debate, less subtle in his reasoning and less dubious in his motives, Bentinck typified the count__ __mbers whose indig__tion __gainst Peel knew __ __ounds. He also epitomised the hearty p__ __cal dilettan__sm __ Peel scorned.

Peel retorted to these atta__ __ that he __s p__ the welfare of __ nation abo__ __se co__ __ns. He rightly claimed t__ __al was c__ __r, and that events had shown that he w__ __only possible minister. His arguments made sense to men who __membered the traditional standards expected of a minister of the Crown. Disraeli's apologia for party looked to the future. Peel's defence of his actions recalled the past. __ __pa__ a generous and __quent tribute to the effo__ __ which __ __en i__ made for the __se of repeal, __nd __ __d some __giving among his supporters, including G__ __one and Aberdeen, who could not forget t__ savagery with __ich Cobden and his companions had deno__ __ the agricultural interest. Peel succeeded in reducing the __corn to a nominal lev__ or June 25th, 1846, when his Bill __ n its third reading in the L__ds, but he had depended on Whig and Radical votes. On the same evening the Protectionists in the Commons gained their revenge by going into the lobbies with their old enemies and defeating Peel on a coercion Bill for Ireland. Four days later Peel resigned.

It was the end of an era, for Peel never held high office again. He still dominated public life, but it was as if the greatest of actors was permanently in the wings. Four years later he died, and his followers spent twenty years looking for a party. English politics reverted to a fluid and confusing state. The Peelites formed one party, the Protectionists another. Old-fashioned Whigs such as Palmerston had little in common with impatient Radicals such as Bright. Within five years the Protectionists had abandoned protection, Disraeli—ever a realist—confessing that politically it was dead and buried. But their quarrel with Peel and his followers was never made up, and while Gladstone moved slowly and hesitantly towards Liberalism, Disraeli set about educating his party. The economic advantages enjoyed by England in the mid-nineteenth century meant that the country reaped all the benefits of Free Trade without incurring its hardships. Both sides had exaggerated the results of repealing the Corn Laws. Although the nation prospered for a generation, Free Trade did not inaugurate an era of peace and brotherhood. But neither did it ruin the farmers, for another twenty years passed before the opening up of the American prairies exposed English agriculture to competition more fierce than any that had been anticipated during the 'forties. Once the Corn Law issue had been settled, men turned their attention to other problems—to Parliamentary reform, to the condition of the people, to religion, science and education. Later still Gladstone led a Liberal party dedicated to peace, retrenchment and reform, while Disraeli Conservatism sought to combine reform of a different sort with a regard for traditional institutions and a new awareness of the opportunities and responsibilities of Empire, but this realignment of political forces took place only after the death of Palmerston and the enfranchisement of the urban working class.

Distress in Ireland

Cheap corn and a programme of public works did not of themselves solve the Irish problem, as Lord John Russell found to his cost when he succeeded Peel. The disaster of 1845 was followed by an even worse blight in 1846, after all the signs had pointed to a good harvest. Men were dumbfounded, for it was unusual for one bad year to be succeeded immediately by another. Once more the Irish starved, as death and pestilence ravaged the land. Hunger inspired crime, and when the famine ended Ireland languished in the grip of agrarian distress and reciprocal outrage. Nothing was done to protect the tenants, and too many landlords resorted to eviction in a desperate effort to cut their losses. In November 1847 Lord John Russell lamented that murder and eviction were as common as ever, and in the following year Smith O'Brien, angered by the sufferings of the people and weary of the ineptitude of the government, led the Young Irishmen in revolt. The rising was a trivial affair, being put down without difficulty, and O'Brien and his accomplices were transported. But the war between landlord and tenant went on, breeding new woes for succeeding generations. The famine of 1845-6 did more than topple Sir Robert Peel and abrogate the Corn Laws. It was the decisive event of Irish history in the nineteenth century, marking a new epoch in the dismal and tragic story of England's attempt to pacify Ireland. It left a permanent scar on Anglo-Irish relations and precipitated the exodus of the Irish from their doomed island. In the fifteen years succeeding the famine two million Irish emigrated. Some came to England, others to Scotland, but an increasing number went to America, to that New England which Puritan pioneers had settled in the grim days of the seventeenth century. The Irish-Americans never forgot their cousins over the water, or the sorrows—real and imagined —which England had brought upon their country, and the hatred of Britain which they carried to the United States had important effects on American policy. When nationalist movements in Ireland looked to America for aid they were not disappointed: Irish rebellion was financed by Americans who never ceased to think of themselves as Irishmen. This was as true of Sinn Fein and the I.R.A. in the twentieth century as it had been of the Fenians in the 1860s.

But Englishmen were in no mood to lose themselves in the complexities of Irish politics, nor could they foresee the dire consequences of their folly and indifference. During the next twenty years they became conscious of their economic power, of Britain's status as the workshop of the world, of her unquestionable superiority in matters of domestic tranquillity and civil peace to the quarrelsome and fickle nations of the continent. These assumptions of insular supremacy found a provocative and colourful exponent in the effervescent and frequently outrageous figure of Palmerston, a bright and breezy sixty-year-old, whose jaunty self-confidence denoted that he was a living link with the days of Canning. Foreign statesmen might shake their heads ruefully, Queen Victoria might deplore his latest indiscretion or lapse of taste, but ordinary Englishmen took Palmerston to their hearts. For a generation he delayed parliamentary reform, and baffled the statesmen of Europe—until he met his match in Bismarck. When the age of Peel gave way to the age of Palmerston a more-spontaneous, less-deliberate character came over English politics, and while public life was confused and perplexing, it was undeniably exciting.

8 : The Supremacy of Palmerston

Although Palmerston was the dominant figure in English public life after the death of Peel, he was not always in sympathy with contemporary developments, and frequently he failed to understand them. Some historians have gone so far as to describe him as the last great representative of the eighteenth century, and fanciful as this is, it emphasises the curious relationship between the supreme politician of the age and the ideas and movements which were reshaping the world in the mid-nineteenth century.

Social and Economic Developments

The pace of change was becoming more and more intense. As the harvest of industrialism was gathered, so new techniques were discovered and applied with ever-increasing skill. Iron manufactures expressed the triumphs of ingenuity, brawn and machinery. The railways were booming, and within the next quarter of a century their tentacles spread throughout the country. Despite the recklessness which had tainted railway development in the 1840s, promise ripened into achievement. In 1853, 7,000 miles of track were open. Twenty years later this figure had doubled. In the same period the number of passengers carried by the railways rose from 100 million to 439 million per annum. A social revolution had been carried through. Men could now travel more quickly and more cheaply than ever before. Labour became more mobile. The distance between town and country diminished. Markets which were once too remote could now be exploited. Shipping also kept abreast of commercial expansion. In 1853, 5 million tons of goods were carried from British ports in British ships. By 1873 this had almost trebled. The number of ships grew and steam-ships accounted for a bigger proportion of the nation's merchant fleets. Foreign trade reached immense proportions. In 1830 the annual value of exported goods had been £38 million, and ten years later this stood at £50 million. But within the next thirty years the rate of growth multiplied at a fantastic rate. In 1873 the annual value of exports was £240 million. The textile industries accounted for much of this trade, but as time went on their share of the total earnings fell. In 1842 cotton and woollen exports had earned 58 per cent of the national income from overseas trade. By 1873 the percentage had dropped to 42. During the same period iron, coal and machinery exports rose from 11 per cent of total overseas sales to 24 per cent. The money gained from these exports was spent on a relatively bigger amount of imports, especially foodstuffs such as cheese, butter, bacon and eggs. The Protectionist's dream of a self-sufficient Britain had vanished for good, and the Free Trader proudly pointed to the cheap breakfast-table as evidence of the utility and worth of his doctrine.

During the years 1850–75 the standard of living of the common people improved. It was a period of prosperity, for there were only two recessions of any importance: one in 1857, the other in 1866. Of course, many people still lived in conditions which would be thought intolerable today. Towns were often dingy and insanitary. Too many houses were unfit for human habitation. Hours of work were long and exhausting, while employment was insecure and poorly remunerated. Life was haunted by poverty, disease and hunger, and many men and women—and especially children— lived out their lives without beauty, leisure or any of the comforts of civilised existence. But although much remained to be done, conditions were improving and the social conscience was becoming more sensitive to injustice and exploitation. The progress of humanitarianism is one of the great themes of nineteenth-century history. It was accomplished through the courage and devotion of innumerable individuals who dedicated themselves to fighting degradation, cruelty and crime, and who challenged indifference, apathy and neglect. Here the trade unions, Co-operative movement and Friendly Societies played a noble part.

After the collapse of Owen's grandiose plans the trade unions entered upon a less-dramatic but more rewarding period in their history. They had still to face the hostility of those advocates of extreme *laissez-faire* who thought collective action on the part of the workers was a sinister interference with the laws of supply and demand and the freedom of the market. *Laissez-faire* seems a strange doctrine today. The idea that all state interference with economic activity was a threat to the welfare of the community looks too much like a doctrine to enable the strong to get stronger at the expense of the weak for us to take much comfort in it. But men who had worked hard and long to better themselves were suspicious of governmental intervention, while the thought of combinations among working men was tarnished with secrecy and fears of revolution. The age was never an age of *laissez-faire* in an absolute sense, however, for the government did not relinquish control over all economic activity, and legislation such as the Factory Acts and the Poor Law was in itself a defiance of pure *laissez-faire* doctrine. But the workers knew that they would have to rely on their own efforts. The government could not be expected to take action on their behalf. Wisely the unions devoted themselves to the cautious and patient improvement of wage-rates and working conditions and the provision of benefits for their members. Organisation followed the trades and crafts of the workers involved. In 1841 the Miners' Association of Great Britain and Ireland was founded. Soon it was able to pay a solicitor a salary of £1,000 per annum to safeguard its interests and tender legal advice. Although badly hit by the depression in the coal industry in 1847, it had set the pattern for future development. In 1851 the Amalgamated Society of Engineers was established. Its executive committee exercised a scrupulous control over its branches, and by publishing its reports it proved that the old charge of secretiveness was outmoded. Despite a setback in 1852, when the employers locked out the engineers and exacted an ineffectual promise from them to give up the union, the Society survived. Other crafts organised themselves on similar lines. The builders, carpenters and bricklayers formed the Amalgamated Society of Carpenters and Joiners, and by 1860 this had survived a lock-out, had gained a great measure of success through a strike and had amply demonstrated the value of organisation on a national scale. By carefully eschewing political commitments, and preferring patient negotiation to sensational action, the unions gained much ground.

But they still suffered from time to time from the rash actions of extremists, and these often gave magistrates the excuse to penalise unions. The legal position of the unions was insecure. It was held that they did not come within the scope of the Friendly Societies Act of 1855, and consequently their funds were not protected from dishonest officials. Legally they were still associations in restraint of trade. The unions continued to agitate against this state of affairs, and in 1871 the Trade Union Act finally conceded full legal recognition and a measure of security for union funds.

But the trade unions were not the only evidence of the willingness of the working classes to help themselves. The Co-operative movement sought to ameliorate the effects of capitalism by sharing the profits made in the course of normal business. The Rochdale Pioneers of 1844 are usually regarded as the founders of the modern Co-operative movement. By 1851 there were over a hundred Co-operative Societies with a total membership of 15,000. Members of the societies received dividends in proportion to the purchases which they had made. After much trial and error the societies embarked upon production as well as selling. Perhaps more important were the Friendly Societies, which offered their members benefits covering sickness, accident and death, and which were pledged to spreading the principles of fraternity and benevolence. The Oddfellows were reorganised in 1833, the Foresters in the following year, but in addition to the big societies there were many small, local clubs. In 1846 the establishment of a Registrar of Friendly Societies helped to protect the more responsible societies from the dangers of fraud. By 1850 the total membership of the Friendly Societies had grown to one and a half million. Yet another sign of working-class thrift was the success of the savings-bank movement: by 1844 there were over a million depositors with £27,000,000 to their account. The majority of these were wage-earners.

As trade swelled and profits rose the nation became confident of its role as workshop of the world. This confidence was given unique expression in the Great Exhibition of 1851, which has become legendary for its buoyant optimism, its hopes for peace and plenty, its pride in what had been achieved and its conviction that greater triumphs had still to be won. The overwhelming tastelessness of much of what was displayed should not obscure the initiative and imagination which were also duly rewarded. Yet there was a naïvety about the affair which is both sad and touching. The hopes for peace were ill founded, for within three years the nation was at war with Russia. Nor did Free Trade bring in a golden age of international understanding. Britain was still benefiting from her early start in industrialisation. She was not competing on equal terms with her neighbours. Neither Germany nor the United States for example, had as yet undergone their own Industrial Revolutions. The dream of a peaceful world in which the nations would co-operate in commerce and trade gave way to doctrines of economic nationalism. But it is misleading to see 1851 as the year which marked the peak of British industrial achievement. When compared with the developments which took place in the second half of the nineteenth century the accomplishments of 1851 seem puny in comparison.

Palmerston and the Queen

Palmerston's foreign policy mirrored the economic confidence of the British people, but the 1840s and 1850s were also years of anxiety and fear. On the continent revolutions broke out in 1848 in France, Austria, Germany and Italy. Palmerston sympathised with the nationalist movement in Italy. He thought that Charles Albert of Piedmont had little choice but to challenge the Austrians, and he would have been content to see a strong Piedmont ruling a north Italian kingdom. But although he favoured a liberal solution to the Italian problem, Palmerston had no wish to weaken Austria as a great power. Indeed, he believed that she would be all the stronger without her Italian entanglements, and he was incapable of appreciating Schwarzenberg's advice, when the Austrian reminded him that just as Austria did not meddle in Irish affairs, so England ought not to dabble in Italian politics. Palmerston tried to mediate in the quarrel between Austria and Piedmont, and although he failed to persuade Austria to hand Lombardy over to Piedmont his intervention probably prevented a clash between Austria and France. The 1848 revolution in France had

had the effect of bringing Louis Napoleon Bonaparte, a nephew of the great Emperor, to power, and although the Crimean War was fought in alliance with France against Russia, the 'fifties and 'sixties were clouded by suspicions of French intentions, suspicions which were to embarrass Palmerston on more than one occasion.

When Peel resigned Russell took over as Prime Minister, with Palmerston as Foreign Secretary. Palmerston was the ablest and most popular member of the Cabinet, but his relations with the Queen and the Prince Consort were strained. He offended Queen Victoria by his disdain for what she regarded as her constitutional rights, as well as by his conduct of foreign policy. The Queen disapproved of his tendency to act without consulting or informing his sovereign. She expected to be told of what had passed between the Prime Minister and Foreign Secretary, and to be shown dispatches in good time. She wanted to have all drafts sent to her for approval before they were released. She wanted to know precisely what it was that she was authorising, and she saw no good reason why a decision which she had sanctioned should be arbitrarily changed by a minister acting on his own initiative. Victoria also distrusted the sympathy which Palmerston showed for liberal and nationalist movements on the continent, for her own feelings naturally lay with her fellow monarchs. Later, when the Queen sympathised with German nationalist aspirations, Palmerston chose to be sceptical. He described Bismarck as 'crazy' and thought that in any clash of arms France would beat Prussia. Palmerston's undisguised approval for the drubbing administered by the London draymen to Haynau, an Austrian general who had played a brutal part in the suppression of the Italian revolt, and his ostentatious welcome to Kossuth, the Hungarian patriot, only made the Queen more angry. Palmerston's attitude was typified by the famous 'Don Pacifico' incident in 1850, when he brought the full weight of English diplomacy to bear upon the Greek government in order to enforce the payment of compensation to a shady moneylender of Portuguese extraction, who claimed British citizenship by virtue of being born in Gibraltar. It was a hollow victory, for it involved offending the French government as well as tyrannising over the Greek, but

Palmerston carried it off in splendid style. His peroration in the Commons has become famous as a statement of the principle underlying his foreign policy: 'As the Roman, in days of old, held himself free from indignity, when he could say "Civis Romanus sum", so also a British subject, in whatever land he may be, shall feel confident that the watchful eye and the strong arm of England will protect him against injustice and wrong.'

The Russell ministry managed to survive, despite the stresses which hampered its conduct of public affairs, but it was first weakened and then brought down in consequence of events in Paris. Louis Napoleon had been elected President of the French Republic in 1848, but he had his eye on a more glamorous title and a more permanent office. In December 1851 he arrested his opponents, overthrew the constitution and declared himself Prince-President. (A year later he declared himself Emperor of the French, assuming the title of Napoleon III.) Palmerston acted quickly on hearing of the *coup d'état* and sent a message of congratulation and approval to Napoleon. But he had gone too far. He had not consulted his colleagues in the Cabinet, and worse still he had ignored the Queen. Russell's patience was exhausted, and the latest breach of etiquette was the last straw. Palmerston was forced to resign. But he was not prepared to suffer this indignity in silence. Early in 1852 he seized the chance to defeat the government in the Commons by challenging Russell's proposals for the militia. This was Palmerston's famous 'tit for tat'. Russell resigned, but although Derby formed a Conservative administration, this was speedily defeated, and Aberdeen, a kindly, well-meaning man, headed a coalition ministry of Whigs and Peelites.

On the face of things the government was a powerful one. Palmerston was installed at the Home Office, where it was thought that his talent for offending the Queen would be less embarrassing than at the Foreign Office. His old colleague and rival, Russell, was Foreign Secretary, while Gladstone, the ablest of the Peelites, became Chancellor of the Exchequer. But the ministry suffered from lack of leadership. Aberdeen was a feeble Prime Minister, and he was incapable of resolving the feuds which divided the members of his administration. Despite Gladstone's good work at the Exchequer, the ministry collapsed because of its inept handling of the Crimean War—a war which might have been averted if Aberdeen had been more decisive and more determined.

The Crimean War

The manner in which the country drifted into war with Russia and the incompetence with which the war was fought should not divert attention from the more profound problems which were involved. The essential difficulty was the perennial question of what would happen when the Ottoman Empire finally broke up. Unhappily for the Powers the Turkish Empire—like England's Charles II—was an unconscionable time in dying. Russia, France, Austria and Britain were all interested in the future of the Near and Middle East. Nicholas I of Russia harboured plans for expansion towards the Mediterranean. Russia needed an ice-free port, and Constantinople would fit the bill admirably. The part played by Russia in winning independence for the Greeks, the special relationship of the Tsar and the Orthodox Church, the vision of the Tsar as the protector of the Christian subjects of the Porte—all of these helped to inflame Russian ambitions in the eastern Mediterranean. But Nicholas could not make up his mind as to the best way of securing Russian interests. Sometimes he thought of partitioning the Ottoman Empire in friendly collabora- tion with the other Powers. Sometimes he contemplated keeping the Turkish Empire alive, in order to advance his schemes under the guise of benevolent alliance. There were occasions when he even thought that Russia could satisfy her demands without consulting the other Powers at all. He went so far as to drop hints to the British ambassador about 'the sick bear of Europe', sug- gesting that preparations should be made in order to meet the situation which would arise if the Sultan's imperium finally disintegrated. But the British Cabinet could not make up its mind as to whether the Ottoman Empire was doomed or not. Aberdeen preferred to prop it up, hoping that the situation would not worsen in the meantime. Nicholas felt that his gestures of co- operation had been spurned, but for the present he was prepared to wait upon events.

The accession of Napoleon III changed the situation. Napoleon was determined to reassert French prestige in the Near East and to undo the reverses which Louis Philippe had endured during the 1840s in connection with Mehemet Ali's vain bid for an independent empire of his own in Egypt and Syria. Napoleon came forward as the spokesman for the Latin monks in Palestine and demanded that the keys of the Church of the Nativity should be handed over to them. In justification of his action he cited concessions which the Turks had made to the Bourbons as long ago as 1740. Nicholas replied by invoking the treaty of Kutchuk Kainardji in defence of his pretensions as protector of the Christian subjects of the Sultan and supported the rights of the Greek monks as custodians of the Holy Places. The Sultan tried to please both parties. He ordered the keys of the Church of the Nativity to be given to the Latin monks, while assuring Nicholas that his own privileges were not infringed in any way. But both Napoleon and Nicholas were angry at what had been accorded to the other. The Tsar once more talked of the sick bear of Europe and the need to make provisions for his decease. He dangled Egypt and Crete invitingly before Britain, hoping thereby to separate Britain from France. Aberdeen and Russell were unsure of their next move, for they suspected Napoleon III as much as the Tsar. Meanwhile Nicholas demanded formal recognition from the Sultan of the protectorate, which he claimed had been conceded by the treaty of Kutchuk Kainardji. When the Sultan refused, the Russian mission left Constantinople.

The British government doubted Nicholas's good faith, and their misgivings were fully shared by Napoleon III. But Aberdeen was incapable of formulating a coherent policy. Neither he nor his colleagues wanted war, but they did not want to see Russia winning control of the Near East. In the Commons Bright and the Radicals vehemently opposed any policy which would lead to war. Meanwhile the Russians decided to invade the Danubian principalities of Moldavia and Wallachia in order to force the Sultan to concede all their demands. Aberdeen was sympathetic to Russian claims regarding the guardianship of the Holy Places, but he felt that the demand for the protectorate over all Greek

14 WILLIAM COBBETT   **15** ROBERT OWEN

16 RICHARD COBDEN   **17** JOHN BRIGHT

28 A Staffordshire colliery in the mid-nineteenth century

Christian subjects of the Porte was excessive. In June 1853 a British fleet was sent out to the Dardanelles as a precaution. The next month the Russians invaded the principalities. Meanwhile the British ambassador at Constantinople, Stratford de Redcliffe, a good friend of Turkey and an advocate of reform, was trying to secure peace. He had advised the Sultan to give way on the Holy Places while standing firm with regard to the Tsar's claim to protect all Christians within the Ottoman Empire. He attempted to draft a note which would be acceptable to the Tsar while respecting the Sultan's rights, but when Stratford's version was submitted to a conference of the Powers which had assembled at Vienna it was amended to such an extent that the Turks were convinced that to accept it would be to submit to French and Russian tutelage. The Sultan therefore rejected the Vienna Note, and his own amendments were in turn rejected by the Russians as inadequate. The Turks then attacked the Russians in the principalities, but when the Russians destroyed the Turkish fleet at Sinope even those who had thought the Turkish declaration of war foolish and provocative were alarmed. The 'massacre of Sinope' provoked an outcry. The drift to war became irreversible. Ultimatums sent from Paris and London were ignored by the Tsar, and in the spring of 1854 the Crimean War—a war which almost nobody wanted—began.

Even when the war started it was difficult to know where or how to fight it. Austria and Prussia remained neutral, which meant that Russia was alone, but in any case Napoleon III remembered his uncle's greatest mistake and was determined not to be drawn into continental Russia. Ideas of fighting in the principalities were scotched by virtue of the fact that by the time the allies had arrived the Russians had withdrawn. The French and British then decided to attack their enemy in the Crimea. This would allow them to make good use of their advantage in sea-power and communications. But immense inefficiency prevented the campaign from reaching an early conclusion.

The war exposed shocking deficiencies in the British army. Forty years of peace had allowed all the abuses of the eighteenth century to be perpetuated, and the army's organisation had

M

become more rusty with every year that passed. The higher command was dominated by venerable but incompetent old men. The practice of buying and selling commissions still prevailed, and although this made it possible for young men to take the place of older men who would otherwise have been unable to afford to go into retirement the system was grossly inefficient. Opportunities for reform had been missed during Wellington's long tenure as Commander-in-Chief, and peacetime economies had prevented much-needed improvements in conditions of service. The men were badly paid, appallingly housed, poorly fed and badly clothed. Hygiene in the barracks was neglected and sanitation primitive. The elementary decencies were often better observed in the prisons. Flogging was the usual punishment, and there was no provision for the off-duty needs of the troops. The horrors of the Crimea were the natural consequences of the army's peace-time habits.

The clumsy diplomacy which had produced the war was excelled by the stupidity with which it was fought. Raglan, the British commander, was a veteran of the Peninsular War, and could not cure himself of the habit of referring to the enemy as 'the French'. Although he did his best, he was too old and too mediocre. St Arnaud, the French commander, was a dying man, and his disagreements with Raglan embittered relations between the allies. At the Alma the allies won their first victory, but failed to follow it up. They had lost their chance of ending the campaign. Todleben fortified Sebastopol, and what had been envisaged as a bold decisive stroke to destroy Russian power in the Black Sea declined into a wearisome siege, for which neither the French nor British armies were prepared. The Russians tried to capture the British base at Balaclava, but were driven off. The battle was fought with colossal incompetence on both sides. It was distinguished by the charge of the Heavy Brigade and the futile courage of the Light Brigade, but it settled nothing. During the winter the troops—many of them inexperienced recruits who were little more than boys—suffered terribly in the camps and trenches. Hospital arrangements were disgraceful, and Florence Nightingale, 'the lady with the lamp', won undying glory for her ceaseless efforts to improve the lot of the soldiers. During the ghastly winter the Russians made a second attempt to crush the British base, but the dawn battle of Inkerman, in which the bravery of the troops was relatively unencumbered by the stupidity of the higher command, foiled their plans.

The folly of the government and its generals was fully brought home by the mortality rate among the troops, and Aberdeen's ministry was discredited. In January 1855 the Commons demanded an inquiry into the army's supply services. Aberdeen resigned. He was too much a man of peace to wage a war: he had never forgotten the heaps of slain and wounded he had seen on the field of Leipzig in 1813. He gave way to the indomitable Palmerston, whose heart was in the fight, and a new energy characterised the direction of hostilities.

The losses sustained by both sides had been grievous. The French and British had suffered heavy losses, the Russians more so. Thousands of Russian soldiers died on the long march to the Crimea. But Napoleon III was determined to gain what would pass for military glory. Canrobert, who had succeeded St Arnaud, was replaced by Pélissier, a rough, vigorous soldier with little sense of the finer points of the military art but amply endowed with tenacity and courage. When Raglan died, disappointed with the miserable results of the campaign and exhausted by the strain of command, the government replaced him by General Simpson, an unimaginative officer, well fitted to collaborate with the ferocious Pélissier. The allies attacked the forts of the Malakoff and the Redan, the keys to Sebastopol. The British were driven off with heavy casualties, but Pélissier, utterly indifferent to the cost, took the Malakoff after much slaughter. During the night the Russians withdrew: Sebastopol had fallen (September 1855).

During the fighting various attempts had been made to end the war by negotiation, but these had failed. Piedmont joined the allies, while Sweden became a passive supporter. Prussia and Austria held themselves aloof from the conflict, though they could not overlook any alteration in the balance of power. The death of Nicholas I in March 1855 changed the situation. Though his successor, Alexander II, continued the struggle, he gave way to the demands of the allies after the fall of Sebastopol. The neutralisation clauses of the treaty of Paris (1856) forbade the Russians to refortify Sebastopol or to maintain a battle fleet in the Black Sea. The Tsar abandoned his claim to exercise any protectorate over the Christian subjects of the Sultan, while the Sultan promised to grant constitutions to the Danubian principalities, as well as to introduce other reforms. The Straits Convention of 1841 was reaffirmed, the Dardanelles being closed to foreign warships in time of peace. The Russians also gave up southern Bessarabia, thus losing control of the mouths of the Danube. These concessions might seem small reward for the cost in blood and treasure of the Crimean War, but Russian ambitions had sustained a sharp check. Yet the reverse was only temporary. During the Franco–Prussian War of 1870 the Russians denounced the neutralisation clauses of the treaty of Paris, and the 1870s saw the revival of their designs in the Balkans.

Chinese Affairs: the Indian Mutiny

When the Crimean War ended Palmerston's attention was soon taken up with other matters. In the Far East Britain became involved in another quarrel with China over the rights of ships flying the British flag. The Chinese wished to exclude foreigners from their country. They neither desired the presence of the European nor did they envy his civilisation. The westerners were eager to open up and develop the Chinese market. On the one hand the Chinese were capable of great cruelty when dealing with illegal traders or unwelcome missionaries. On the other, unscrupulous racketeers were only too willing to exploit the trade in opium and coolies. In 1856 the Chinese seized the *Arrow*, a small vessel flying the British flag. They claimed that the ship was carrying a well-known pirate and imprisoned the crew. Later the men were released but no apology was made. When no satisfaction could be obtained from the Chinese the British bombarded the forts at Canton. The Chinese retorted by putting a price on the head of every Englishman. Negotiations were of no avail. The Chinese refused to permit the establishment of a British diplomatic mission at Peking. Further expeditions were sent to China in

1858 and 1860, and on the latter occasion the Summer Palace of the Emperor was burnt in retaliation for Chinese atrocities against Europeans. Palmerston was jubilant. The Chinese were forced to open several ports to western trade, including Tientsin. They also received diplomatic missions at Peking and agreed to the regulation—instead of the suppression—of the opium trade. Palmerston's triumph seems vain and empty today, for the west is now paying the price for its crude handling of the Chinese question during the nineteenth century. Although there was a good case for trade between China and the west, the dubious character of so much of the commerce in dispute, and the disreputable methods used to implement it, have tainted western relations with China in ways which have had lasting ill-effects.

Although China remained on the periphery of western influence, British power was expanding in other regions. In 1819 Britain acquired Singapore. In the 1820s she took Assam from Burma and in the 1850s she annexed Pegu and Rangoon. British rule in India had been extended under several able and ambitious Governor-Generals. The incapacity of native rulers, and their inability to maintain law and order, compelled the British to assume the direct administration of additional provinces. In the 1840s Sind and the Punjab were annexed after fierce fighting. Despite setbacks such as the disastrous retreat from Kabul during the first Afghan War, British fortunes flourished, but there was still little sense of an imperial mission. Commerce was the main preoccupation, not the white man's burden. But men were jolted out of their complacency by the outbreak of the Indian mutiny in 1857, which had the effect of terminating the East India Company's rule in India and substituting that of the Crown. The mutiny was not a war for independence, nor was it the first time that sepoys had refused to obey orders. Large areas of India were undisturbed, and only one of the three principal armies was affected. But the mutiny was on a bigger scale than previous military revolts, and the atrocities and crimes committed during its course shocked Victorian public opinion and shattered illusions that western culture was gradually and irresistibly permeating Indian life. The causes of the mutiny are still obscure. Rumours of the imposition of Christianity by force, and tales which alleged that bullets issued to the native troops had been oiled with the fat of swine and cows, helped to inflame the sepoys. Both the Hindu, who holds the cow to be sacred, and the Moslem, who despises the pig as unclean, were offended by the possibility that they were handling bullets greased with animal fat. The early reverses suffered by the British exposed military deficiencies in stark fashion, but if their commanders had shown greater initiative the rising might have been speedily suppressed. British prestige was restored by the ruthlessness with which the mutineers were vanquished and their outrages revenged, but although the mutiny heralded an era of improved administration, it left a dark legacy of hatred and distrust on both sides. It stiffened religious fanaticism and superstition among the Indians, while heightening the haughty disdain for Indian ways which was already common among the British.

The Orsini Plot

Just as his premature congratulations after the *coup d'état* of December 1851 had brought about his fall, so Palmerston was thrust out of office a second time because of another incident connected with Napoleon III. In his younger days the French Emperor had had sympathies with Italian nationalism, and Italian patriots were bitterly disappointed when he did nothing for Italy. In 1858 an Italian called Orsini sought to remind his imperial majesty of his days in the carbonari by throwing a bomb at his carriage. Napoleon survived the attempt, but Orsini paid for his rashness with his life. (Characteristically Napoleon wanted to spare him but dared not do so.) Unfortunately Orsini had laid his plans in London and had manufactured his bombs in England, and in order to silence the clamour in France Napoleon demanded some action by the British authorities to prevent a repetition of the episode. Both Napoleon and Palmerston kept their heads, but when Palmerston introduced legislation to prevent foreign refugees using British asylum to prepare assassination he was accused of licking the French Emperor's boots. His critics in the Commons denounced the Conspiracy to Murder Bill as sure evidence that Palmerston was allowing a French tyrant to regulate English domestic policy. When he was defeated by a motley collection of enemies in the House Palmerston resigned. Derby and Disraeli formed a minority government, but they misjudged the mood of the Commons when they introduced a moderate Reform Bill in 1859, and although they gained a number of seats at the general election, they had no alternative but to go out of office. Palmerston then returned, forgiven for his lapse. He remained Prime Minister until his death in 1865. But men did not forget the Orsini affair. Napoleon was soon dabbling in Italian politics and indulging in his ill-fated Mexican adventure, but Englishmen still resented what they regarded as his insolent attempt to dictate to the British government. The truth was that the nation had rather lost its nerve: suspicions of France had provoked the excesses of the invasion scare, when men ostentatiously joined the Volunteers in order to repel the French. These fears lurked in men's minds throughout the 1860s.

Palmerston's Second Ministry

Palmerston's ministry was a strong combination. It embraced Whigs, Peelites, even a handful of Radicals. Gladstone returned to the Exchequer, and was now moving from an advanced Peelite position to the Liberal outlook with which his name is identified. (The slow pace of Gladstone's political development should not be forgotten.) But Palmerston himself remained the Canningite he had always been. He was opposed to further parliamentary reform, whatever the more youthful or daring members of his Cabinet might think of it, and he regarded the vote as a privilege to be conferred on the deserving, not a right. He had little desire to embark on an ambitious programme of legislation, and listened to demands for government action with cynical impatience. His interests still lay in foreign affairs, but his conduct of them during the 'sixties is more open to criticism than at any other period of his career.

Palmerston's last ministry saw the final triumph of Free Trade. Richard Cobden negotiated a reciprocity treaty with France in 1860, by which the French undertook to reduce duties on British manufactures in return for concessions on French wines and spirits. Meanwhile Gladstone completed the transition to Free Trade, every year seeing further reductions in customs duties. In 1860 Gladstone abolished the tariff on 371 articles and reduced the levy on many more. In 1861 he did away with the tax on paper. In 1863 he cut the duty on tea and in 1864 that on sugar. In 1865 he halved the tea duty. Within six years he succeeded in lowering the income tax from tenpence in the pound to fourpence in the pound, though he had now given up his old hope that one day he would be able to abolish the tax altogether. Trade flourished, and Gladstone and Cobden could rest content with their work, but Gladstone's desire for economies, and his preference for low taxation, brought him into conflict with Palmerston, who thought some of the reductions in tariffs dangerously novel, and whose ideas on foreign policy and defence were likely to lead to additional expenditure. As it was, Gladstone's passion for retrenchment held up some much-needed improvements in barrack accommodation for the army.

Palmerston's popularity remained as high as ever, except among the working men of the north, who felt that he was the biggest obstacle to their getting the vote, but his policy was fraught with difficulty and frustration. During the last six years of Palmerston's life the limitations of the Canningite tradition in British diplomacy were cruelly revealed. Brave words proved incapable of transforming situations which sea power alone could not handle. Palmerston and Russell were in sympathy with the Italians in their struggle for independence, and the popular imagination was fired by Garibaldi's exploits, but England's principal contribution lay in restraining other Powers from intervening in the tangled events which led up to the establishment of the kingdom of Italy in 1861. Palmerston and Russell were suspicious of Napoleon III's plans for Italy, while their anti-Austrian prejudice brought them into conflict with the Queen, who was favourably disposed towards a legitimate and Germanic Power. When the 'two dreadful old men' lectured her on the relevance of the Glorious Revolution of 1688, she tartly replied that she could not see what William of Orange had to do with Italian affairs. But English sentiment was overwhelmingly pro-Italian. Aristocrats and literary men favoured a free and rejuvenated Italy, while middle-class Dissenters were happy to see the Pope take a nasty knock. If verbal encouragement and emotional commitment are taken as the test of political involvement, then Britain merited the traditional praise awarded to her for her part in creating a free and united Italy. Yet one cannot refrain from wondering what England could have done to help the Italians if Napoleon III had come down on the side of the Habsburgs. Despite appearances, English policy could not be directed in total independence of the desires and interests of her European neighbours.

The Italian War of Liberation allowed Britain the luxury of seeing her hopes fulfilled without the embarrassment of having to exert herself to attain her desires. The outbreak of the American Civil War in 1861 created more complex problems for the British Cabinet. British sympathies were divided. Most men condemned slavery in the southern states of the United States, but the right of the southern states to secede from the union impressed upper-class opinion in particular as a weighty argument. Initially Lincoln affirmed that he was fighting to preserve the union, not to abolish slavery, and this helped to focus attention on the technical rather than the ultimate reason for the secession of the Confederacy. But the middle and lower classes, which were strongly influenced by Nonconformist opinion, sympathised with the north, and this became more pronounced after Lincoln committed himself to the abolition of slavery throughout the rebel states in 1863. Several factors confused British opinion. There was a certain preference for the more aristocratic south as against the brash and bustling north, though to talk of links with a fellow aristocratic culture is a gross exaggeration. Men who hated slavery were unhappy about compelling states to remain in a union which they felt threatened their own interests. How could one balance a detestation of slavery with a belief in the right of self-determination claimed—on impressive technical grounds—by the Confederacy? By the usual standards of judgment the southerners ought to have belonged to those who were rightly struggling to be free, but the slavery issue threw all normal moral criteria out of joint. England's liberals were thrust into a dilemma, and they spent most of the war avoiding the issue. With opinion divided in such a fashion it is not surprising that Palmerston was preoccupied with staying out of what was emphatically an American quarrel. But several incidents brought the British government into conflict with the Federal administration. To begin with, Britain recognised the southern states as belligerents. Although this was tactfully worded in order to avoid recognising the independence of the Confederacy, the north was offended, while the hopes of the south were prematurely —and as it turned out, falsely—raised. The Confederates put a high value on full recognition of their status, and they planned to send envoys to England to plead their case. Two of their representatives, Mason and Slidell, were on their way to Britain on the English ship *Trent*, when they were taken off by a northern cruiser. Tempers were inflamed. While the Yankees boasted of their achievement the British were angry at the insult to their flag. Arrogance on both sides helped to create an ugly situation. One of the last services rendered by the Prince Consort before his death was to suggest the toning down of the dispatch demanding the return of the two southern envoys. After much wrangling Mason and Slidell were allowed to proceed on their mission to London. On their arrival they were given a cold reception. Both belonged to the more intransigent school of thought among the Confederates, and they did little for their cause.

The dispute over the *Alabama* was more serious. The south laid orders for several armed ships in British yards, despite the fact that this was a technical violation of British neutrality. Of these ships the *Alabama* was the most famous, and she had a successful career as a commerce raider until she was captured in 1864. Attempts to stop her sailing from Liverpool failed, partly because of Russell's dilatoriness, and the Federal government held Britain responsible for the losses which the *Alabama* inflicted on northern shipping. Palmerston and Russell refused to accept responsibility, though they were more vigilant in preventing further evasions of the law. Later, during his first ministry, Gladstone agreed to take the quarrel to arbitration and in 1872 Britain paid £3,000,000 compensation to the United States.

Though Britain was involved in these disputes with the north, there was no question of British intervention on the side of the south. Palmerston was always emphatic in his insistence that Britain should stand aside from the conflict: 'the only thing to do seems to be to lie on our oars and to give no pretext to the Washingtonians to quarrel with us'. Russell toyed with the notion of acting as mediator between the combatants, but when the Federal government indicated that this would be interpreted as an unfriendly act he dropped the idea. Meanwhile, every month that passed imposed a bigger strain upon the south's economy, for the northern navy tightened its grip upon the Confederate ports. The success of the Federal blockade demonstrated how delusory the south's hopes had been, that countries which bought cotton would intervene on the Confederacy's behalf. But while the south fought on against overpowering odds, and in a futile cause, the northern blockade inflicted great hardships upon the cotton workers of north-west England, who were thrown out of work because their supply of raw material dried up. Here the American Civil War made its contribution to the development of English democracy, for the mature and self-controlled behaviour of the Lancashire mill-hands during a time of great misery and suffering did much to convince advanced Whigs and cautious Peelites that the urban working classes were worthy of the franchise. Despite their own troubles, the workers of the north remained true to their advocacy of the anti-slavery cause, refusing to condemn the Federal government for the blockade which was ruining Lancashire as well as forcing the Confederacy to its knees. Such constancy won the workers golden tributes. The editor of the *Spectator* affirmed that 'the working classes have a livelier sympathy with the popular feelings and the lives of other nations than the classes now most influential in politics', while Gladstone confessed that it was 'a shame and a scandal that bodies of men such as these should be excluded from the parliamentary franchise'. Bright was exultant and spoke ecstatically of the moral superiority of the unfranchised people, whose perception of the ethical nature of the American struggle had been so clear and unshakable. However rhetorical the commendations, the workers had nobly earned them. British diplomacy, on the other hand, scarcely covered itself with glory.

Palmerston was wise in keeping out of hostilities, but it was not easy to enforce neutrality fairly and equably.

Other events brought home the weakness of Britain's diplomatic position, a weakness which was obscured by her economic pre-eminence and her command of the seas. But Palmerston was too fond of bold gestures, even in situations where sea-power was impotent. His unreflecting sympathy for liberal and nationalist movements on the continent betrayed him into assuming postures which brought him only embarrassment and humiliation. In 1863 the Poles rose against the Russians. The Tsar's decision to introduce conscription in his Polish dominions was the last insult to a proud and oppressed people. British sentiments were with the Poles, for all shades of political opinion were agreed in regarding Russia as the most brutal and backward of the great Powers. But sentiment was not enough. Both Austria and Prussia were happy to see the Polish revolt crushed, and Bismarck, the recently appointed Chancellor of Prussia, willingly co-operated with the Tsar in putting down the rebellion. Palmerston and Napoleon III protested against the savagery with which the Tsar restored order in Poland, and both talked vaguely of a reappraisal of the Polish situation. The Tsar owed his position as the legitimate ruler of Poland to the Vienna settlement, and Russell felt that the Powers which had collaborated in formulating that settlement should call Russia to account for her actions. Napoleon was less interested in perpetuating the Vienna settlement, and thought more seriously of a congress to deal with the Polish question. But though these verbal exchanges raised Polish hopes, they were empty gestures. Even when Austria joined France and England in protesting against the brutality which the Russians had shown in suppressing the revolt, the Tsar made no concessions. Neither France nor Britain could give any practical assistance to the Poles, and neither wished to antagonise the Central Powers as well as the Tsar. Palmerston and Napoleon III had to sit idly by while the Russians dealt with the Poles with customary cruelty, and both Britain and France lost prestige.

But Palmerston had not learned his lesson. In the following year Prussia and Austria took advantage of the complex Schleswig–

Holstein question in order to impose a settlement on Denmark by which they each took one of the provinces. (This was their means of preventing the Danish King from merging Schleswig with the kingdom of Denmark.) The Prince of Wales had married Princess Alexandra of Denmark in 1863, and the Danes therefore looked to England for help. Public opinion rallied to the Danish cause, and agitators and journalists demanded that something should be done for the Danes. The result was a repetition of the sort of thing which had occurred over the Polish revolt. Palmerston called a conference of the Powers at London, but the intransigence of the Danes thwarted hopes of agreement, and when the meeting broke up without achieving anything Prussia and Austria went ahead with their plans. After the failure of his attempted mediation Palmerston could only bluster. When Napoleon III revived his idea of a European Congress to settle all matters in dispute among the Powers, Palmerston suspected a trap and contemptuously rejected the proposal. Napoleon was offended and turned to those dreams of compensation in the Low Countries and the Rhineland which finally proved his undoing in 1870. Without an ally on the continent there was nothing that Britain could do. It was unthinkable for her to challenge Austria and Prussia. She lacked the necessary military resources, and sea-power alone could not retrieve the situation. Palmerston would have been wiser if he had refrained from using ambitious and provocative language. The Danes were bitterly disappointed. They had hoped for something more tangible and effective than 'honourable sympathies'. Britain was humiliated a second time. She was learning the lessons of power. High moral sentiments were valueless unless some practical means of enforcing them existed. For too long Englishmen had assumed that moral rectitude was enough, and Palmerston's habit of giving vivid expression to such feelings perpetuated the error. Derby denounced the Cabinet's foreign policy as one of 'meddle and muddle'. To European statesmen, mindful of England's Irish policy and her tendency to encourage subversive movements on the continent, Palmerston's talk of the rights of small countries and emergent nationalities seemed little more than hypocrisy. But Radical politicians remained addicted to eloquent perorations as the solution for international tension, and it is still one of the weaknesses of democracy to assume that clashes of interest can be resolved by impressive pieces of rhetoric or pious avowals of pacific intent.

It is a great mistake to look back nostalgically to the heyday of Palmerston and so-called gunboat diplomacy. Too much of its success rested on sheer bluff and chance. It was powerless to influence the course of events in Europe, and even when it was successful, it looks spurious from the vantage point of the twentieth century. The isolation which England endured in the last thirty years of the nineteenth century was the outcome of Palmerstonian diplomacy, and its consequences were unfortunate for both Britain and Europe. In reality Britain's isolation was far from splendid, for while she could not ignore developments on the continent, she was prevented from helping to shape decisions which affected her well-being. Much of the disappointment which Palmerston experienced during the final years of his life was an apt commentary on the diplomacy which had dominated English foreign policy since the death of Castlereagh. Palmerston was simply unable to understand a world increasingly dominated by Bismarck, the most subtle exponent of *Realpolitik*.

When Palmerston died in October 1865 a new alignment took place in English politics. Though the other of 'the two old boys' —Russell—took over, his ministry soon collapsed. Parliamentary reform was in the air once more. The age of Whigs, Peelites and Protectionists had passed away with the intrepid aristocrat who had bewitched the English public for so long. The age of Gladstone and Disraeli had dawned. Shortly before his death Palmerston let slip his fears for the future: 'Gladstone will soon have it all his own way, and, whenever he gets my place, we shall have strange doings.' The two men had never understood each other. Gladstone had joined Palmerston's government only after much heart-searching. As late as 1857 he toyed with hopes of a reconciliation with the Conservative party, but as the years slipped by he found himself in idle isolation. Whatever Palmerston's faults, Gladstone preferred working with him rather than with Disraeli, and although he distrusted the general tendency of Palmerston's foreign policy, he was in agreement with him on Italian affairs. Most important of all, the prospect of handling the nation's finances proved irresistible. But while Palmerston's liberalism was a matter of phrases and sentiment, Gladstone was prepared to carry principles into action, not only in finance but also with respect to parliamentary reform and Irish affairs. Again his conversion was accompanied with much subtlety of thought: in 1859 he was defending rotten boroughs as 'nurseries of statesmen'. But throughout the 1860s Gladstone writhed under Palmerston's reluctance to embark on an ambitious programme of legislation, and during these years Gladstone's stock rose among the Radicals. Palmerston's fears were justified. The old man's death precipitated intense political controversy and another instalment of what he would have undoubtedly regarded as dangerous innovation and hasty reform.

9 : The Leap in the Dark

THE long predominance of Palmerston and the prosperity of the country during the 1850s and 1860s diverted the attention of all but a minority of far-sighted men from the need for further reform. But even before Palmerston's death there had been signs of impending change. In 1864 the Prime Minister had been given a rowdy reception by a crowd of working men at Bradford, and when he died men thought that an era had come to an end. The old politicians were passing away: Herbert, Aberdeen and Graham were all dead, and whatever positions they had assumed in the past, men such as Gladstone and Disraeli were less committed than their predecessors to the maintenance of the *status quo*. Men who could not recall the abuses of the old electoral system, or the struggle for reform in 1832, concentrated their energies upon exposing the anomalies of the contemporary political structure. Conscious as they were of the vagaries of the franchise, the persistence of corruption and the continued existence of proprietary boroughs, the reformers could not share the feelings of those who regarded the post-1832 Parliament as a nearly perfect institution. Indeed, they found the outlook of their opponents difficult to grasp and impossible to respect. Many Radicals had studied the working of American democracy, and although democracy was still viewed with caution if not with downright distaste, a growing number of reformers were advocating universal manhood suffrage. As we have seen, the conduct of the working men of Lancashire during the cotton famine caused by the American Civil War had impressed the middle classes and had shown that the working classes of the towns were mature enough to be trusted with the vote. The case for extending the franchise and revising the constituencies was winning more converts. Despite delays and disappointments, the reformers sensed that time was on their side.

Gladstone's Conversion: the Demand for Change

The most famous conversion was that of Gladstone in 1864. In his case the splendid qualities displayed by the cotton workers probably meant more than any theoretical arguments. Although he shuddered at the prospect of sudden, or violent, change he told the Commons that every man who was not incapacitated by some consideration of personal unfitness or political danger was morally entitled to come within the pale of the constitution. He even supported a Bill to reduce the franchise qualification in the boroughs from £10 to £6, and his adherence to what had previously been a Radical cause won the confidence of the more staid, but nevertheless reformist, members of the middle class. Gladstone was rebuked by Palmerston, who denied that every sane man had the moral right to vote, and Gladstone's rashness caused him to be defeated at Oxford in 1865, but his words, echoing as they did the Englishman's obsession with the moral aspect of political behaviour, focused men's attention on the state of the country's representative institutions. Others had toiled harder or longer, for the cause of parliamentary reform, or had courted unpopularity with a greater disdain for public approval, but when Gladstone talked of morality it was time for his opponents to prepare their own statements of faith, and for aristocrats to look to their privileges.

But other figures were flirting with the idea of change. Nor were they necessarily notorious apologists for reform, such as John Bright. The controversy over parliamentary reform cut across many of the conventional divisions of political life. Once again the variety of Victorian loyalties and the absence of anything like a modern two-party system are forcibly brought home. Disraeli, always eager to respond to the realities of politics providing that they were clothed in suitably romantic terms, talked of the 'mechanic' whose 'virtue, prudence, intelligence, and frugality, entitle him to enter the privileged pale of the constituent body of the country'. That was in 1859, before Gladstone had taken the plunge, and before the self-control of the Lancashire mill-hands undercut still further doubts about the trustworthiness of the working classes.

N

The Radicals sought to organise agitation through the Reform Union, which was set up in Manchester in 1864, and the Reform League, which was established in London in the following year. The League was a motley affair, comprising ex-Chartists, trade unionists and well-meaning middle-class sympathisers. Although the immediate response was disappointing, a growing number of middle-class thinkers felt that the existing political structure did not give them sufficient power, for the landed interest retained too many of its privileges. The working classes were increasingly conscious of their exclusion from the constitution and wanted the recognition which they thought had been denied too long. The middle classes were now so confident of their strength that they were less frightened of the workers. The workers realised that their own objectives could not be attained without the co-operation of the middle classes. But although men were willing to contemplate reform, they were not willing to fight for it. There was little enthusiasm for reform among the general public until hopes had been raised by attempted legislation and bitter controversy at Westminster, and until the recession of 1866 had added an economic motive for agitation. Only when events at Westminster had created the atmosphere of crisis was the prospect of reform enough to inspire men to call meetings and address rallies: even so, there was no repetition of the agitation of 1832. The Second Reform Bill was essentially the product of shifts of power within Parliament itself. The most able and gifted men in the Commons tended to support reform, but the opposition to innovation was still powerful and should not be underrated. In Robert Lowe it had an able exponent and doughty fighter, fully capable of holding his own in debate and able to draw upon a wealth of political experience.

Robert Lowe and the Case against Reform

The fact that Lowe was a Liberal throws an illuminating light upon the reform controversy. Any simple division of men into progressives and reactionaries neglects the truth that those who have advanced ideas in one sphere of public life may be conservative in another. Lowe typified those Victorians—perhaps a trifle over-earnest for our taste—who wanted good government, that is to say government by the enlightened for the benefit of the unenlightened. To men of his frame of mind democracy would jeopardise liberty by imperilling order. By placing a greater value upon popularity than upon wisdom it would lead to irresponsible government and thence to chaos. Even from a narrow party standpoint it would be fatal for the Liberals to identify their fortunes with democracy. If they failed they would be ruined as a political party, while if they succeeded they would have the sorry consolation of knowing that they were ruining their country. Lowe claimed that all that had been achieved by the Parliaments which had sat since 1832 was ample proof of the excellence of the system under which they were elected. It was for the reformers to show, beyond all reasonable doubt, that what they proposed would result in legislative assemblies of equal excellence.

Lowe was also worried about the stability of government in a democracy: 'The end being good government, in which of course I include stable government, before I give my assent to the admission of fresh classes, I must be satisfied that this admission will make the government better or more stable.' And here Lowe's intensity of feeling betrayed him. He foolishly described the working classes as venal, ignorant, drunken, impulsive, indecent, immoral and violent. He outdid the Radicals in hot-tempered zeal. He talked of the dangers of levelling down, and emphasised the need to retain the vote as a privilege of citizenship. He denounced the tyranny of numbers, and drew upon his experience in both the United States and Australia for examples of corruption and demagogy. He lamented that a democratically elected legislature would be incapable of giving the country the statesmanlike leadership it required. He maintained that democracy would endanger property, for the working classes—and here he was completely mistaken—were already committed to socialism. If the workers were granted political power free trade would be wrecked, strikes would increase and the country's peace would be threatened by class war. Property would be violated, and the country's institutions would perish.

All this seems extravagant and melodramatic today. It is as if

Lowe took the most irresponsible radical propaganda and the most ignorant popular literature and constructed his image of the working classes from them. He ignored the stability of the English working classes. Duped by the few extremists who talked wildly of revolution and socialism, he ignored the majority, who preferred the Bible to Karl Marx and the chapel to atheism. It could be claimed that the surest way of preventing working-class aspirations leading to violence was to bring the workers within the pale of the constitution, where they could give legal expression to their desires, rather than driving them to excess by excluding them from political life. In theory Lowe's case was a powerful one: any honest democrat will admit that the majority can tyrannise as effectively as the minority and that unscrupulous men will seek to win votes by promises, just as others sell them for bribes. But its greatest weakness was that despite its theoretical consistency and its measure of wisdom, it neglected current political realities. It was reminiscent of the Tory viewpoint in 1832. It had similar virtues and similar defects. All Lowe's objections to the working-class franchise had been made against the enfranchisement of the middle classes two generations earlier. Further, Lowe's experiences in the United States and Australia were a mixed blessing. Both he and his opponents were too fond of generalising about British politics from the experience of newer states. They forgot that English society was more complex and more stable, and they overlooked social factors which would limit the immediate consequences of democracy in Britain, factors which did not operate in new countries without deep social roots and established patterns of social behaviour. Lastly, the most serious refutation of Lowe's arguments was one which he himself would be the first to concede if he was alive today: despite all the controversy and the conflicting prophecies, democracy in Britain worked. There was no collapse of government. If anything, governments since 1867 have been more firmly based than ever before.

The Passing of the Second Reform Bill

When Russell succeeded Palmerston the scene was set for another attempt to reform Parliament. On March 12th, 1866

Gladstone introduced a Reform Bill which proposed that the county franchise should be amended to include tenants-at-will paying an annual rent of £14, and that the qualification in the boroughs should be lowered from £10 to £7. He also suggested that men who had had £50 in a Savings Bank for two years should get the vote. Gladstone was seeking to enfranchise the respectable working men, but it is worth noting that despite his 1864 speech he was giving the vote as a reward for working-class thrift. Although Bright supported the Bill, many of the Radicals were dissatisfied. They thought that the government's proposals were too cautious and feared that once they were made effective they might become a barrier to further reform. Thus Russell and Gladstone lacked the united support of those who wanted parliamentary reform. They also faced the opposition of the Conservatives, despite Disraeli's own confession that some measure of reform was necessary. The Conservatives wanted to determine the scope of any reforms, while Disraeli wished the Conservatives to get credit for any extension of the franchise. In addition, the government had to withstand the opposition of Lowe and other like-minded Liberals and Whigs, who were determined to do all they could to thwart reform. Bright christened them the Adullamites, likening them to David and his followers in the cave of Adullam. When the government tried to redistribute several constituencies they found that the Adullamites were strong enough to tip the scales against them. Russell then resigned (June 1866).

Derby and Disraeli took office once again at the head of a minority Conservative administration. The situation was confused and uncertain. Few hazarded a guess at what the future would bring. Lowe distrusted Disraeli even more than he despised Bright and the Radicals, and he and his friends found little comfort in the defeat of the Liberal government. Disraeli certainly favoured reform, but the sincerity of his motives has been questioned. He never forgot that he and his party had been out of office for virtually twenty years. He was as keenly interested in political advantage as in parliamentary reform. He wanted to re-establish the Conservative party as a powerful force in the nation's life, and to embark on a long tenure of power, instead of the brief ministries which he and Derby had enjoyed during the past twenty years. Disraeli was fully prepared to carry a sweeping Bill, more dramatic in content than that Bright and his associates envisaged, if he thought that this would prepare the way for a long and secure Conservative ministry. The prospect of shocking Liberal opinion by outdoing his opponents in innovation appealed to his sense of humour as well as to the romantic Radicalism which was so important an ingredient in his Toryism. But the Conservatives were in a minority in the Commons. Disraeli would have to win the confidence, or at least the support, of several groups. He was also aware of the importance of working-class support, and he did not overlook the effects of the current industrial recession. He had followed the campaign of the Reform League with shrewd concern. Both Disraeli and his Prime Minister, Derby, wanted to settle the reform question. If allowed to drag on it would embitter politics for years, but if the Conservatives could end the wrangle they anticipated that they would reap the rewards. This made Disraeli all the more eager to catch the Whigs bathing and steal their clothes. But even within the Conservative Cabinet opinion was divided. Not even the prospect of a lengthy term of office could still the doubts harboured by Lord Cranborne and other cautious Tories.

In February 1867 the government announced its intention of extending the franchise 'without unduly disturbing the balance of political power'. Their resolutions were couched in the most general terms, for within the Cabinet Cranborne and his supporters were stolidly opposing anything resembling the bold measure which Disraeli had in mind. Disraeli sought to satisfy both the moderates and the Radicals. In addition to the reduction of the franchise qualification in both the counties and the boroughs, he produced his fancy franchises as an insurance against democracy. University graduates, members of the learned professions and those who held £50 in government stock, or who had a similar amount in a Savings Bank, were to have a second vote. But the government lacked the strength to carry the original Bill, and Disraeli soon shocked his less-enthusiastic supporters by displaying a cynical willingness to accept almost every amendment which had the backing of a majority in the Commons. Cranborne and Carnarvon resigned in protest. One by one the fancy franchises were dropped, and even the safeguards on the borough vote, such as the rating qualifications, were swept away. The Bill ended up by giving the vote to all householders who had been resident for a year or more, and all lodgers laying a rent of £10 a year or more, in the towns, while in the counties the vote was given to all £12 householders and to leaseholders of property worth more than £5 a year. Forty-five seats were redistributed, which had the effect of over-representing the counties and bigger towns at the expense of the smaller towns. The final version of the Bill was a significant commentary on the confusions of current political allegiances, yet it is astonishing that Disraeli should have passed a Bill at all. Although his fancy franchises had perished, he had succeeded in getting a Tory Bill through a House in which he was in a minority, and despite the opposition of an important section of his own party. Small wonder that he could not disguise his glee. But his hopes that the newly enfranchised working men would immediately vote Conservative were dashed. Disraeli climbed to the top of the 'greasy pole' when he succeeded Derby as Prime Minister in February 1868, but at the general election later in the year the Liberals were returned and Gladstone—idealistic, high-minded and hard-working—formed his first ministry. Disraeli had to wait until 1874 for confirmation of his belief that his party would eventually make an appeal to the 'Conservative working man'.

The Significance of the 1867 Act

At the time the Second Reform Act seemed a drastic measure. Pessimists were numerous. Men thought of it as a leap in the dark —a phrase coined by Disraeli himself and used by Derby—while Carlyle talked of 'shooting Niagara'. The Act brought great changes. Almost a million voters were added to the register, bringing the total number up to two million. In the towns almost all who were settled at a regular address had the vote, and in the counties the agricultural labourers were virtually the only class which remained outside the political order. Those who moved regularly in their employment were still voteless, unless they also owned property. In the counties the rural districts counted for more politically than the smaller towns. While democracy triumphed in the boroughs, aristocracy still ruled the shires. In some of the small towns, such as Dorchester and Hertford, the electorate was little different from the old one. The biggest impact was made in the provincial towns, such as Cambridge or Ipswich, where the electorate was doubled or even trebled. The greatest change in the political balance took place in the industrial towns. In 1866 Gateshead had 1,165 electors, of whom only 110 were artisans. By 1872 the electorate had increased to 9,191, of whom the vast majority were working men. Similarly, in Newcastle upon Tyne only 1,559 out of 6,630 qualified voters in 1866 were working men. By 1872 the electorate had swelled to 21,407, and once again the majority of the new voters were artisans.

But although the balance of power within the industrial towns had now swung emphatically to democracy, the redistribution of seats which took place in 1867 was far from ironing out the imperfections of the system. There were still too many glaring inconsistencies. Liverpool had a population of half a million; Marylebone of 447,000; yet each returned the same number of M.P.s—two—as Tiverton, with a population of 10,000. The south and west were still over-represented, while the boroughs and agricultural counties were better off than the industrial counties. Wiltshire and Dorset returned a grand total of 25 M.P.s. Their population numbered 450,000. The West Riding of Yorkshire— an industrial area—had a population of 2,000,000, but returned no more than 22 M.P.s for all of its constituencies. Even London, with a population of 3,000,000, returned no more than 24 M.P.s. The effect of the new franchise qualifications and the redistribution of seats was to heighten the contrast between the counties and the boroughs.

In the boroughs a new political order emerged. The large electorates in the industrial towns necessitated new forms of political organisation. In Birmingham, Chamberlain and Schnad-horst showed what could be done. Working through the local Liberal caucus, they skilfully controlled the distribution of

Liberal votes in proportions sufficient to elect all three members, thus evading the intentions behind the provision that no man could cast more than two votes in a three-member constituency. A limitation meant to secure the representation of minorities was thereby exploited to further the plans of the majority. Corruption was not dead—the Ballot Act was not passed until 1872, and legislation was necessary in the 1880s to deal with continued abuses—but large electorates meant that old-fashioned bribery and influence were less effective. Instead, party organisation on the Birmingham model was needed to direct and manipulate votes. In 1867 the National Union of Conservative and Constitutional Associations was founded, and ten years later the National Federation of Liberal Associations was established. National parties now emerged, each with an organisation, a national policy and a national leader. Democracy was not the savage monster many of its critics had anticipated, for it could be disciplined and controlled through party organisation. English politics could never return to the old habits of Pitt, Peel and Palmerston. The future lay with men like Joseph Chamberlain. At long last, after a travail of half a century, the political structure and representative institutions of the country reflected in some measure the social groupings expressive of the distribution of economic power, but the implications of this momentous event had still to be worked out.

10 : Faith and Anxiety

A GENERATION ago the Victorians were the butt for facile satire and malicious humour. Their achievements were decried and their failings ridiculed. The adjective 'Victorian' was synonymous with complacency, hypocrisy, greed, prudery and pride. The sneers of Lytton Strachey showed little understanding of the problems of the age and less compassion for the men who faced them. Pseudo-Marxists earnestly denounced what was fondly thought to have been a period of unrestricted *laissez-faire*. The disillusionment of the First World War and the troubles of the post-war years prompted the rejection of all that the Victorian Age seemed to represent. But recent historians have been both more tolerant and more perceptive. The blithe generalisations of an earlier epoch have been questioned. Research has revealed an astonishing degree of variety in Victorian attitudes and habits of mind, in the scope and pace of industrialisation, in social conventions and religious belief. Qualities which were once regarded as typically Victorian are seen to have their roots in the Regency. The age of *laissez-faire* covers the period of the first Factory Acts. The Industrial Revolution is vindicated as the means whereby the standard of living for the common people was raised, and the privilege of leisure made possible for all. Despite the horrors of urban development, the amenities previously enjoyed by the few came to be shared by the many. The Victorian era—with all its energies, faults and skills—is one of paradox, conflict, doubt and hope.

The Victorians are usually remembered for their solid and useful virtues: thrift, hard work, self-help, temperance and respectability. But it would be foolish to accept these at their face value. There were brutal and violent elements in society which could be ignored but not forgotten. Prostitution in London was notorious. Drunkenness disgraced the large towns. Although there was much sentimentality about children, there was much cruelty to them in all classes of society. The Victorians were reacting against the excesses of the Regency, on the one hand, and the impersonal factors in their midst, on the other. Even their prudery was a genteel attempt to cloak the extent and prevalence of vice. They were trying to create an ordered society, and many of them were becoming increasingly aware of the need for a just society as well. They knew and feared the forces of disorder, whether these were political and economic, or moral and social. In their attempt to evolve worthy standards of public behaviour they lacked an adequate understanding of the relationship between man and society. They were ignorant of psychology and sociology. They thought of conduct in individualistic terms, and had no conception of the significance of heredity and environment in assessing personal responsibility. They sought to establish morality by exhortation, and to deter men from unorthodox conduct by venting the full weight of social ostracism upon all guilty of any moral lapse. Admirable in intention, they were deficient in insight and sympathy. Worse still, it was too easy for their attitude to degenerate into a harsh Pharisaism, where the dutiful observance of externals did service for true purity of heart.

Victorian Religion: Dissenters, Evangelicals, Tractarians

Victorian religion mirrors these strengths and weaknesses. Similar attitudes towards the moral and social problems of the time linked the Evangelical, the Tractarian and the Dissenter. The appalling scale of drunkenness united even Protestants and Catholics on a common temperance platform. Total abstinence from alcohol became a doctrine of the Victorian Age, but it would certainly have seemed strange to the reformers of the sixteenth century, or the Puritans in the seventeenth. It was, however, a genuine response to a distressing social problem whose vast scale was just being realised. Life in the slums of a Victorian town was a grim business, and violence and crime were often precipitated by excessive drinking. The surest way of reducing excess is to remove the conditions which drive men to the bottle to forget their woes, but this is a long-term solution, and the Victorians wanted a prompt and effective answer to their problem.

At the same time, the persistence of drunkenness in the twentieth century, when so many of the more primitive incentives have been curtailed if not destroyed, vindicates the Victorian concern to bring home to all men their personal responsibility for their actions as citizens.

Victorian religion centred round family prayers, and family prayers centred round the Bible. Religious experience was communicated through conventional forms of phrase, usually derived from passages of scripture. This practice gave colour and intensity to the devotions of ordinary folk, but on occasion it clouded important differences of emphasis and meaning, while at other times the phraseology broke down under the weight of emotion which was laid upon it. This failing became more serious as the Victorians lost their grasp on the objective truths of the Christian faith. Their hymn-books reflect the substitution of individual emotion for the more classical approach of the eighteenth century. Reminiscences of Wordsworth and Shelley mingled with echoes of the Bible. Assertion took the place of argument, but this was scarcely surprising when geology and Biblical scholarship were undermining the old certainties. The chronology of Genesis was shown to be deficient, while the order of creation did not tally with that indicated by the study of fossils. These developments stimulated the rise of the religion of feeling, which ignored the discipline of theology while reaffirming individual responsibility. Nature, not grace, became the primary consolation, and such a subjective faith easily degenerated into what one modern writer on science and Christian belief has criticised as the concept of 'a god of the gaps'. Society and science drifted helplessly out of religion's ken.

Certainly there was little social commitment, in any systematic sense, in Victorian religion. Neither the Church of England nor Dissent manifested the more radical implications of Christianity with regard to the structure and values of society. Later in the century this neglect was followed by an intense reaction which laid excessive emphasis upon what came to be called 'the social gospel'. The established Church was committed to the *status quo*, and was too closely identified with the Conservative party for it to bear any sustained witness against the wrongs and injustices of contemporary society. The Nonconformists were too closely linked with the successful middle classes for them to challenge the rampant individualism of the age. Indeed, it may be said that this period sees the substitution of a religion of individual salvation for that of world redemption. Even when they sent out their missionaries, the Victorians tended to think in terms of multiplying the number of individual conversions. The consolations of the hereafter would compensate for the sorrows of the present world order. Anglicans counselled obedience within the pattern of existing social obligation, each man in his station giving due honour to those fortunate enough to be born in more resplendent circumstances. The Dissenters were less submissive to the squire, and less respectful towards the aristocracy, but suggested that by self-help and application one could rise in the scale, and that by doing so the individual could demonstrate his own election. Religion was too much an affair of conformity and success, but even beneath the outward forms there lurked sinister realities. The working classes of the towns were scarcely touched by any denomination, except by the Primitive Methodists in the north. Yet the gibe that Nonconformity was middle class needs some qualification. Thrift, hard work, abstinence and fidelity were the virtues lauded by Dissent. Any man who practised them (with any success) was certain to become bourgeois, and this undoubtedly represented an advance on the disordered and primitive life which was the fate of too many of the workers in the industrial towns. Nor were the Nonconformists happy with their limited appeal. While the Congregationalists admitted that their destiny seemed to be to minister to those of the middling sort, they lamented that they were not making a bigger impact upon the working classes. They were disturbed by the prevalence of coarse sensuality among the poor in the towns, and distressed at their own failure to combat it. It may be objected—and Matthew Arnold voiced the criticism —that a religion such as Dissent was hardly likely to make any impression upon the working class, but at least the charge of complacency can be overcome. Similarly, despite the identification of the Church of England with the established social order, there were many men, usually convinced Evangelicals or dedicated disciples of the Oxford Movement, who spent their lives in the grim slums of the great towns. History has so often been written by anti-clericals that it is all too rarely just to the parson.

Nor is it true to imply that the churches were in a state of torpor. Though Nonconformity saved most of its energies for bitter and vindictive battles with the Establishment over such matters as church rates and education, it was not dead intellectually. The Dissenters were sympathetic to German scholarship, and this softened the insularity which Arnold made so much of in his celebrated denunciation of their failings. Later in the century English Nonconformity responded to German liberalism with remarkable speed, but modern scholars have shown that orthodox belief about the Person of Christ and traditional interpretations of Baptism and Holy Communion persisted among Dissenters until the middle of the nineteenth century. In organisation some important changes took place. Presbyterianism was re-established in England as an independent and Trinitarian denomination in 1836. In 1832 the old Independency was replaced by modern Congregationalism, when the Congregational Union of England and Wales was inaugurated to facilitate co-operation between Independent congregations. Methodism suffered several schisms during the first half of the nineteenth century, but the Wesleyans and Primitive Methodists remained the two major branches of the denomination.

Whatever the deficiencies of the Dissenting Churches, they brought culture, comfort and inspiration to the lower-middle and respectable working classes of the north. Arnold decried the illiberal and stifling nature of Dissent, its excessive emphasis on what he cared to call the Hebraic side of Christianity—that is to say the moral and ethical aspects of the faith. He scoffed at tea-meetings and sermons and endless exhortations to do something practical, but despite its measure of truth, it would be misleading to take Arnold's account as either a complete description or a fair one. He himself knew that he was exploiting irony and wit to expose those faults which he thought particularly dangerous. The importance of Dissent in firing the consciences of reformers, radicals, trade unionists and pioneer socialists can never be over-emphasised, while the structure of the Dissenting Churches gave many men of humble origins valuable experience in public speaking, in committee work, in handling financial matters and in conducting meetings and conferences. The Bible gave these men whatever culture they possessed and taught them to fight injustice wherever they saw it. The Authorised Version was no mean primer, and the imagination of many self-educated men was roused by the Psalms, the Prophetic Books, the Gospels and the Epistles. Later they might prefer to read Mill or Spencer or perhaps Arnold himself, but whatever culture there was in most mining villages emanated from the ugly Methodist or Baptist or Congregationalist chapel on the main street. It might not have represented 'sweetness and light'; it was undeniably imperfect; and it was incapable of educating the whole man. But it was the primary source of enlightenment and the greatest challenge to unrelieved materialism and the wearisome monotony of toil. It brought fire and strength into the lives of men who needed a faith by which to steer.

Evangelicalism remained the greatest driving force in the Church of England during the first third of the nineteenth century. Like Nonconformity, it laid particular stress upon individual commitment, personal morality and the domestic virtues. Like Nonconformity, it was too individualistic, while its concept of the Church was less fully developed. But the intensity of conviction which inspired people such as Wilberforce and Ashley proved a powerful agency in the betterment of society. The Evangelical laid great emphasis upon changing the world by changing the individual, and if he did not possess a coherent picture of the sort of society he wanted to create, this was virtually unavoidable, given the circumstances of the time. He usually stuck to a literal interpretation of the Bible and a penal-substitutionary doctrine of the Atonement. He was often weak in theology, taking traditional statements of faith more or less on trust, and this explains the panic provoked by Darwinism. After Darwin published his *Origin of Species* in 1859 the Evangelicals were loudest in challenging his hypotheses, but they were not alone. Samuel Wilberforce, the Bishop of Oxford, rushed into controversy with little knowledge of the subjects he was debating and little regard for the decencies of debate. Huxley soon exposed the Bishop's ignorance, and the Church had to suffer the ill-effects of Wilberforce's rashness for many years. Darwin himself was more cautious than many of his followers about the theological or sociological implications of his theories of biological evolution. He never shared the uncompromising agnosticism of Huxley. But the Evangelicals never recovered from the discredit which their rather pathetic sophistries brought upon them. Suggestions that the appearance of fossils might be delusory were brushed aside by the counter-assertion that if this was so God must have planted them in the earth in order to baffle and deceive humanity.

Further, the Evangelicals were uncharitable and short-sighted when dealing with those members of the Church of England who tried to restate their faith in the light of scientific discoveries. The publication of *Essays and Reviews*, a collection of articles by seven distinguished Anglicans, provoked another tempestuous controversy, following, as it did, less than a year after the issue of *Origin of Species*. Indeed, to contemporaries the second dispute was even more sensational than the first, for the Church was divided against itself. Accusations of dishonesty were hurled at scholars who had dared to question accepted formulations of religious belief, and doctrines such as the literal inspiration of the Bible and the historical accuracy of the Pentateuch. That they had arrived at their views before Darwin published his theories relating to the evolution of species is a reminder that Darwin's work was the culmination of an intellectual movement covering a quarter of a century. It is also a tribute to the determination of Pattison, Jowett, Temple and their associates to meet a contemporary need in a contemporary style. But the bishops and clergy were bewildered by their honesty of thought. The innovators failed to reshape the thinking of the Church, although a generation later their views had passed into general circulation. Ecclesiastical discipline was invoked in order to defeat a party which was guilty of reprehensible originality: the majority of churchmen preferred to reaffirm imprecise and questionable notions in well-remembered if perplexing language. Ultimately several of the authors gained the accolade of respectability: Jowett became Master of Balliol and

Temple Archbishop of Canterbury. But the controversy was a sorry commentary on the attitude of the ecclesiastical hierarchy towards scholarship. Despite all the advantages of a monopoly of higher education, the Church of England produced only a handful of first-class theologians. No one emerged who was capable of assimilating the findings of continental scholarship in order to translate revealed truths into the language of the age.

At first it had seemed that the Oxford Movement might meet the need. Keble, Pusey and Newman originally protested against attacks on the privileges of the Church of England in the 1830s, but in stating their beliefs in order to combat national apostasy they found that they had to diverge from the accepted interpretation of several of the Thirty-nine Articles, though they claimed that the conventional reading was not the only valid one. They deplored the attacks which the Dissenters and Radicals made upon the Established Church, but they writhed under the domination of the state, and in vindicating the claims of the Church as a divinely instituted society they reaffirmed doctrines of extreme episcopalianism derived from the theory of Apostolic Succession. They wandered farther from the Protestant path. They looked back beyond the Caroline divines and the Elizabethans to the English Church of the late Middle Ages. They were more enamoured of the Church of Augustine, Anselm and Becket than of the Church of Henry VIII and Cranmer. They sensed the inadequacy of identifying the Church with the nation. They made great claims for the Church as a supernatural institution, and their historical imagination (it was hardly historical scholarship) led them to deal ever more sympathetically with the Church of Rome. Soon they were displaying a disturbing fondness for what most Englishmen regarded as Popish superstitions: the doctrine of Purgatory, masses for the dead, the veneration of the Virgin and the Saints. Their views on the nature of the priesthood and the meaning of Baptism and Holy Communion brought them into conflict with both conservative Evangelicals and traditional Broad Churchmen, whose distaste for dogma ensured that they had scant use for doctrines reminiscent of Rome. Although much controversy later took place over the attempts of the Anglo-Catholic party within

o

the Church of England to revive what they presumed were the ritualistic practices of the medieval Church, the Oxford Movement was not primarily an attempt to change accepted habits in worship. It was much more ambitious. Newman and Pusey dreamed of creating a renewed Church of England, with a theology, discipline and worship worthy of its status as the historic Church of the land. The leaders of the Oxford Movement lacked the intellectual stature and spiritual courage necessary for such a task. Although too much attention has been paid to their temperamental weaknesses and psychological problems, their deficiencies of character and mental instability were too great. Their appeal to history was not based on any thorough study of the past: it was too dilettante, too fanciful, too poetic. Instead of working out a restatement of faith in contemporary terms they issued apologias for their personal beliefs and actions. They were as obscurantist as the Evangelicals when dealing with the challenge of science, while liberalism had frightening connotations for them, both in politics and scholarship. Some historians have seen them as comprising the last ecclesiastical movement produced by pre-scientific Oxford. At the same time they suffered from the Englishman's aggressive dislike of the Church of Rome, a prejudice which was roused to fury in 1850, when the Pope decided to set up a diocesan hierarchy in England. In the following year Lord John Russell's Ecclesiastical Titles Act—passed against the opposition of Gladstone and the Peelites—forbade the Catholic Bishops to take titles already used by those of the Church of England. It was a mean piece of legislation, John Bright condemning it as 'little, paltry, and miserable—a mere sham to bolster up Church ascendancy'. Twenty years later Gladstone repealed the Act, which had never been more than a truculent gesture, but Russell had taken care to attack the 'Puseyites' as well as the Catholics, and in the minds of many people a sinister connection was established between the two. The Anglo-Catholics were popularly regarded as a fifth column within the Church of England.

The most gifted of the Tractarians, John Henry Newman, found the logic of events irresistible, and in 1845 he was received into the Catholic Church. He lived the rest of his life in seclusion, justifying in elegant prose his own integrity when this was challenged with characteristic energy by Charles Kingsley. But Newman never found the total spiritual peace for which he yearned. He never quelled the sceptical bent of his mind, although he sidestepped the Darwinian controversy and ignored the questions raised by Biblical scholarship. The Catholic Church appealed to his imagination, his feeling for history, his preoccupation with the doctrine of development, but it never quite stilled the doubts which lay in his mind. He would not admit this, saying that ten thousand difficulties did not make one doubt, but language such as this was evasive enough for Kingsley and others to denounce Newman as a sophist, an over-subtle controversialist whose fondness for splitting hairs made any sincere exchange of views impossible. Newman was honest, however, in dealing with his critics. He was less candid in dealing with himself.

Those who tired of the obstinacy of the Evangelicals or the preciosity of the Oxford Movement turned to something more in tune with the spirit of the mid-Victorian age: muscular Christianity, typified by the bluff, vigorous, kind-hearted, sentimental Charles Kingsley. This reflected the weariness of the middle classes with dogma and doctrine and all the traditional concerns of theology and ecclesiastical controversy, as well as their obsession with utility. The advocates of 'muscular Christianity' fled from the problems of belief by throwing themselves enthusiastically into inculcating moral living and good works. Kingsley dabbled in Christian Socialism, and many like-minded men distinguished themselves by their efforts for the working classes and the poor. It has been suggested that Kingsley's Christianity was little more than the cult of a healthy outdoor life, expressive of a schoolboy enthusiasm for high spirits and outdoor pursuits and a contempt for the allegedly effeminate postures of Oxford and Rome. This is as unfair as the suggestion that all Anglo-Catholics were sickly poseurs, but it contains a germ of truth. Yet a down-to-earth Christianity commended itself to practical men. It eluded the conflict of religion and science, as well as abstruse disputes relating to episcopacy and the Articles. It made a strong appeal to middle-class parents who wanted their boys to grow up as honest

Englishmen, with no nonsense about religion. Its concern for social service gave it a common interest with the earnest agnosticism exemplified by T. H. Huxley and George Eliot. It was finally enshrined in the public schools of the second half of the nineteenth century, with their preoccupation with manliness, athleticism, the team spirit, patriotism and the conventional religion of good form. Thomas Arnold had had a nobler ideal: godliness and good learning, in which scholarship and faith had gone hand in hand. But this was suited only to the minority of boys who were fitted for it intellectually. When the middle classes demanded new public schools for their sons they wanted something less exacting. The English gentleman replaced the Christian scholar as the ideal type.

Literary Responses to Contemporary Problems

The Victorian Age was weak in music, the visual arts and architecture. It preferred spurious imitation or quaint revival to genuine originality, and fussy decoration to bold simplicity. Though changing fashions have led to a more sympathetic attitude towards Victorian art, it would be unfortunate if excessive condemnation was succeeded by exaggerated praise. In literature the mid-Victorians were strong. The range of style and content represented by Dickens, Thackeray, the Brontës, George Eliot and Trollope is immense, and these novelists were all critical of the received ideas of their time. Dickens was a man of his age in his love of death-bed sentiment, his partiality for the grotesque, his belief that most men were decent at heart. But he denounced the contemporary adulation of riches and success, and his novels often mirror the social problems of the time—the new Poor Law, the effects of railway development, the harshness of transportation, the evils of imprisonment for debt, the exploitation of children, the consequences of an over-complex legal system. He pilloried the narrow-minded, the avaricious, the hypocritical and the self-righteous. His themes were often powerful, and he vividly portrayed the London underworld, yet he contrived to win the devotion of many readers who ought to have been more shocked than they were. He was so successful a story teller that he probably had less effect than he desired as a social reformer. Similarly,

George Eliot expressed the lofty concern of the Victorians for issues of personal responsibility, loyalty, doubt and faith. In her youth she had been a devout Calvinist, but acquaintance with German philosophy made it impossible for her to remain faithful to Christian doctrine, though she admired the ethics of the Sermon on the Mount. She could not believe in the divinity of Christ, or in the traditional after-life, yet she never fully threw off the effects of her upbringing. Repelled by dogmatic assertion, she was sympathetic to mysticism—to religion as the fruit of personal experience rather than divine revelation. In this, as in her severe and austere devotion to goodness, she represented the wistful rather than the aggressive side of Victorian agnosticism. She sought her consolation amidst the choir invisible, and in the notion that goodness and truth had an eternal value, despite the failure of old faiths.

Tennyson is the poet usually associated with Victorianism, though the more energetic, less melodious and more obscure Browning was as able an exponent of contemporary attitudes. But Tennyson was the more torn by the contemporary struggle between faith and doubt, optimism and pessimism. There were times when he cheerfully wished the world to spin for ever down the ringing grooves of change, confident that fifty years of Europe were better than a cycle of Cathay, and when his vision of the future was filled with dreams of prosperity and peace. But he was also prone to fits of gloom and despondency, when he warned his readers that the onward march of progress was capable of turning back upon itself. His most famous poem *In Memoriam* was written long before the appearance of *Origin of Species*, yet it illustrates the impact of the discoveries of geology and biology upon a sensitive man, broken by grief at the loss of a close friend and struggling to cling to the consolations of religion. Tennyson could not forget the pitiless struggle for existence within the natural order, and the apparent indifference of the universe towards the individual:

> Are God and Nature then at strife,
>   That Nature lends such evil dreams?
>   So careful of the type she seems,
> So careless of the single life;

> That I, considering everywhere
>   Her secret meaning in her deeds,
>   And finding that of fifty seeds
> She often brings but one to bear,
>
> I falter where I firmly trod,
>   And falling with my weight of cares
>   Upon the great world's altar-stairs
> That slope through darkness up to God,
>
> I stretch lame hands of faith, and grope,
>   And gather dust and chaff, and call
>   To what I feel is Lord of all,
> And faintly trust the larger hope.

Tennyson never gave up hope. He confessed that if he abandoned all faith that somewhere in the universe there was a God he 'should not care a pin for anything'. Despite all his misgivings, he looked forward to the time when faith and reason would be at one:

> Let knowledge grow from more to more,
>   But more of reverence in us dwell;
>   That mind and soul, according well,
> May make one music as before,
>
> But vaster ...

However vague his notion of God's existence, he affirmed his poetic conviction that the whole creation was moving towards some divine event. It was dim and far-distant, but Tennyson trusted that it would eventually take place. Again, this was the religion of the heart, of feeling, of personal experience, verified, not by the intellect but by the intensity and refinement of emotional commitment.

John Stuart Mill and the New Utilitarianism

But Christianity was not the only faith which was questioned in the middle years of the century. The long sway of Benthamism was coming to an end. The deficiencies of the classical Utilitarian doctrines were becoming more and more apparent, and this growing scepticism was reflected in the life and work of the son of Bentham's most devoted disciple. John Stuart Mill is another of those wistful mid-Victorians, whose mind was divided between confidence and doubt. He was an anxious Radical, in startling contrast to the bustling and cocksure Bright. Mill had been given an intensive education by his father, and he never recovered from the cramping effects of intellectual precocity, allied to emotional deprivation. He was intellectually honest, sympathetic to new ideas and extremely well intentioned, but there was a priggish, fussy quality about his thought. He was too honest to pretend that Utilitarianism could be sustained with all Bentham's harsh consistency and uncompromising tenacity. Mill softened the doctrine, but in admitting many qualifications he robbed the system of its main asset—its brutal clarity. He recognised differences in the degrees and types of pleasure. Instead of the unflinching application of the pleasure/pain principle, Mill substituted an appeal to majority opinion in order to ascertain a pleasure's worth or desirability, and brightly talked of the superiority of being Socrates dissatisfied to being a fool satisfied. But in doing so he betrayed an attitude radically different from that of Bentham. While Bentham's energies were dedicated to the attainment of happiness, by securing the free and unhindered operation of the pleasure/pain mechanism, Mill's first loyalty was given to liberty.

Mill valued liberty more than any other ideal. He interpreted it in terms of the spontaneous development of each individual's faculties, and he felt that this was threatened not only by legislation and traditional social conventions but also by the tyranny which could be exercised by the majority. Social tyranny could be as confining as legal tyranny, and the tyranny of opinion could bear heavily upon the enlightened minority. Though in his essay *Utilitarianism* Mill had come very close to advocating majority opinion as the surest way of deciding a controversy, he became increasingly worried by the dangers of democracy. He knew that the majority could err, and that the imaginative few—upon whom the future progress of humanity depended—were easily exposed to persecution and injustice. Thus, although he believed in representative government, he sought some means of protecting the progressive minority. In *On Liberty*, which was first published in 1859, he tried to resolve the conflict between the claims of the individual and those of society.

He wished to preserve as large a sphere of activity for the individual as possible, and he stated his purpose clearly:

> 'The object of this Essay is to assert one very simple principle, as entitled to govern absolutely the dealings of society with the individual in the way of compulsion and control, whether the means used be physical force in the form of legal penalties, or the moral coercion of public opinion. That principle is, that the sole end for which mankind are warranted, individually or collectively, in interfering with the liberty of action of any of their number, is self-protection. That the only purpose for which power can be rightfully exercised over any member of a civilised community, against his will, is to prevent harm to others. His own good, either physical or moral, is not a sufficient warrant.'
>
> *On Liberty*, Chapter I

But the application of this principle was fraught with difficulties. Mill immediately added that the doctrine was to apply only to those 'in the maturity of their faculties'. He was not speaking of children or young people, for these were still in a state to require being taken care of by others, and they therefore had to be protected against their own actions as well as against external injury. He conceded that compulsion was necessary at certain stages of historical or political development, but civilisation implied that it should be kept to a minimum. He distinguished between actions which concerned only the individual and those which affected society: when a person disabled himself, by conduct which was purely self-regarding, from the performance of some duty which he owed to the public, he was guilty of a social offence—'No person ought to be punished simply for being drunk; but a soldier or policeman should be punished for being drunk on duty.' Mill was aware of the limitations of this distinction between self-regarding and other regarding actions, but he maintained that in practice it was the safest standard by which to justify action by the authorities with respect to the behaviour of individual members of society.

Mill was at his best when defending the right of free speech. His sincere respect for truth, and his earnest desire that men should come to a deeper apprehension of it, led him to plead the case for liberty of discussion. His defence of the free exchange of ideas has not been bettered:

'We have now recognised the necessity to the mental well-being of mankind (on which all their other well-being depends) of freedom of opinion, and freedom of the expression of opinion, on four distinct grounds; which we will now briefly recapitulate.

'First, if any opinion is compelled to silence, that opinion may, for aught we can certainly know, be true. To deny this is to assume our own infallibility.

'Secondly, though the silenced opinion be an error, it may, and very commonly does, contain a portion of truth; and since the general or prevailing opinion on any subject is rarely or never the whole truth, it is only by the collision of adverse opinions that the remainder of the truth has any chance of being supplied.

'Thirdly, even if the received opinion be not only true, but the whole truth; unless it is suffered to be, and actually is, vigorously and earnestly contested, it will, by most of those who receive it, be held in the manner of a prejudice, with little comprehension or feeling of its rational grounds. And not only this, but, fourthly, the meaning of the doctrine itself will be in danger of being lost, or enfeebled, and deprived of its vital effect on the character and conduct: the dogma becoming a mere formal profession, inefficacious for good, but cumbering the ground, and preventing the growth of any real and heartfelt conviction, from reason or personal experience.'

On Liberty, Chapter II.

This was well said, and remains a priceless statement of liberal belief, but Mill was, nevertheless, too individualistic in his approach. He distrusted the state too much to realise that it could be the agent of a fuller life, not merely the enemy of the individual's right to self-fulfilment. One modern critic has expressed this as the difference between a negative, as distinct from a positive, concept of liberty. Mill tended to think that the individual was in conflict with society, but it is impossible to talk of one without the other. The individual is born into a society whose standards of conduct and forms of belief influence his whole development.

There must, inevitably, be tension between the desires of the individual and the pressures (both for good and ill) laid upon him by society, but it is only in society that the individual can be said to have any rights at all. A later generation of liberals, of whom the most convincing was T. H. Green, sought to retain Mill's regard for the rights of the individual, while recognising that the state could play a more positive role in creating the conditions in society which made a fuller and more satisfying life possible for the members of the community. Mill shrank from state action—even in the field of education—and preferred to see certain tasks performed by voluntary organisations. He failed to understand that many tasks in an industrial and urban society had become too great to be adequately performed by voluntary action. He also failed to anticipate the great problem of the twentieth century: what is to be the attitude of the democrat or liberal towards those factions in society which seek to exploit democracy only in order to destroy it? The dilemma created for all lovers of freedom by the ruthless abuse of liberty by Fascists and Communists is still a live issue today. Mill lacked the vision to perceive that here lay the greatest of all threats to that free interplay of ideals which he cherished so passionately. In other matters, such as the emancipation of women, he was in advance of his time, and whatever his faults, he remains an impressive and attractive figure. He never understood Christianity, and his discussion of it is usually inadequate. Like many mid-Victorians, he substituted hope for faith as the inner principle of his life, but hope is none the less a theological virtue.

Matthew Arnold and the Plea for Sweetness and Light

Ruskin devoted himself to the effort to arouse his contemporaries to a more sensitive and less moralistic appreciation of art, while Carlyle, the rhetorical and verbose admirer of the strong, silent men of history, castigated the pettymindedness of an unheroic age. But the most perceptive of the Victorian critics of Victorianism was Matthew Arnold, whose *Culture and Anarchy* is the classic statement of the case against so much of nineteenth-century life. The son of the famous headmaster of Rugby, and distinguished as a poet and literary critic, Arnold had also had experience as a schools inspector. He knew the England which he wrote about at first-hand, for his work had taken him into many of the most depressing, and most typical, of the new towns. With wit, irony and a shrewd eye for the exploitation of detail, he exposed the materialism, selfishness and ignorance of English society. He did not share Carlyle's romantic illusions about the aristocracy, but he was equally scornful of Bright's cheerful optimism concerning the middle and working classes. He attacked the failings of all sections of society, using the terms Barbarian for the aristocracy, Philistine for the middle classes and Populace for the working classes.

> 'All of us, so far as we are Barbarians, Philistines, or Populace, imagine happiness to consist in doing what one's ordinary self likes. What one's ordinary self likes differs according to the class to which one belongs, and has its severer and its lighter side; always, however, remaining machinery and nothing more. The graver self of the Barbarian likes honours and consideration; his more relaxed self, field-sports and pleasure. The graver self of one kind of Philistine likes fanaticism, business, and money-making; his more relaxed self, comfort and tea-meetings. Of another kind of Philistine, the graver self likes rattening; the relaxed self, deputations, or hearing Mr Odger speak. The sterner self of the Populace likes bawling, hustling, and smashing; the lighter self, beer.'
>
> *Culture and Anarchy*, Chapter III.

Arnold shuddered at the insularity of English life. He was well versed in French and German literature as well as the classics, and he was acquainted with the French and German systems of education. He deplored the tendency to reiterate ideas without thinking about them, and he pleaded for men 'to allow their thought and consciousness to play on their stock notions and habits disinterestedly'. This he called 'the belief in right reason and in a firm intelligible law of things', and he hoped to persuade men 'to try, in preference to staunchly acting with imperfect knowledge, to obtain some sounder basis of knowledge on which to act'. He was appalled by the provinciality of Dissent, by the bitterness of sectarian passion, by 'hole-in-corner' religion, by the mutual antagonisms between ecclesiastical denominations and the classes of society. He lamented the self-satisfaction of all three social classes:

> 'The Barbarians remain in the belief that the great broad-shouldered genial Englishman may be well satisfied with himself; the Philistines remain in the belief that the great middle class of this country, with its earnest common-sense penetrating through sophisms and ignoring common-places, may be well satisfied with itself; the Populace, that the working man with his bright powers of sympathy and ready powers of action, may be well satisfied with himself . . .'

Arnold despised any concept of education as a useful commodity which could be dispensed in quantities sufficient to ensure affluence, commercial success or technological efficiency. Like Mill, he was preoccupied with the full and complete development of the individual: 'perfection . . . is a harmonious expression of *all* the powers which make the beauty and worth of human nature, and is not consistent with the over-development of any one power at the expense of the rest'. But this ideal clashed with the growing materialism of the age, a materialism which was all the more dangerous because it was disguised under the trappings of nominal religion:

> 'The idea of perfection as an *inward* condition of mind and spirit is at variance with the mechanical and material civilisation in esteem with us, and nowhere, as I have said, so much in esteem as with us. The idea of perfection as a *general* expansion of the human family is at variance with our strong individualism, our hatred of all limits to the unrestrained swing of the individual's personality, our maxim of "every man for himself". Above all, the idea of perfection as a harmonious expansion of human nature is at variance with our want of flexibility, with our inaptitude for seeing more than one side of a thing, with our intense energetic absorption in the particular pursuit we happen to be following.'
> *Culture and Anarchy*, Chapter I.

The nation's wealth had corrupted the nation's soul—'Never did people believe anything more firmly, than nine Englishmen out of ten at the present day believe that our greatness and welfare are proved by our being so very rich.' Arnold commented on the attitude of the rest of the world towards Britain's achievements; though industrial power was envied, there was little love or admiration for Britain, and in Arnold's view this was a judgment on her sense of moral values:

> 'British freedom, British industry, British muscularity, we work for each of these things blindly, with no notion of giving each its due proportion and prominence, because we have no ideal of harmonious human perfection before our minds, to set our work in motion, and to guide it. So the rest of the world, desiring industry, or freedom, or bodily strength, yet desiring these not, as we do, absolutely, but as means to something else, imitate, indeed, of our practice what seems useful for them, but us, whose practice they imitate, they seem to entertain neither love nor admiration for.'
>
> *Culture and Anarchy*, Chapter V.

Against the utilitarianism of the age Arnold stood out for 'sweetness and light'.

Of course there were weaknesses in his argument. Like his father before him, he thought too much in terms of the Church as the nation on its spiritual side, and much of his defence of the Establishment looks like highly sophisticated special pleading. He never grasped the force of Dissenting objections to the state Church, or the thinking which lay behind Tractarian denunciations of the Church of England's subjection to the state. Recent historians have placed much more emphasis on the economic and social factors which produced the provinciality of so much English middle-class life, rather than simply blaming the Dissenters. The fact that the Dissenters were still virtually excluded from the universities when Arnold wrote reminds us that they were treated—together with the Roman Catholics—as second-class citizens in some respects. Dissent was often bitter, vindictive, brash and aggressive—but the Church of England was no pure apostle of sweetness and light. There was also an element of intellectual condescension in Arnold's discussion of modern innovations, such as the railways, and in his reaction to the objections which Cobden and Bright made to the limitations of the conventional classical education. But, despite his faults, his criticism of contemporary values and practice was a much-needed corrective to superficial encomiums on improvement.

Envoi

The mid-Victorians were proud of their technological and material success, and for many people this bred a complacent satisfaction with things as they were. Even when the aroma of religion was retained this was little more than the deification of success. But many profound thinkers and sensitive spirits were appalled by the increasing lure of financial gain and the glorification of things temporal. However immense the problems which they faced, the Victorians never ceased to grapple with them. A society threatened by shallow materialism from within and by aggressive totalitarianism from without can ill afford to sneer at the efforts made in the nineteenth century to resolve the recurring problems of faith and doubt, individual responsibility and social freedom. Despite their disillusionments, and their awakening consciousness that knowledge could enslave as well as liberate the human mind, the Victorians never gave up their resolve

> To follow knowledge like a sinking star,
> Beyond the utmost bound of human thought.

They doubted the consolations of traditional religion, but there were other consolations:

> Though much is taken, much abides; and though
> We are not now that strength which in old days
> Moved earth and heaven; that which we are, we are;
> One equal temper of heroic hearts,
> Made weak by time and fate, but strong in will
> To strive, to seek, to find, and not to yield.

Chronological Table

Date	Home	Abroad
1793	Repression in Scotland	France declares war on Britain
		First Coalition
		Flanders campaign opens
1794	Habeas Corpus suspended	'Glorious First of June'
	Treason Trials in London	Fall of Robespierre: Directory set up in France
		Holland an ally of France
1795	Seditious Meetings Act	
	Treasonable Practices Act	
1796		Spain joins France
		Bonaparte's Italian campaigns
1797	Cash payments suspended	St Vincent
	Mutinies at Spithead and the Nore	Treaty of Campo Formio
		Camperdown
1798	Irish Rebellion	Bonaparte's Egyptian Expedition
		Battle of the Nile
1799	Anti-Combination Laws	Second Coalition
		Brumaire
		Bonaparte First Consul
		Marengo
		Hohenlinden
1801	Union of British and Irish Parliaments	Treaty of Lunéville
	Pitt's resignation	Armed Neutrality of the North
	Addington forms his ministry	Copenhagen
1802		Peace of Amiens
1803	Volunteer Movement	Outbreak of War between France and Britain
		Bonaparte plans invasion of England
1804	Pitt's second ministry	Napoleon Emperor of the French
		Pitt sets about forming Third Coalition
1805		Ulm
		Trafalgar
		Austerlitz

Date	Home	Abroad
1806	Death of Pitt	Fox initiates abortive peace negotiations
	Ministry of 'All the Talents'	Jena
	Death of Fox	
1807	Prohibition of the Slave Trade	Treaty of Tilsit
	Portland ministry	Berlin Decrees
	Orders in Council	
1807		Napoleon invades Portugal
1808		Napoleon intervenes in Spain
		Baylen
		Vimiero
		Convention of Cintra
1809	Perceval Prime Minister	Corunna
		Walcheren Expedition
		Talavera
		Wagram
1810	George III's last bout of insanity	Torres Vedras
1811	Regency	Fuentes d'Oñoro
		Albuera
1812	Assassination of Perceval	Napoleon's Russian campaign
	Liverpool Prime Minister	Storming of Cuidad Rodrigo and Badajoz
		Salamanca
		War with the United States
1813		Vittoria
		Leipzig
1814		Abdication of Napoleon
		Peace with the United States
		Congress of Vienna opens
1815	Corn Laws	'Hundred Days'
		Waterloo
		Vienna Peace Settlement
		Quadruple Alliance
		Holy Alliance
1816	Abolition of Income Tax	
	Spa Fields Riot	
	March of the Blanketeers	
1818		Congress of Aix-la-Chapelle
1819	Peterloo	Acquisition of Singapore
	Six Acts	
	Renewal of Cash Payments	
1820	Death of George III	Revolutions in Spain, Portugal, Naples, Piedmont
	Accession of George IV	
	Cato Street Conspiracy	Congress of Troppau
1821		Congress of Laibach
		Greek Rebellion

Date	Home	Abroad
1822	Castlereagh's suicide Canning Foreign Secretary Liverpool reforms his ministry	Congress of Verona
1823	Peel begins his reform of the Penal Code Huskisson initiates reforms at Board of Trade	
1824	Anti-Combination Acts repealed	
1825		Greeks recognised as belligerents Ibrahim Pasha in the Morea
1827	Huskisson's Sliding Scale Liverpool's stroke Canning's short Premiership and death Wellington Prime Minister	Navarino
1828	Corporation and Test Acts repealed	
1829	Metropolitan Police Force set up Catholic Emancipation	Treaty of Adrianople
1830	Death of George IV Accession of William IV Agrarian disorders Grey forms Whig ministry	Greek independence recognised Revolutions in France, Poland, Belgium, Germany, Italy and Portugal Louis Philippe King of the French
1831	Struggle for Reform Bill	Mehemet Ali revolts against Sultan
1832	First Reform Bill passed	
1833	Factory Act Abolition of slavery throughout British Empire	Treaty of Unkiar Skelessi British intervention in Portugal
1834	Poor Law Amendment Act Tolpuddle Martyrs Melbourne Prime Minister Peel's short-lived ministry Tamworth manifesto	Franco–British intervention in Spain
1835	Melbourne returns to office Municipal Corporations Act Irish Tithe Act	
1836	Registration of births, deaths and marriages	
1837	Death of William IV Accession of Victoria	Rebellions in Canada
1839	First Chartist Petition Bedchamber Crisis Anti-Corn Law League founded	The Powers guarantee Belgian independence and neutrality Opium War Durham Report
1840	Penny Post	

P

Date	Home	Abroad
1841	Peel's Second Ministry	Straits Convention
1842	Second Chartist Petition Peel reduces duties Peel's income tax Sliding Scale Mines Act	
1844	Bank Charter Act Companies Act Factory Act	
1845	Maynooth Grant Irish famine	
1846	Peel amends Corn Laws Fall of Peel Russell Prime Minister Potato famine in Ireland	Spanish Marriages Crisis
1847	Fielden's Factory Act	
1848	Third Chartist Petition Smith O'Brien's rebellion in Ireland	Revolutions in France, Austria, Germany and Italy Louis Napoleon Bonaparte President of French Republic
1849	Repeal of Navigation Acts	
1850	Death of Peel Ecclesiastical Titles Bill	'Don Pacifico'
1851	Great Exhibition Fall of Palmerston	Louis Napoleon Prince-President
1852	Palmerston's 'Tit-for-Tat' Fall of Russell Derby–Disraeli ministry Aberdeen ministry	Napoleon III Emperor of the French
1854		Crimean War begins
1855	Palmerston's first ministry	Fall of Sebastopol
1856		Treaty of Paris *Arrow* incident
1857		Indian Mutiny
1858	Conspiracy to Murder Bill Resignation of Palmerston Second Derby–Disraeli ministry	Orsini's plot
1859	Palmerston's second ministry Volunteer Movement	Italian War of Liberation begins
1860	Gladstone's Free Trade policy at Exchequer	Cobden Free Trade Treaty with France Garibaldi's Sicilian Expedition
1861	Death of Prince Consort	Italy united under House of Savoy American Civil War begins
1862	Cotton famine in Lancashire	*Trent* affair *Alabama* escapes

Date	Home	Abroad
1863		Polish revolt
1864		Schleswig–Holstein Crisis
1865	Death of Palmerston	End of American Civil War
	Russell Prime Minister	
1866	Attempted Reform of Parliament	Austro–Prussian War
	Fall of Russell's government	
	Third Derby–Disraeli ministry	
1867	Second Reform Bill passed	
1868	Disraeli Prime Minister	
	Gladstone's first ministry	

THE NEAR AND MIDDLE EAST

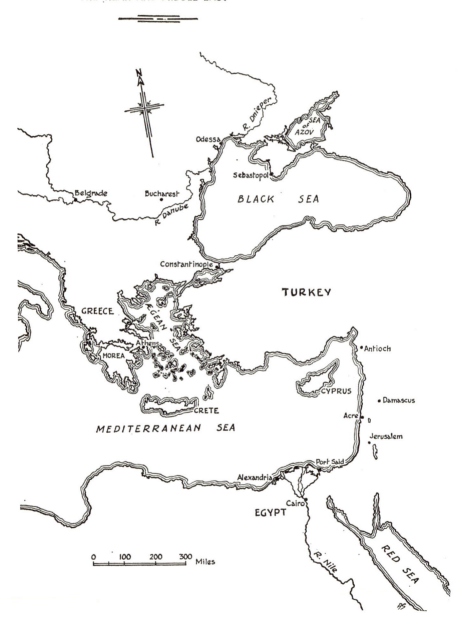

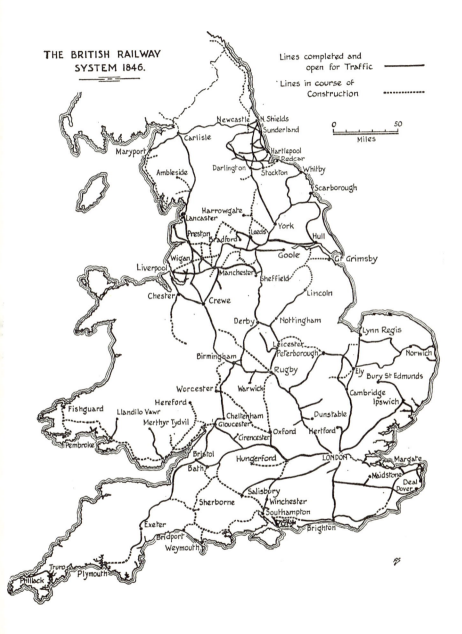

THE BRITISH RAILWAY
SYSTEM 1846.

Lines completed and
open for Traffic ————————

Lines in course of
Construction ----------------

0   50
Miles

Newcastle N. Shields
Carlisle   Sunderland
Maryport   Hartlepool
                              Redcar
Ambleside   Darlington   Stockton   Whitby
                                                  Scarborough
               Harrowgate
        Lancaster
    Preston   York
        Bradford   Leeds   Hull
Wigan
Liverpool   Manchester   Goole   Gt Grimsby
Chester   Sheffield
          Crewe   Lincoln
              Derby   Nottingham
                                            Lynn Regis
      Birmingham   Leicester   Norwich
                       Peterborough
                   Rugby   Ely Bury St Edmunds
   Worcester   Warwick   Cambridge
Hereford   Ipswich
Fishguard Llandilo Vawr   Dunstable
       Merthyr Tydvil   Cheltenham
                        Gloucester
Pembroke   Cirencester   Oxford   Hertford
                Bristol   Margate
                   Bath   Hungerford   LONDON   Maidstone
                                                  Deal
                        Salisbury   Dover
              Sherborne   Winchester
        Exeter   Southampton
           Bridport   Brighton
         Weymouth
   Truro
Phillack Plymouth

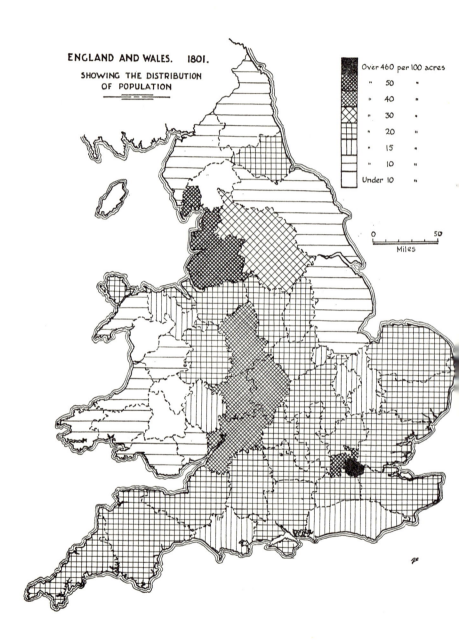

ENGLAND AND WALES. 1801.

SHOWING THE DISTRIBUTION
OF POPULATION

Over 460 per 100 acres
"   50   "
"   40   "
"   30   "
"   20   "
"   15   "
"   10   "
Under 10   "

0   50
      Miles

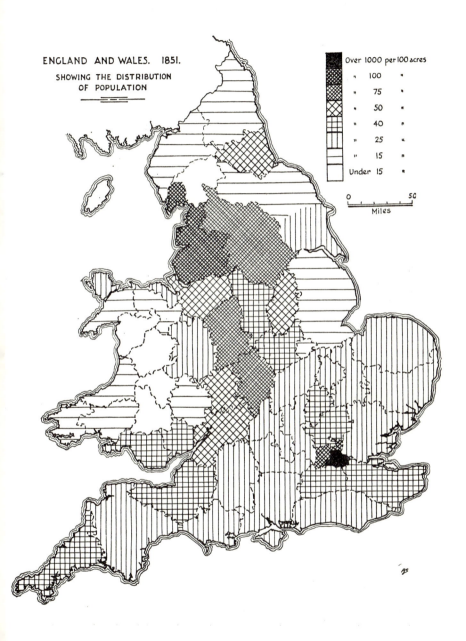

ENGLAND AND WALES. 1851.

SHOWING THE DISTRIBUTION
OF POPULATION

Over 1000 per 100 acres
" 100 "
" 75 "
" 50 "
" 40 "
" 25 "
" 15 "
Under 15 "

0   50
Miles

Books for Further Reading

THIS list of books is not intended to be a complete and comprehensive bibliography of the period: such a book list would overwhelm the student. Rather it is to be regarded as an indication of the principal works which will fill out the picture created in the preceding pages, and which will, in turn, provide the student with the necessary information for further study. The bibliography is arranged under chapters, in the hope that this will prove convenient, but several books recommended cover more than one chapter, and in order to minimise repetition, chapters have been grouped together wherever suitable, while no book is listed more than once.

General Works

E. L. Woodward: *The Age of Reform* (Oxford, 1962).

A. Briggs: *The Age of Improvement* (Longmans, 1960).

E. Halevy: *A History of the English People in the Nineteenth Century* (First Four Volumes, Benn, 1949–51).

G. M. Young: *Victorian England, Portrait of an Age* (Oxford, 1957).

G. Kitson Clark: *The Making of Victorian England* (Methuen, 1962).

G. D. H. Cole and R. Postgate: *The Common People* (Methuen, 1961).

C. R. Fay: *Life and Labour in the Nineteenth Century* (Cambridge, 1947).

Crane Brinton: *English Political Thought in the Nineteenth Century* (Benn, 1954).

John W. Derry: *The Radical Tradition* (Macmillan, 1967).

Chapters 1 and 2

C. Hobhouse: *Fox* (Constable, 1934).

John W. Derry: *William Pitt* (Batsford, 1962).

A. Cobban: *The Debate on the French Revolution* (Kaye, 1950).

Arthur Bryant: *Years of Endurance* (Collins, 1942).

Arthur Bryant: *Years of Victory* (Collins, 1944).

Oliver Warner: *The Glorious First of June* (Batsford, 1962).

Oliver Warner: *The Battle of the Nile* (Batsford, 1960).

Oliver Warner: *Trafalgar* (Batsford, 1959).

H. Butterfield: *Napoleon* (Duckworth, 1957).

H. A. L. Fisher: *Napoleon* (Oxford Home University Library, 1953).

Christopher Hibbert: *Corunna* (Batsford, 1961).
John Naylor: *Waterloo* (Batsford, 1959).
Elizabeth Longford: *Wellington, the Years of the Sword* (Weidenfeld and Nicolson, 1969).

Chapter 3

Dorothy George: *England in Transition* (Penguin Books, 1962).
T. S. Ashton: *The Industrial Revolution* (Oxford Home University Library, 1961).
J. L. and B. Hammond: *The Town Labourer* (Guild Books, 1949).
J. L. and B. Hammond: *The Village Labourer* (Guild Books, 1948).
F. A. Hayek (Editor): *Capitalism and the Historians* (Routledge & Kegan Paul, 1954).
J. Plamenatz: *The English Utilitarians* (Blackwell, 1958).
Jeremy Bentham: *A Fragment on Government*
An Introduction to the Principles of Morals and Legislation (Blackwell, 1948).
W. Cobbett: *Rural Rides* (Everyman Library, Nos. 638–9).
Margaret Cole: *Robert Owen* (Batchworth Press, 1953).
E. E. Thompson: *The Making of the English Working Class* (Penguin Books, 1968).

Chapters 4 and 5

H. Nicolson: *The Congress of Vienna* (Methuen, 1961).
W. R. Brock: *Lord Liverpool and Liberal Toryism* (Cambridge, 1941).
R. J. White: *Waterloo to Peterloo* (Heinemann, 1957).
Arthur Bryant: *The Age of Elegance* (Collins, 1950).
C. Webster: *The Foreign Policy of Castlereagh* (3 Volumes, Bell, 1950–8).
C. R. Fay: *Huskisson and his Age* (Longmans, 1951).
C. M. Woodhouse: *The Greek War of Independence* (Hutchinson, 1952).
N. Gash: *Mr Secretary Peel* (Longmans, 1961).
N. Gash: *Politics in the Age of Peel* (Longmans, 1953).
G. M. Trevelyan: *Lord Grey of the Reform Bill* (Longmans, 1952).
J. R. M. Butler: *The Passing of the Great Reform Bill* (Longmans, 1914).

Chapters 6 and 7

Lord David Cecil: *Lord M* (Constable, 1954).
G. Kitson Clark: *Peel and the Conservative Party* (Bell, 1929).
J. L. and B. Hammond: *The Bleak Age* (Penguin Books, 1947).

Asa Briggs (editor): *Chartist Studies* (Macmillan, 1959).
R. Fulford: *From Hanover to Windsor* (Batsford, 1960).
N. McCord: *The Anti-Corn Law League* (George Allen & Unwin, 1958).
N. Gash: *Reaction and Reconstruction in English Politics* (Oxford University Press, 1965).

Chapter 8

P. Guedalla: *Palmerston* (Benn, 1926).
C. Webster: *The Foreign Policy of Palmerston* (Bell, 1951).
A. J. P. Taylor: *The Struggle for Mastery in Europe* (Oxford, 1954).
J. D. Chambers: *The Workshop of the World* (Oxford Home University Library, 1961).
Arthur Bryant: *English Saga* (Collins, 1940).
C. Woodham-Smith: *The Reason Why* (Penguin Books, 1958).
W. Baring Pemberton: *Battles of the Crimean War* (Batsford, 1962).

Chapter 9

D. Southgate: *The Passing of the Whigs* (Macmillan, 1962).
H. J. Hanham: *Elections and Party Management* (Longmans, 1959).
P. Magnus: *Gladstone* (John Murray, 1954).
Walter Bagehot: *The English Constitution* (Oxford World Classics, 1955).
F. B. Smith: *The Making of the Second Reform Bill* (Cambridge University Press, 1966).
R. Blake: *Disraeli* (Eyre and Spottiswoode, 1966).
J. R. Vincent: *The Formation of the Liberal Party* (Constable, 1966).

Chapter 10

G. Faber: *Oxford Apostles* (Penguin Books, 1954).
J. H. Newman: *Apologia Pro Vita Sua* (Fontana Books, 1959).
J. S. Mill: *Utilitarianism*
On Liberty
Representative Government (Everyman Library, No. 482).
Matthew Arnold: *Culture and Anarchy* (Cambridge, 1960).
Basil Willey: *Nineteenth Century Studies* (Chatto & Windus, 1955).
David Newsome: *Godliness and Good Learning* (John Murray, 1961).
Raymond Williams: *Culture and Society* (Penguin Books, 1961).

INDEX